The
EVERYTHING.
Guide to Magazine Writing

Dear Reader,

I love writing for magazines. The work offers chances to create short, funny blurbs as well as long, hard-hitting features. Magazines focus on everything from celebrity gossip to do-it-yourself bathroom remodeling. They are staffed by some of the most creative, intelligent, and inquisitive people on the planet.

On the flip side, magazine writing today offers increasing challenges for writers. Contracts are so complicated that you sometimes need a lawyer just to sign them. Accounting snafus make it tough to get paychecks on time. Demands for total copyright ownership can force writers to work longer hours just to earn the same amount of money.

In my years as a magazine writer and editor, I've learned a lot of things that can ease the nitty-gritty of getting the job done—and that can help to bring extra jobs your way. I hope this book gives you all the insights you need to build a successful magazine-writing career, whether you want to see your byline in print a few times or plan to launch a full-time freelance magazine-writing business.

May your nut grafs be strong, your quotes meaty, and your query letters accepted. I look forward to seeing your work on newsstands everywhere!

Kim Kavin

The EVERYTHING® Series

Editorial

Publisher	Gary M. Krebs
Director of Product Development	Paula Munier
Managing Editor	Laura M. Daly
Associate Copy Chief	Sheila Zwiebel
Acquisitions Editor	Lisa Laing
Development Editor	Katie McDonough
Associate Production Editor	Casey Ebert

Production

Director of Manufacturing	Susan Beale
Associate Director of Production	Michelle Roy Kelly
Prepress	Erick DaCosta
	Matt LeBlanc
Design and Layout	Heather Barrett
	Brewster Brownville
	Colleen Cunningham
	Jennifer Oliveira
Series Cover Artist	Barry Littmann

Visit the entire Everything® Series at *www.everything.com*

THE
EVERYTHING®
GUIDE TO MAGAZINE WRITING

From writing irresistible queries to landing
your first assignment—all you need
to build a successful career

Kim Kavin

△

Adams Media
Avon, Massachusetts

For my sister, Michelle Kavin, one of the truly great writers

An Everything® Series Book.
Everything® and everything.com® are registered trademarks of F+W Publications, Inc.

Published by Adams Media, an F+W Publications Company
57 Littlefield Street, Avon, MA 02322 U.S.A.
www.adamsmedia.com

ISBN 10: 1-59869-241-0
ISBN 13: 978-1-59869-241-9

Printed in the United States of America.

J   I   H   G   F   E   D   C   B   A

Library of Congress Cataloging-in-Publication Data
available from the publisher.

This publication is designed to provide accurate and authoritative information with regard to the subject matter covered. It is sold with the understanding that the publisher is not engaged in rendering legal, accounting, or other professional advice. If legal advice or other expert assistance is required, the services of a competent professional person should be sought.

—From a *Declaration of Principles* jointly adopted by a Committee of the American Bar Association and a Committee of Publishers and Associations

Many of the designations used by manufacturers and sellers to distinguish their products are claimed as trademarks. Where those designations appear in this book and Adams Media was aware of a trademark claim, the designations have been printed with initial capital letters.

This book is available at quantity discounts for bulk purchases.
For information, please call 1-800-289-0963.

Contents

Top Ten Magazine-Writing Mistakes to Avoid / x

Introduction / xi

The Magazine Writer's Role / 1
You're a Content Provider **2** • More Demands Every Day **4** • Contract Issues **6** • Your Competition **7** • The Best of the Best **10** • Tricks of the Trade **11**

Is Magazine Writing for You? / 15
Assessing Your Skills **16** • Financial Considerations **19** • Being in Control **20** • Professional Recognition (Or Not) **21** • The Challenge of Awards **22** • Psychological Demands and Rewards **24**

Starting Your Business / 29
You're an Entrepreneur **30** • Setting Goals **31** • Starting Out Right **32** • Your Home Office **34** • Accounting Issues **35** • Administrative and Marketing Materials **37** • Legal Considerations **39** • Protecting Yourself **40** • Opening for Business **42**

Magazine Markets / 43
The Universe of Magazines **44** • Consumer Titles **44** • Trade Titles **47** • Academic Titles **49** • Technical Titles **50** • Online Titles **51** • Competing Titles **53** • Creating Your Stable of Titles **54** • Using Corporate Consolidation to Your Benefit **55**

Query Letters / 59

The Editor's Crowded Desktop **60** • How Queries Are Formatted **61** • Inside Query Components **61** • Two Points You Must Make **66** • Helpful Suggestions **68** • Beginner Mistakes to Avoid **70**

Cementing Your Base / 73

Getting on Mastheads **74** • Typical Masthead Deals **75** • Should You Specialize? **78** • Working for Promotion or Barter **80** • The Importance of Networking **82** • Making Contacts **83**

Assignment Letters / 85

What Is an Assignment Letter? **86** • Why You Should Insist on Them **87** • What Assignment Letters Should Include **91** • Breaking It Down **92** • When Your Editor Won't Write One **95** • Taking the Initiative **95**

Negotiating and Signing Contracts / 99

Contracts 101 **100** • First North American Serial Rights **101** • Work-for-Hire and Hybrid Contracts **102** • Scary Clauses to Consider **104** • How to Negotiate Effectively **110** • When to Walk Away **112** • When to Use an Attorney or Agent **112**

Juggling Multiple Assignments / 115

A Successful Magazine Writer's Day **116** • Every Client Is Your Only Client **118** • Setting Your Own Deadlines **120** • Keeping Updated To-Do Lists **123** • Making Time for Valuable Last-Minute Work **125** • Having Resources Ready **127**

Copyrighting Your Work / 129

Copyright Basics **130** • Why Bother to Register? **132** • Finding Forms Online **134** • The Benefits of Filing Quarterly **135** • If Your Copyright Is Violated **137** • Getting Help **140** • Moving On **141**

Marketing Yourself / 143
It's a Race to Win Work **144** • The Challenge of Self-Promotion **146** •
Query Letters and Introductory E-mails **147** • Entering Writing Contests
150 • Being Active in Writers' Groups **151** • Attending Industry
Conferences **152** • Joining Magazine Staff Meetings **153** • Creating
a Web Site **154**

Making Time to Improve Your Craft / 157
Remember, You Love to Write **158** • Reading for Fun **159** • Attending
Writers' Conferences **162** • Creative-Writing Exercises **164** • Adding
to Your Skills **167** • Reviving Your Commitment to Downtime **169**

Expanding Your Base / 171
Should You Grow Your Business? **172** • Repurposing What You Already
Own **174** • Entering New Markets **177** • Copywriting **179** • Partnering
with Photographers and Illustrators **181** • Creating Alter Egos **183**

Increasing Your Income / 185
How Much Is Enough? **186** • The $1-per-Word Question **188** • Per-
Project Versus Per-Hour Pay **190** • Adding Little Extras **192** • Getting
Raises from Longtime Clients **194** • Dropping Your Lowest-Paying
Clients **196** • Cutting Expenses **197**

Working with Editors / 199
You're Part of a Stable **200** • Making and Keeping Allies **202** • Being
Helpful Without Being Suckered **204** • Protecting Yourself with New
Editors **206** • When to Take the Kill Fee **207** • Five Tips for Keeping
Editors Happy **209**

Collecting Your Due / 213

Money Matters **214** • When the Check Isn't in the Mail **215** • Assuming the Best **218** • Understanding the Worst **219** • Is Fighting Worth Your Time? **221** • Strategic Techniques **224** • Legal Options **226**

Managing Your Future / 227

A Life of Sporadic Cash Flow **228** • Retiring Without a Pension or 401(k) **230** • Health Care **231** • Your Network of Colleagues **234** • Balancing Work and Play **236** • Getting Help at Home **238**

Dealing with the Doldrums / 241

Boredom and Loneliness **242** • Adding Travel to Your Work **243** • Creating a Network of Writer Friends **245** • Taking Small Vacations **246** • Taking Big Vacations **247** • Ten Tips for Getting Back on Track **248**

Adding to Your Repertoire / 255

Using Magazine Writing As a Launch Pad **256** • Taking Photographs **256** • Illustrating Your Work **258** • Editing and Proofreading **259** • Writing Books **260** • Building a Web Presence **263** • Giving Speeches **264** • Teaching **265** • Consulting **265**

Writing Stronger Stories / 267

Better Reporting **268** • Improving Your Leads **270** • Strengthening Nut Grafs **272** • Hansel and Gretel **274** • Meaty Quotes **275** • Authority and Voice **277** • Memorable Endings **278**

Appendix A: Magazine Writers' Organizations / 281

Appendix B: Must-Have Reference Books / 291

Appendix C: Magazine Marketplace / 295

Index / 299

Acknowledgments

Literary agent Jacky Sach of Bookends LLC brought me this project and helped me to see it through. She never fails to think of me when writing opportunities arise, and I am always grateful for chances to work with her.

This is my third book for Adams Media, and everyone at the company continues to impress me with their hard work and collegial attitudes. Lisa Laing, in particular, has been a terrific supporter of mine.

Virtually all that I know about magazine writing is thanks to my work over the years with excellent writers and editors. I have learned as much from the people whose copy I edit as I have from the people who edit my copy. In particular, I would like to thank Richard Thiel, Diane Byrne, and Elizabeth Ginns Britten at *Power & Motoryacht* and *Voyaging*; Tom Richardson, Joe Myerson, and Rick Eggleston at *Offshore*; Tim Sayles at *Chesapeake Bay*; Dave Funkhouser at *The Hartford Courant*; Dan Nott at NJN Publishing; and freelancers Betsy Frawley Haggerty, Heather Freckmann, and Michael Verdon.

My parents, Marc and Donna Kavin, and my sister, Michelle Kavin, are wonderful supporters of everything I do—and excellent distractions when I need a break from writing. I love and appreciate them dearly. Last on this list but first in my heart is Sean Toohey, who always understands when I am still typing long past midnight. He is the partner of my dreams.

Top Ten Magazine-Writing Mistakes to Avoid

1. **Missing deadlines:** Always make your deadlines, and beat them when you can.

2. **Existing in the shadows:** Half of being a successful magazine writer is marketing yourself through contests and writers' groups.

3. **Failing to recycle your notes:** Most assignments can be spun into several stories for various magazines, with minimal effort by you.

4. **Giving away your rights:** Magazine-writing contracts want more and more from writers, including indemnity from lawsuits. Protect yourself legally.

5. **Settling for low pay:** Getting an assignment is exciting, but it's also a business proposition. Don't just accept the offered paycheck. Negotiate for more.

6. **Reporting inaccurately:** You may be the finest wordsmith since Longfellow, but if you can't keep the facts straight, you'll be out of business in a flash.

7. **Keeping messy files:** Being an editor's writer of choice means having all your notes and previous articles at the ready for answering questions quickly.

8. **Working for free:** Magazine editors on tight budgets may try to get extra work from you without extra pay. Insist on compensation.

9. **Being a squeaky wheel:** There's nothing wrong with befriending an editor, but nobody likes a writer who calls daily with complaints.

10. **Writing badly:** If you can't keep readers' attention, editors will stop calling. Develop a voice, know your subject matter, and tell your stories well.

Introduction

▶ READERS BUY ABOUT 360 million copies of magazines in the United States each year. Considering that there are just shy of 300 million people living in the country, that's an awful lot of reported newsstand and subscription sales.

You know a lot of the titles well, from *Fortune* to *Entertainment Weekly* and *Woman's Day*. Studies show that nearly 85 percent of people above the age of eighteen read magazines, with celebrity news, fashion, and home furnishings among their favorite subjects. What you may not know, though, is that consumer magazines make up just one-third of the total magazine market. There are more than 18,000 magazines being published in the United States as of this printing, and only about 6,300 of them are titles you might find in your local supermarket or bookstore. The rest are trade, academic, technical, and online titles, publications such as *Human Resources Magazine, Professional BoatBuilder,* and *Diabetes Forecast.*

If you're an aspiring writer, this information could not be more encouraging. There are countless opportunities to get your words into print, and reader demand has never been stronger for your insights on everything from politics to needlepoint. Even better, while it may be challenging to break into the best-known magazines, fully two-thirds of the titles out there have circulations of less than 500,000 readers. That means there are literally thousands of editors seeking to grow their circulations by publishing interesting articles. Offer these editors well-thought-out ideas, and you're likely to win assignment after assignment.

What prevents many talented wordsmiths from making the most of this situation is a failure to recognize that magazine writing is a business. Make no mistake about this fact: Magazine advertising brought in an estimated $23 billion in 2005, the last year for which statistics are available. Publishers produce magazines to earn a profit, plain and simple.

You, the writer, fit into this equation by filling the magazine's pages with compelling content, which in turn draws a readership base that gets advertisers excited. You may be called a freelancer, a stringer, or a contributing editor, but at the end of the day you are an independent contractor hired as part of the magazine's overall economic plan. Every assignment you agree to write is, at its core, a business deal between you and your editor.

To be a successful magazine writer, then, you need to know as much about your business as you do about your craft. There are contracts to be vetted, pay rates to be negotiated, and copyright issues to be debated. Every magazine's mission statement, style, and competition are different, and you need to know how your writing fits into the mix. Editors have unique personalities, and you must get the attention of those who control the best assignments. When all of that is done, you need to actually produce the stories. And you'd better do so eloquently, accurately, and on time.

Indeed, a lot more goes into being a magazine writer than knowing how to turn a catchy phrase. By reading this book, you will learn about the realities that combine the craft and the business of getting words into print. You will discover not just how to be a better writer, but also how to be a financially successful one.

Remember: Readers buy about 360 million magazines in the United States every year. Here's hoping your sentences are among those they find most memorable in the issues to come.

Chapter 1

The Magazine Writer's Role

You may want to be a magazine writer because you're good at writing stories. That's a fine place to start, but more and more magazines are demanding that writers do far more than just write stories. As the companies that own magazines diversify into Internet, television, and other forms of media, they are insisting that magazine writers diversify, too. There are a lot of writers out there who can do so, and they are your competition.

You're a Content Provider

The job of a magazine writer used to be fairly straightforward: Find an interesting topic, interview people about it, and then put everything you learn into a compelling feature that will keep readers turning the magazine's pages. The work required a solid foundation in journalism, summed up as the ability to report and write. End of story.

Those reporting and writing skills are still a huge part of the magazine writer's role today, but they have become more of a foundation than a total job description for the most successful writers in the business. Increasingly, magazine publishers are referring to writers as "content providers." They see the magazine writer as more of an information collector, someone whose work they can use in multiple ways.

What a Content Provider Does

Consider the role of a writer for a magazine like *In Style*, which covers celebrity news and fashion. Say the writer gets a scoop about a hot celebrity's new boyfriend. The writer may still land an assignment to write an article that runs in the monthly magazine on newsstands everywhere, but that same writer may also be asked to create a "teaser article" that will run on the magazine's Web site as a promotion before the article appears in print. And, since we're talking about a celebrity, the writer may also be asked to discuss her article on one of the many television shows that feature movie-star news, such as *Entertainment Tonight*. The magazine may even ask the writer to attend a star-studded movie-premiere cocktail party and mingle among the guests, promoting the upcoming feature in the process.

QUESTION?

Why do more and more magazine publishers think of writers as content providers?
Because huge media corporations own and control more magazines than ever. These same corporations also own television shows and Internet companies, and they want writers to put their stories to work not just for the magazine, but for all of the corporation's media outlets.

At this point, the magazine writer is not only tasked with crafting a full-length feature article, but also with writing an advertorial-style, Web-friendly snippet; with being able to speak articulately and look fashionable on camera; and with being able to socialize as a human advertisement for the upcoming feature. These are not exactly the skills most journalists possess or even have in mind when they set out to write for magazines, nor are they the kinds of things you're likely to learn in a typical journalism school.

Adapting to This New Approach

Indeed, if you are like most would-be magazine writers, you simply enjoy the job of writing. You probably have a few favorite magazines that you like to read more than any others, and you believe that you can contribute to the ongoing conversation that those magazines have, in print, with their readers.

Sometimes you can do just that, and nothing else. Not every magazine writer, after all, becomes a darling of the publisher and is asked to speak on camera and attend glitzy events. (Or even less celebrity-studded parties, if you're talking about a publication like *Fine Woodworking Magazine* that doesn't typically have movie-star red carpets at its gatherings.) And not all magazines have gone this path of pushing writers into ever-expanding roles. In some cases, you can be a writer and nothing else.

The day is coming, though, when you may no longer have that choice—and as you enter the magazine-writing business, you need to understand that probability. Many, many magazines have found financial success by following the business model that turns writers into content providers, which means that ever more magazines are likely to follow the same path. Most magazines will no longer be standalone entities that have readers. Magazines are becoming components in multimedia packages that have users—users who want to receive the content that writers provide in new and different ways, be it online, in a cellular phone text message, or in an iPod download.

FACT

Time Warner is one corporation changing the way magazines do business. It owns magazines plus Warner Brothers Entertainment, Home Box Office, and America Online. The company wants to use stories in other media—say, by creating a *Sports Illustrated* special that premieres on HBO and is promoted on America Online.

You may not feel these multimedia pressures when you start out as a magazine writer, but the legal and financial implications they create will absolutely be a part of your life. Even if a magazine you write for has no intention of putting your words on the Internet any time soon, the magazine's parent company will want to reserve the right to do so in the future. Even if a magazine you write for has no intention of putting you on television any time soon, the magazine's parent company will want to reserve the right to use your image on television later. Even if a magazine you write for has no intention of running your story anywhere but in its own pages, the magazine's parent company will want to reserve the right to reprint your story in its other magazines and multimedia outlets whenever it so chooses. Legally and financially speaking, all of these things make the job of being a magazine writer more demanding than ever—and they require you to know not only what you are writing, but also how you are selling it.

More Demands Every Day

Many of the older editors still working in the magazine business today can remember a time when they gave out story assignments through friendly conversations. A writer would call the editor on the telephone, or the two would meet for a drink in a local bar. The story idea would be discussed, the editor would offer a fee and a deadline, and the writer would accept with a smile. The story would appear in the magazine's pages, and then all rights to the reported material would go back to the writer, who might try to sell the exact same story, or a revised version, to another editor at another magazine.

It was all very gentlemanly, and the system allowed writers to earn a decent living by re-selling their reporting and writing several times over. The magazine got what it wanted, too, and the writers and editors often felt they were on the same side, both working toward the common goal of making a great story for the magazine's readers.

Today, the multimedia pressures bearing down on magazine editors make it harder and harder for these gentlemanly types of agreements to exist. Editors are often tasked not just with helping a writer make a terrific story for readers, but also with getting the writer to sign contracts that demand increasingly more rights for the same amount of pay—and that, as a result, make it harder for the writer to earn a living or even control what happens to her writing.

E ALERT!

Some magazines now force writers to sign contracts that not only give the magazine the right to do whatever it wants with an article, but that also insist on the writer handing over all of her notes and research to the magazine—so that she can never use them again, in any form, for any other publication or media company.

Of course, the magazine writer-editor relationship remains strong at many magazines, mostly because many editors dislike having to make these stronger contractual demands on the writers they have known for many years. For new magazine writers, though, there is often little leeway. While a longtime contributor to a magazine may be allowed to amend contracts, retain more rights, and receive appropriate compensation for extra services, new writers are often given an ultimatum along the lines of "sign it and do it, or we'll find another writer who will." In other words, if you want to work for some magazines nowadays, you often have no choice but to go along with their contractual demands—no matter how difficult they might make it for you to succeed as a magazine writer overall.

Contract Issues

You will learn more about legal considerations in Chapters 7 and 8, but for now, consider this list of things that a magazine may demand of you in exchange for a $500 or $1,000 story assignment:

- The right to use your image or likeness however it wants, whenever it wants, without so much as notifying you
- The right to sell your article to other parties, including advertisers, without giving you a percentage of the sale income
- The right to make you pay all of the magazine's legal expenses should someone file a lawsuit regarding your article
- The right to reprint your article, or parts of it, in other media outlets the magazine's parent company owns without compensating you for the additional use of your work

These demands appear in magazine writers' contracts every day. They are insulting at best and terrifying at worst.

Imagine signing away the right for a magazine to use your image in exchange for writing an article about mental-health institutions. Then imagine that a major mental-health news story breaks a few months after your article appears. You just may find your words, and your photograph, on the nightly news under the headline "Schizophrenia Stabbing"—only because you happen to tune in to that channel. The magazine would not even have to alert you to the fact that it was going to use your image, and your words, to gain publicity. And you certainly won't be receiving any royalty checks for the additional income the magazine generates through this extra publicity.

It is imperative that when you sign a contract with a magazine, you understand not only what you are agreeing to write, but also what rights you are giving away to the magazine's parent company.

If that's not enough to get your attention, imagine that you sign a contract stating that your work will not violate the rights or agreements of your sources or anyone else with whom they have third-party agreements. Say your story is about the fancy new home of a professional athlete. You visit the home at a marketing director's invitation, take a tour with the marketing director, and write an article about the work the interior designer has done. It all seems very routine until a few weeks after your story appears, when you are served with a subpoena—because the interior designer claims the marketing director had no right to show you the home. Now you have to hire a $300-an-hour attorney (and perhaps pay for the magazine's legal expenses, too) because your story—spoon-fed to you by a legitimate marketing director—may have violated a third-party agreement the director had with the interior designer. An agreement you had no way of knowing, or even suspecting, existed.

It's easy to see how the new structure and contractual demands of magazine parent companies make scenarios like this not only possible, but probable. And it's therefore easy to see why you, the magazine writer, need to understand the business of writing as well as the craft. You also need to understand that you are part of a greater universe of magazine writers, one that includes a good bit of congeniality but also a great deal of competition.

Your Competition

Countless people want to write for magazines. Some never get much farther than sitting back in their easy chair, reading their favorite magazine, and thinking to themselves, "I could write one of these articles." Yet for every few dreamers out there, there's at least one dedicated writer who will make the real effort it takes to get published. This is your competition, and there's plenty of it.

Networking Is Essential

Becoming a magazine writer means entering into a loose network of writers all over the country and, in many cases, the world. Even if your goal is to publish a single article in a magazine you have read for years, your story idea and writing samples will be compared with those sent in by professional, full-time freelance magazine writers, like the hundreds upon hundreds of writers who are members of the American Society of Journalists and Authors (ASJA). ASJA members earn their livings by researching magazines and pitching story ideas, sending query letter after query letter to editors of all kinds. Your ideas and query letters will fall onto the same magazine editors' desks, which means that even if you don't aspire to be a full-time freelancer, you need to understand just how stiff the competition for magazine-writing assignments can be.

There are 1,100 members of the American Society of Journalists and Authors, the leading professional organization for nonfiction writers in the United States. The standards for gaining membership are high, including submitting multiple articles you have published in various magazines within a strict, recent timeframe. Thousands of people who write for magazines never make it into this elite group.

Most professional writers work for the same magazines again and again, getting to know their editors the way you might know a sister or brother. They speak with their editors several times a month; they know what ideas the editors already have versus what they are seeking for upcoming issues; and they know the style and tone the editors prefer when it comes to actually writing articles. In many cases, these writers and their editors become personal friends, meeting for lunches on weekends and even attending each other's weddings. They exchange quick e-mails during the day about industry gossip, and they trade printed cards and sometimes even gifts during the holidays.

The Value of Research

All of this, of course, gives the professional writers a huge advantage over first-time magazine writers—but the relationships can also work in your favor if you are new to a magazine. Yes, a magazine's editor is going to give plum assignments to the writers she knows, but she also is going to grow accustomed to the way her regular writers sound in print. Their tone, voice, and word choices will become second nature to her ears, the way comfortable slippers feel ready-made for her feet. Your ideas and words can offer a refreshing change of pace if you've done your homework and suggested a story that's a good fit for the magazine.

ALERT!

Never, ever send a story idea to a magazine without first asking for the magazine's writer's guidelines, also known as submission guidelines. You should research not just the appropriate editor to contact, but also the sections of the magazine that accept freelance queries and the format in which editors want those queries to be sent.

You'll have to do the same kind of pre-query research the pros do, such as going online and researching the magazine's content and target audience. Many magazines post their writer's guidelines on their Web sites, with clear explanations of sections that are open to freelancers and the topics those sections cover. Many magazines also have online archives of previous issues, which will let you search through stories that have already run—so that you don't duplicate another writer's idea and, in the process, show that you don't read the magazine for which you hope to write.

All of this background work isn't likely to land you a regular columnist's slot, even at the smallest of magazines, but it will offer you a chance of getting hired for that all-important first assignment.

Remember: This is how even the best-known regular writers at any given magazine started out in their careers, and there's no reason that you can't follow the same path. If you can fulfill the editor's demands after you get your first query letter accepted, you will have a chance of becoming one of the magazine's regular writers. The editor will be more likely to look at your future queries, or even to bring story ideas to you. Stay on the editor's good side and continue to do your best work, and you may even get the nod when a coveted columnist's position opens up.

So you see, while the competition is definitely tough in the magazine-writing business, there are openings for newcomers who have good ideas, strong writing skills, and the business sense to see where they fit into a magazine's big-picture business plan. If you're a good writer who is willing to look beyond the basics of stringing words into sentences, then you, too, can make a career out of working for magazines. In every sense, writers who understand that their true role encompasses more than just writing are the most likely to be successful at landing assignments. In fact, you can learn a lot about how to become a successful magazine writer by understanding how the best of the best do their jobs every day.

The Best of the Best

If you were to take a look at a brochure for a writers' conference, you might find that only one-third of the seminars had to do with the actual craft of writing. Another third of the seminars are likely to focus on networking and building writer-editor relationships, while another third are about the business of dealing with contracts and pay negotiations.

These are the kinds of conferences the best magazine writers attend year after year, always keeping abreast of the newest developments and opportunities. All the while, they nurture the contacts they already have at their favorite magazines, and they continue to submit queries for future work even when they are fully booked with assignments for the next few months.

Why do the professionals devote so much time to worrying about their magazine-writing futures if they are successful in the present? Because they know that to truly be among the best of the best—to continually land assignments—they must always stay at least a few steps ahead of new-comers like you.

Tricks of the Trade

One trick of the trade is getting hold of a magazine's editorial calendar, a list typically sent to advertisers describing the topics that will be covered in each issue. A monthly dog magazine's editorial calendar, for instance, may start out something like this:

- January: Training Tricks
- February: Leashes and Harnesses
- March: Best National Parks for Dog Walking
- April: Grooming
- May: Toys and Treats

And so on, filling out a year's worth of issues with general topics that adver-tisers can count on. A company that makes leashes, for instance, would probably be most interested in advertising in the February and March issues, where leashes are likely to be discussed. A company that makes dog treats, by contrast, will probably want to advertise in the January and May issues.

QUESTION?

How can you get a copy of a magazine's editorial calendar?
Sometimes, magazines post their editorial calendars online. If not, you can call the magazine's main number and ask for a copy. If the assistant can't help you, ask for someone in the marketing or sales department. They rely on editorial calendars to sell ads daily and always have them at hand.

The editor's job then becomes finding actual articles that fit within these topics, and the best magazine writers are ready to answer the call for queries. In fact, many top-notch magazine writers pitch story ideas with these specific topical guidelines in mind, sometimes sending their queries more than a year in advance. Their note to the editor may read something like this: "Hi Diane. I know you just finished shipping the March issue to the printer, but I recently found out about this great park for dog walking, and I'd be happy to keep the idea for you until next year's issue on the same topic. Please let me know if you think it might be worth a feature."

If the idea is good, the editor will make a note in her files—and when it comes time to assign stories a year later, that writer will be first to get the call.

The best freelancers also pay attention to which magazines their chosen editors are competing with, and they look to submit story ideas that will help those editors look good in meetings about beating competing titles. For instance, if you were submitting a query about a new four-wheel-drive vehicle to a car magazine, it would help your chances greatly to know that the magazine's main competitor just ran a twenty-page spread about four-wheel-drive vehicles—and left out the important model that your story would discuss. Your note to the editor could read something like this: "Dear John. In reading the most recent issue of *Horrible Car Magazine*, I couldn't help but notice that the recent spread on four-wheel-drive vehicles overlooked a major new model. I propose writing about that new model for your *Awesome Car Magazine*, so your readers will have the information first."

In those first two sentences of your query letter, then, you will have established not just that you can put sentences together, but also that you have expert knowledge of the topic, that you understand the magazine's market, and that you are eager to help the magazine editor defeat his competition on the newsstand.

These are the kinds of things the best of the best magazine writers do: They go beyond the craft of actually writing the story to ensure their pitches get noticed. Of course, being able to report accurately and write well are key parts of the job, too, and you'll learn more about those things later in this book. You can know everything there is to know about the business of writing, but if you fill your copy with clichés and rely on weak verbs surrounded by flowery adjectives, you're not likely to land any assignments at all.

Spend as much time as possible researching a magazine's competition before sending a query letter. You can often learn exactly how a magazine tries to differentiate itself simply by leafing through similar titles at your local newsstand.

Still, the most important thing to remember when you consider becoming a magazine writer is that the ability to write is just the beginning of the job. Knowing that your role is part of a bigger enterprise can only add to your chances of landing assignments. You need not be afraid of being called a content provider instead of a writer. Simply be aware that the probability of this happening exists, and know what you need to do to keep yourself worry-free and well paid as you get the job done.

You can start by making sure you have the right skills, personality, and financial standing to do the job in the first place. Magazine writers come in all shapes and sizes, of course, but in general they have a few similar traits that help them to succeed. Chapter 2 will help you figure out whether you share these common traits of successful writers and then allow you to answer the all-important question, "Is magazine writing for you?"

Chapter 2

Is Magazine Writing for You?

Writers get published in a variety of ways, from pamphlets to screenplays to books. Being a magazine writer requires a certain set of journalistic skills, plus the ability to handle the financial and psychological demands of the job. You may be a gifted writer, but that doesn't necessarily mean you will be a good magazine writer. You need to fully understand your personal and professional strengths (and weaknesses) before leaping into the magazine-writing business.

Assessing Your Skills

The odds are that if you're considering becoming a magazine writer, somewhere, somebody in your life told you that you have a way with words. It may have been all the way back in grammar school when you wrote an essay about Dr. Seuss that left your first-grade teacher teary-eyed, or it may have been in college when you published an op-ed piece in the campus newspaper that led to real change in the community.

Either way, you believe that you can write—in a way that makes other people want to read your words. This is one of the key skills of the magazine writer. It's one that many people think they possess but that relatively few writers actually do.

A lot of people are good writers, but far fewer people are writers whose work other people actually want to read. Unless you plan to write for educational magazines that are required reading among students, you need to be able to write in a way that grabs people's attention and keeps it.

In reality, successful magazine writers tend to be skilled at two different things: reporting and writing. The best writers have the ability to ferret out information, spot trends, and arrange facts in unique ways, all so that when it comes time to write the actual story, they are including the most interesting information and insights possible. This is what editors want to publish and readers want to buy on the newsstand: stories they cannot find anywhere else. Good reporting is often the key to making those kinds of stories. After all, building an article is just like building anything else. If you start with good materials, your finished product is likely to turn out better.

Being a Good Reporter

So reporting, then, is a key skill for any magazine writer. This includes the ability to conduct interviews by telephone or in person, not just getting the information you need from a source, but also getting the source to speak in interesting sentences that you can quote. You need to know how to ask open-ended questions, the kinds that sources cannot answer by simply saying "yes" or "no," the kinds that keep sources talking until they feel comfortable giving you the information they won't give to anybody else. You need to know how to get the best story out of the source, as opposed to making the source's information fit into your preconceived notion of the story.

Reporting also involves the ability to do research. Many beginning magazine writers think doing good research means typing a few words into Google and seeing what turns up. On the contrary, the best magazine writers do research in myriad ways:

- By reading the minutes of city council meetings and asking for copies of any legislation that is discussed
- By reading dense, technical books that help them better understand their article's subject matter or their interviewee's work
- By reading police reports and court documents from pending lawsuits and trials
- By researching their subject's history in library microfilms and other historical documents
- By reading other magazines and newspapers on a daily basis, not just for fun, but to spot trends and new information

As with good reporting, solid research can often turn a so-so article into a must-read feature. Even if your writing is mediocre at best, having great material that nobody else possesses is a surefire way to elevate your articles to the publishable level.

You shouldn't aspire to be a mediocre writer, of course. As with anything, it's not just what you say but also how you say it. Even if you have the best reporting and researching skills in your field, your job as a magazine writer is to put that information into a form that makes other people want to pick it up off the newsstand and read it.

Being a Good Writer

This means that you need to know the mechanics of crafting good articles, such as writing compelling leads, strong nut grafs (a nut graf is your thesis paragraph—the point of your article), meaty middles, and memorable endings.

More and more often, it also means that you need to know how to write eye-catching headlines and cover blurbs, informative captions, and relevant sidebars. Your skills as a magazine writer include making your research and reporting fit into the format that any given editor requests. This may mean short, snappy blurbs in one magazine and long, meandering paragraphs in another.

Being a Good Colleague

All of which leads to another skill that every successful magazine writer possesses: the ability to work well with editors. You can't expect to get along with every editor you encounter—some personalities and working styles simply don't mix—but to survive in the magazine-writing business, you do need to be adaptable. You must have a flexible style of working that allows you to fit into several different magazines' molds at once, not to mention a personality that will allow you to bend to whatever demands your various editors impose.

ALERT!

Some editors like to be extremely involved with their writers' work, going so far as to question specific word choices, while other editors take a more hands-off approach, letting the writer's own voice come across on the page. Know how much editing you can tolerate, and try to work with editors who have complementary personalities.

So, then, the main skills you need to have as a magazine writer are reporting, researching, writing, and working with editors. These are all things you can learn. You may have natural instincts for doing some of these things better than others, but in most cases you can find instruction should you need to improve in any particular area. There are other considerations you need to keep in mind, though, when deciding whether magazine writing is for you—and they have more to do with your personal life and psychological makeup than with anything you might learn from a teacher.

Financial Considerations

Whether you're just getting out of school and entering the workforce or considering a transition from a full-time position into magazine writing, you need to understand the financial considerations that go along with the job. Many people enjoy having full-time staff positions because the jobs make them feel financially secure. Receiving a paycheck that's the same amount on a weekly basis makes it easy to pay bills, prioritize spending, and anticipate income. Plus, many full-time staff positions come with benefits, including health insurance and retirement-savings plans like 401(k)s, all of which add to the sense of comfort that makes people work for one employer in the first place.

Full-time magazine writers lead a different financial lifestyle, and you may or may not have the type of personality and money-management skills that lifestyle requires. For starters, work often comes in spurts. You may receive three paychecks totaling $5,000 one month, but only one paycheck worth $500 the following month—none of which has had taxes withheld.

FACT

Full-time freelance magazine writers are responsible for paying income taxes on a quarterly basis, in January, April, June, and September. Taxes are not taken out of your paycheck the way they are for staff members. It is your responsibility to ensure you are squared away with the Internal Revenue Service.

Acquiring Health Insurance

You also are responsible for finding and financing your own health insurance as a full-time writer. This is a major challenge, especially if you are single or cannot buy into a spouse's existing health-insurance plan. Some writers' groups, including the online site *www.mediabistro.com*, offer access to health insurance companies with group discounts, but for the most part, your choices for health insurance will be more expensive and less plentiful than they would otherwise be in a full-time staff position.

In fact, many writers are moving into whole new arenas of health care, such as health savings accounts. In this scenario, you agree to accept a high annual deductible—say, $2,500 or $5,000—in exchange for bringing your monthly premium payments down to $100 or $200 (far less than you would pay with many "regular" plans). There are no co-pays with many health savings accounts, which means that if you get a $700 blood test, you will have to pay that $700 out of your own pocket, unless you have met that high annual deductible. Of course, this affects your income and savings, and you need to be the kind of person who can plan and prepare for rainy-day needs.

Saving for Retirement

An additional financial consideration that full-time writers must weigh is saving for retirement. There are no "matching funds" coming your way when you are a freelance writer the way there are for staff members, and you are ineligible for staff-only 401(k) plans. You need to be the kind of person who can take responsibility for your own retirement savings through IRAs or other investment vehicles, lest you end up spending every penny you earn and having to work literally until the day you die.

QUESTION?

Do magazine writers need an accountant to ensure their finances are in order?
Many writers do employ accountants, simply because writers are creative people by nature and thus not necessarily good at numbers and money management. Plus, being a magazine writer who works from home also means you are entitled to write-offs of which you may not be aware.

Being in Control

If you group these financial considerations together, what you find is an overarching theme of self-reliance. That is the quality that magazine writers need to make their jobs work from an economic standpoint. If you're the kind of person who can be smart about savings, not spend every penny in your bank account, and keep good track of your incoming and outgoing cash flow on a monthly basis, then you should have little trouble with the financial realities of being a full-time freelance magazine writer.

On the other hand, if you live hand-to-mouth and tend to spend every penny you are given, you are likely to run into trouble—because the pennies won't all come in the same amounts every week, and you may fall well short at tax time or when a large, unexpected medical bill comes your way.

These are some of the practical realities of being a magazine writer, and they are considerations just as real as your abilities to report and write. You can sell 300 articles a year, make all your deadlines, and keep your editors coming back for more, but if you can't manage the money that you earn along the way—if you can't ensure your own health care and retirement savings—then you will end up learning the hard way that magazine writing simply is not the best career choice for you. This has nothing to do with your ability to put nouns and verbs in the right order. It's simply the way the world works, and you need to think hard about whether you have what it takes to survive.

You also need to put serious thought into whether you will be happy with the professional realities of being a magazine writer. They are a world apart from the professional realities that go along with working as a full-time staff member at a magazine, and in fact are far different from the professional realities that come with almost every other full-time job out there.

Professional Recognition (Or Not)

One of the reasons many people enjoy working full-time for companies and corporations is that they feel like they are part of a team. Yes, you may sometimes feel as though you are an island unto yourself in a sea of cubicles, but your cubicle is almost always attached to another cubicle, and it to another cubicle, and so on. The work you do is directly supported by other members of your immediate team, and that team is directly supported by other teams in your division, which in turn is supported by other divisions within the company.

A Sense of Camaraderie

Through these connections, you and your coworkers develop a sense of professional camaraderie that often finds rewards in the form of plaques, certificates, and even the occasional financial bonus. Many companies have internal awards ceremonies where they give annual recognition to the "Hardest-Working Employee" and the "Best-Performing Manager." Even better, a lot of companies reserve entire tables at expensive industry awards ceremonies, inviting you and your colleagues to help represent your team even if you're not winning an award at all.

FACT

The American Society of Magazine Editors has presented the National Magazine Awards for the past forty years. It costs $400 for nonmembers to enter the contest, and that fee does not include a seat at the awards ceremony. If you're not on staff at a magazine, this is the type of expense you will have to shoulder yourself.

In short, one of the perks of being a full-time company employee is the structured attention devoted to giving you professional recognition from time to time—little ego boosts, so to speak, that keep you moving forward in your career path. You usually have something to hang on your cubicle wall that makes you feel at least a little bit appreciated and recognized for your contribution to the whole. At the very least, there is always a promotion opportunity looming on the horizon.

Being Out on Your Own

That type of professional recognition is far harder to come by for magazine writers. There are occasional compliments from the editors you work with, and there are awards to be had from national writers' associations. However, if you are going to win one, you need to be much more proactive than an employee who simply responds to a company-wide e-mail soliciting entry forms.

The Challenge of Awards

As a magazine writer, you need to handle all writers'-contest entry forms yourself. You need to know when they are due, make the photocopies of your articles to send in, and keep track of the submissions you've made. You also have to pay the contest entry fees along with extra costs to actually attend the awards ceremonies. If you decide to attend the ceremonies, you will no longer sit at a table full of your coworkers. Instead, you will find yourself at a table full of other magazine writers—many of whom are very collegial, but who are also your competitors for assignments at various magazines.

All in all, instead of being on the receiving end of invitations to enter and attend awards competitions at your employer's expense, you have to generate your own professional recognition. This can be incredibly intimidating if you're a wallflower type, and it can be a debilitating reality if you rely on regular professional recognition to buoy your personal sense of self-worth.

ALERT!

Think carefully about just how much you need "professional pats on the back" to keep you excited about your work. Magazine writers who are not full-time staff members usually receive far less professional recognition than full-time company employees. Successful magazine writers are typically self-reliant self-starters.

Considering the number of magazine articles written every year, only a small percentage of writers ever win awards at all. That's not to say there aren't opportunities; countless large and small groups offer writing awards for magazine content every year. Still, the big glory tends to go to "important" articles published in long-established titles such as *Esquire*, *Time*, and the *New York Times Magazine*. If you're new to magazine writing and your biggest feature so far is a holistic health-care article for *Natural Horse Magazine*, you're going to have a tough time going up against features about Iraq written by the well-known Sy Hirsch and published in *The New Yorker*.

Consider this partial list of winning titles from a recent American Society of Magazine Editors competition, and you will see just how stiff the competition is:

- *Harper's Magazine*
- *Esquire*
- *Vanity Fair*
- *Rolling Stone*
- *The American Scholar*

Certainly, you can earn a nice living as a magazine writer without ever seeing your byline appear in any of the aforementioned publications. However, professional recognition (or the lack thereof) is important for you to consider as a magazine writer, to be sure. If you need to see your name in lights, you may very well end up disappointed. There are other psychological demands and rewards that you need to keep in mind, too, as you consider whether magazine writing is right for you.

Psychological Demands and Rewards

In many ways, being a magazine writer involves existing in a vacuum. Most magazine writers work from home offices, where their only social interaction on any given day may be with the family dog. Magazine writers have little worry about office politics, since they're rarely in an office, and their schedules vary along with their workloads. Sometimes, twelve- to fifteen-hour days are required, while at other times, you can simply take an entire Wednesday afternoon off and head out to a movie.

There are good and bad things that go along with this scenario, all of which create psychological demands and rewards. Whether the rewards outweigh the demands in your case is a question only you can answer.

Solitude, or Solitary Confinement?

For starters, take the notion of working from a home office. Many magazine writers find this a liberating experience, one that allows maximum freedom and creativity. A laptop with wireless Internet access is literally a portable work space that you can take to the nearest Starbucks, beach, or local park, wherever you find the most inspiration for your writing. Since the only way that editors can reach you is via telephone or e-mail, you can literally shut out the world if you need a few hours to write. Nobody will come knocking on your office door to interrupt you. There simply isn't anybody else around.

QUESTION?

Has working from home become more acceptable in professional circles?
Absolutely yes, and not just for magazine writers. As of 2005, about 24 million Americans worked from home at least part time—including U.S. Supreme Court Chief Justice William Rehnquist, who telecommuted and read oral arguments from home after being diagnosed with thyroid cancer.

On the flip side for most magazine writers is that working from home comes with new demands. Personal calls in the middle of the day typically increase, since your friends and family know you are at home instead of in an office, where it is harder to talk about private matters. Spouses may assume that since you are home, you will handle more of the domestic chores that need doing, such as laundry washing and lawn mowing. Even your stay-at-home-mom neighbors, while trying to be friendly, can become challenging distractions when they invite you to join them for midday gatherings when you otherwise would be typing a feature article on your computer. If you're a mother or father yourself, your children may have a tough time understanding that even though you are home, you cannot play with them, feed them lunch, or walk them home from the bus stop.

All of these things can add up to an intense pressure to defend what you do—writing magazine articles—as a "real job." Yes, it is a good job, one that comes with the ability to do your work from Starbucks or the beach or the local park whenever you choose, but that degree of freedom is not a secret to the people in your life. The resulting changes in their behavior may become a drag on your productivity.

It's important that your spouse, children, friends, and family understand that working from home does involve working. One of the greatest psychological stresses that magazine writers face is defending their need to actually get work done while at home. Even pets need to adjust. You are in the house, but you are not available to play.

Insider Versus Outsider Status

Another psychological challenge that comes with working from home is the feeling of being "out of the loop." No matter how many assignments you receive from any given magazine, and no matter how much loyalty you may feel toward a certain title, you will never be on par with its staff members when it comes to knowing what's going on inside the office.

A lot of magazine writers enjoy this situation, since it frees you from office politics in all its forms. You can't get caught up in all the employee gossip, for instance, unless you have someone to gossip with. Unless you make the effort to pick up the telephone and involve yourself in that kind of behavior, it will rarely become part of your life.

On the other hand, some magazine writers find that being out of the loop is a bit disconcerting, especially writers who have left regular company jobs to begin new careers as freelancers. When you work in the office, you often have more say about the final product, whatever it may be, while as a writer at home, you rarely even see the final product before it goes out to the public. By the same token, you hardly ever know about the comings and goings of key staff members—meaning you may have trouble figuring out where your editor fits in the pecking order, and whether he can actually support you and your continued assignments should problems arise. Again, these kinds of psychological demands and rewards are problems for some magazine writers but are considered benefits by others. Such is also the case with varying work schedules.

Varying Workloads

When you work as a magazine writer, you are likely to have assignments land on your desk at varying paces. Some weeks you will have more work than you can do in a string of eighteen-hour days, while other weeks you may have just enough work to keep you busy for a few hours. There will be times when you send out a dozen query letters and receive rejection after rejection, and then other times when your ideas seem to hit the mark with every pitch.

Many successful magazine writers enjoy this ebb and flow because it gives them a chance to "go hard" at their work for a while, and then to slow down and recharge their creative batteries when necessary. Most successful magazine writers also like to use their downtime constructively, either to work on ideas they previously had to put aside or to market themselves to new editors and magazines.

Other magazine writers, however, find lulls in their schedules to be an open door to the vices of procrastination. Some of the many distractions writers working at home say they fall prey to when there is not enough work to be done include:

- Overeating
- Watching television
- Sleeping
- Playing video or computer games
- Surfing the Web aimlessly

If you're the type of person who needs a constant stream of work from a supervisor to remain motivated, then you need to seriously consider whether you can handle the psychological demand of having to close the fridge, put down the television remote control, and get back to work on a daily basis—all because you know you have to, not because somebody else is telling you to. It can be very easy to call watching CNN all afternoon "research" if you aspire to write for a magazine like *Newsweek*, but planting yourself on the couch with a bowl of popcorn and listening intently to Lou Dobbs is not going to help land you any assignments.

Chapter 3

Starting Your Business

Now that you know magazine writing is the work you'd like to do, it's time to get yourself organized for the job. You need to set goals, outline a plan to reach them, set up your home office, create an accounting system, develop marketing and administrative materials, and consider forming a legal entity to protect your personal assets. The writing part of your job will come soon enough. First, you need to establish a foundation to support your work.

You're an Entrepreneur

If you've learned anything so far from this book, it's that writing is only part of the magazine writer's job. There's a heck of a lot more going on in the background of most successful writers' lives than thoughts about verbs and adjectives, and it all starts with a real dedication to treating writing as a business.

Yes, if you are crafting articles for magazines, then you are a writer. However, at the core of your everyday work should be the notion that you are an entrepreneur. You are a business unto yourself. You are the information technology department, the accounts payable department, the marketing department, the administrative assistant, and the chief executive officer, all rolled into one.

Jack of All Trades

If your computer suffers a virus attack, then you are the one who has to salvage the files. If a magazine fails to pay you for your work, then you have to deal with recovering invoices. If you want to see your newest article promoted online, then you have to send out e-mails or upload a press release (that you write) to your own Web site. If your voice mail and e-mail inboxes are full, then you have to weed through the messages to find the important details. Perhaps most important, if you see your article sales slipping or your income shrinking, then you have to take a step back, look at the big picture of your business, and figure out how to change course.

QUESTION?

How can you juggle all the details that go along with being a magazine writer?
By setting aside an hour or two a day for handling administrative tasks, marketing queries, and payment problems. Consider being a business-person from 8 A.M. till 10 A.M., and then a writer from 10 A.M. until 5 P.M.

There are plenty of ways to get all of this done without infringing too much on your writing time, and with the growth of home-based businesses in recent years, more and more companies are promoting themselves as ready and able to help. You can sign on for an annual plan with a computer service and repair company, for instance, in case you run into software or hardware problems. You can make a one-time investment in accounting software to keep track of all your invoices, not to mention the information you will need when tax time rolls around. You can hire a public relations firm to help promote you as a writer, if that's important to helping you find more work. You can even hire by-the-hour assistants to help you with administrative tasks such as transcribing notes and returning messages if it all just gets too overwhelming.

Realizing Your Limitations

Yes, you *can* do all of those things, but the more important question is, *should* you?

The answer depends on your goals as a magazine writer. Do you want to earn a six-figure salary year after year, or do you simply want to sell a few stories here and there for a little added income from time to time? If it's the former, then you may be able to pay for lots of extra help. If it's the latter, you're going to be a one-man band. Figuring out your goals will help you determine where you fit along the magazine-writing spectrum, and this self-knowledge will in turn help you organize your business plan accordingly.

Setting Goals

There are a few general models that you can consider when deciding what kind of goals to set for yourself as a magazine writer. Take a look at the following descriptions, and decide which one sounds the most like you.

The Occasional Writer

You want to sell three or four articles a year. You have other sources of income to pay your regular bills, and your magazine writing is more of a hobby or personal dream than it is a career.

The Part-Time Writer

You want to sell an article or two every month. You have other sources of income to pay your regular bills, but magazine writing sounds like an interesting career, so you want to wade into it slowly while keeping your day job.

The Average Full-Time Writer

You want to sell three or four articles every month. Magazine writing will be your main source of income, but you have saved at least six months' worth of mortgage and other life expenses so that you can continue to pay your bills while taking only the magazine-writing assignments that interest you.

The Serious Full-Time Writer

You want to sell as much of your work as possible, perhaps branching out into books and other formats in the future. Magazine writing will be your main source of income, and you aspire to be among the top tier of writers who earn six figures each year. You have set aside money not just for paying bills during periods of slow work, but also for promoting your writing business. You are willing to take on assignments of any kind as long as they add nicely to your bottom line.

Starting Out Right

As you can see, one magazine writer's goals may be vastly different from another's. In every scenario, you will want to seriously consider the advice the rest of this chapter contains regarding administrative, financial, and legal concerns. However, you need to be careful not to overdo things right out of the gate. If, for instance, your entire goal is to sell a couple of stories a year to your favorite gardening magazine, you probably don't need to organize yourself into an S-corporation. Start by deciding what your goals as a magazine writer are, and then make a written outline of the plan that you will follow to achieve them.

Outlining a Plan

Creating a plan for your magazine-writing business is no different from creating a plan for any other kind of business. Your plan should include everything you need to acquire to get started, everything you believe you will need to achieve your goal after your first year, and an idea of where you would like your business to be headed five years down the road.

Start by listing the things you will need to begin working as a magazine writer. No matter your goals, these items will include a computer, an Internet connection, a telephone line, and a quiet space from which to work. A fax machine is probably a good idea, too, because billing and invoices are often handled via fax. (Nowadays, you can buy a decent combination fax/printer/scanner at most office-supply stores for somewhere in the range of $300.) Depending on how serious you want your magazine-writing career to be, you might also consider adding the following things to your startup plan:

- Business cards
- Stationery
- A business telephone/fax line separate from your home phone line
- A high-speed Internet connection for doing research on the Web
- Professional office furniture
- Upgraded computer software

Setting Your Startup Budget

Your budget will of course dictate just how much you can invest in your writing business from the start, but making a list of what you will actually need to get the job done can help you determine whether you've set a realistic budget and plan from Day One. If your goal is to become a six-figure freelancer and you don't have enough money to make a simple business card, then it may be time to reevaluate either your goal or your initial startup budget. On the other hand, if you have $5,000 put aside to invest in your writing business and you already have all the tools you need except for some new computer software, then you probably will be in a better position right out of the gate. No matter what your overall plan ends up including, expect one of your biggest initial costs to be setting up a suitable home office.

Your Home Office

Your home-office setup will be most important if you plan to work full time as a magazine writer, but even the occasional writer needs a quiet, well-organized space that is conducive to getting the job of writing done. Whether you have an entire room that you can dedicate as an office or simply a small section of a studio apartment, your goal in setting up your home work environment should be to make the space as comfortable for your needs as possible.

Tangibles

As you read in the last section, this home-office setup should include a telephone and a fax machine, perhaps working from a separate phone line than your home number. There are other typical items that you should consider, as well:

- **A spacious desk** with room for your computer as well as open notebooks and files
- **Good lighting** that will keep your eyes healthy despite extra computer use
- **A telephone headset** that will keep your hands free to type while conducting telephone interviews
- **A large-format monitor** that you can plug into your laptop, if it has a small screen that hurts your eyes after extended use
- **A file cabinet** for storing contracts, notes, and other important paperwork
- **A bookshelf or bookcase** for holding your dictionary, thesaurus, and other reference materials
- **A desktop or electronic Rolodex** or address book for easy access to sources' contact information
- **A well-built chair** that offers good support for your back and that will remain comfortable even during a twelve-hour workday

Intangibles

As important as it is to outfit your home office with items that you can see and touch, you also need to ensure that your setup includes the intangibles that will help you to be successful. Noise is one such intangible. You can't see it or touch it, but it definitely will affect your ability to write. If you think better with a radio on, then put one in your home office. On the other hand, if you need absolute silence when you are working, consider setting up shop in the part of your home that is farthest from the television and kitchen (where people tend to congregate, and from where noise will emanate if you are working late and your husband feeds the kids dinner while watching reruns of *Everybody Loves Raymond*).

ALERT!

Consider setting up your home office as far away from your refrigerator as possible. Many magazine writers complain that they gained weight in their first year on the job, simply because they were easily distracted by that last slice of pie just a few steps away in the kitchen.

Distractions in general are another intangible to consider. If you are easily distracted, consider having your desk face a wall instead of a window. You will be less likely to begin daydreaming when the sun is shining and you're on deadline. Also consider installing caller ID on your telephone, so that you can see when friends and family are calling and screen them out during your busiest work times. Another good tip is to remove all games, like solitaire, from your computer system. There's no easier way to get distracted than by trying to get hearts, diamonds, spades, and clubs into organized rows.

Accounting Issues

Whether you plan to write six or sixty magazine articles a year, you will need a way to keep track of what work you have done, what income you have received, and what payments are owed. A lot of magazine writers do this by creating a Word or Excel file, and that's a decent solution if your goals are to be less than a full-time freelance writer. However, if you intend to make magazine writing your business, then you will be better off investing in an accounting software program that creates and keeps track of professional-looking invoices.

Accounting Software

Accounting software has become easier and easier to use over the years. Even if you are a wordsmith who has always been horrible at math, you will likely find today's accounting software more helpful than frustrating to use. Some of the programs that magazine writers favor include Quicken, Peachtree, and Microsoft Money for Small Business. Each is relatively easy to understand and offers the basic functions of creating invoices, tracking income and expenses, monitoring received income, and showing business cash flow in numbers, charts, and graphs.

FACT

Accounting software does not take the place of an accountant's advice. While some programs offer helpful tax-time tools, your software's main function should be to help you keep track of work you have done, invoices you have sent, and payments you are owed.

Keeping track of expenses and receipts is especially important if being a magazine writer is your main source of income, because you will be entitled to multiple deductions at tax time. Most magazine writers hire an accountant, at least in their first year, to help them understand all the write-off possibilities, and a good accounting software program will make it easier for your accountant to find your deductions and list them accurately for the Internal Revenue Service.

Possible Tax Deductions

Here are some of the possible deductions you can take as a magazine writer:

- Telephone, Internet, and cable television service
- Business travel and meals not reimbursed by your assigning editors
- Books, magazines, and DVDs
- Some home improvements and repairs
- Educational expenses including attendance at writers' conferences

A good accounting software program will help you keep track of all these things and more. In some cases, you can even coordinate your business paperwork and invoice logo with the one you use on your administrative and marketing materials.

Administrative and Marketing Materials

Your administrative and marketing materials have two purposes: They help you to run your business in an orderly manner, and they give the outside world the impression that you are a serious professional. A lot of entry-level magazine writers try to make do without administrative and marketing materials because they are an additional—if nominal—startup expense. This is a bad idea, because successful writers establish themselves from the start, setting themselves apart from people who dream of writing but don't take the job half as seriously. Take the time and effort to create a basic set of administrative and marketing materials when you start your writing business. Your investment will pay off for years to come.

Administrative Materials

Administrative materials are the tools that you will use for communicating with editors and sources. They include business cards, fax cover sheets, and letterhead. Every professional in every kind of business has these basics in hand, and you, as a professional magazine writer, should have them too.

There are lots of ways to create administrative materials, some more expensive than others. Office-supply stores such as Staples now stock row after row of shelves with do-it-yourself business stationery products that you can design on your home computer and print out in color or black-and-white. You also can order raised-letter business cards at a reasonable rate from the same kinds of stores, along with preprinted stationery that includes a logo you create by selecting from templates.

While you can spend a ton of money having a graphic artist create a logo for you, and then incorporating it into all of your administrative materials, most magazine writers find this to be an unnecessary expense. The do-it-yourself route is the most common, and most editors respect the effort as a sign of professionalism.

Be sure you are making the most of your existing computer software before going out and paying for custom-made stationery products. If you already have a copy of Microsoft Publisher on your machine, for instance, you can create do-it-yourself, professional-looking designs for everything from business cards to invoices.

Marketing Materials

Your marketing materials are an extension of your administrative materials. (After all, when you hand out a business card, you are in essence marketing yourself.) Marketing materials include things such as your resume and the folders in which you mail previous writing clips as samples to editors.

If at all possible, your marketing materials should share the same look and logo as your administrative materials. Your goal, remember, is to present yourself as a professional doing business, and the more you can reinforce your name in the editor's memory, the better chance you will have of succeeding. The best way to reinforce your name or idea is to have a logo or look that is professional and classy and that stands out.

A professional set of administrative and marketing materials has additional benefits, as well. One of the most important is that it helps you to establish to outsiders that you are, indeed, running a business—which can be extremely important should you run into legal problems regarding an article you've written.

QUESTION?

Should you use fluorescent-colored stationery and logos to attract attention?
Probably not. While bright yellows and oranges are certainly attention getting, they don't exactly convey a tone of professionalism. Save them for the next time your grade-school son needs a flyer for a class trip.

Legal Considerations

Protecting yourself from lawsuits and related legal expenses is one of the most important jobs you have in setting up your magazine-writing business. More and more, magazines are putting the onus of legal defense onto their writers, and that can mean tens of thousands of dollars in expenses for you—even if you never do anything wrong.

Today's magazine-writing contracts often include clauses that lay liability for an article, and anyone's response to it, at the feet of the person who wrote it. There are two kinds of clauses, in particular, that are most worrisome nowadays:

- **Indemnity clauses:** These guarantee that you, the writer, will pay all of your own—and all of the magazine's—legal bills should anyone sue the magazine, rightfully or frivolously, concerning a story you wrote.
- **Third-party promises:** These guarantee that you, the writer, have not violated anyone's rights in your story—and that you have not violated any third-party agreements that your sources may have made with other parties, with or without your knowledge.

You will learn more about indemnity clauses and third-party promises in Chapter 8.

Protecting Yourself

Often, you have to agree to these conditions in order to land a writing assignment, since more and more corporate-owned magazines are strong-arming writers into signing these types of contracts. There's nothing good, or even fair, about them in the eyes of most magazine writers, but they are today's reality of doing business.

You need to know how to protect yourself, even if you think your work lacks controversy. You may write an article about tomato plants—an innocuous subject, for sure—only to find that there are several competing tomato-seed producers, and the one you left out of your story feels slighted enough to sue. Or, you may find yourself quoting a company's marketing director about the production of a new kind of adhesive fastener, only to find out later that the scientist who invented the fastener did not give the marketing director permission to take the news public.

FACT

Some insurance companies sell "errors and omissions" policies that will protect you in the case of some lawsuits. However, the policies are pricey—at least $5,000 a year in many cases—and most magazine writers don't have that kind of money to invest in pre-emptive defense strategies.

The point is that even if you're not covering celebrity gossip or insider politics, the possibility of legal problems is very real, and you need to take it seriously—because you will be footing the defense bill should you have to hire a lawyer.

Separating Your Assets

One key to defending your personal assets in a court of law is by showing that they are separate from your writing business, even though you work from a home office. Your administrative and marketing materials are a good first step, proof that you take your job of magazine writing seriously.

What can help you most in a situation like this, though, is having your business assets literally separated from your personal money. If you can do this, then in many cases a legal action will only affect your business income—and not your personal savings account, home equity, and retirement investments.

S-Corps and LLCs

The easiest way to separate your business and personal income is by forming either an S-corporation or a limited liability corporation. Many professional magazine writers do this, and it's far less difficult, expensive, and scary than it sounds.

In most cases, you can form either kind of corporation by filling out online forms or by working through your local Small Business Administration. The fees typically range in the hundreds, not thousands, of dollars—a small price to pay to protect yourself in the long run. You can also pay a little extra to have companies such as *www.legalzoom.com* form these entities for you, although most magazine writers have no problem with the do-it-yourself method, especially if they already work with an accountant on an annual basis.

If you decide to form an S-corp or an LLC, go online to *www.sba.gov*, the official site of the Small Business Administration. There are a host of tools that will help get you started, including a section called "Forms of Ownership" that will help you determine which type of business entity is best for you.

There are legal and tax distinctions that differ between S-corps and LLCs—your accountant can help you figure out which is best for you—but most writers describe the basic practical difference as one of accounting. With an S-corp, you typically have to be more diligent in keeping your business expenses separately notated from your personal expenses than you do with an LLC. As many magazine writers are "creative types" instead of "numbers people," they are willing to pay a smidge more in taxes each year if it means less accounting and bookkeeping on a daily basis.

The Name Game

One last note about creating a corporation as a legal protection: Do not name your company Jane Smith, Inc., or Jane Smith LLC. Many magazine writers are tempted to do this, but remember that the entire purpose of creating the corporation is to separate your business life from your personal life. If the name of your company is the same as your personal name, you will be making it harder to prove your case later in a court of law.

Use your creative writing skills and come up with a corporate name such as those used by magazine writers today, including Write On, LLC, Imagine Media, LLC, and The Write Stuff, LLC. Try not to be corny, but do make sure your business title has something to do with the craft of writing. A good name will only enhance your professional appearance to the outside world, and it may even become an idea for a logo that you can create to go along with it.

Opening for Business

Once you have your business organized—from your home-office setup to your administrative and marketing materials, accounting software, and legal protections—it will be time to start seeking magazine-writing assignments. You could send out query letters willy-nilly to titles here and there, but a smarter approach is to take a step back and look first at the entire universe of magazines. After that, you can select the specific titles from which you are most likely to win assignments, and then you can plan a strategy to help you get your magazine-writing business established through repeated assignments from those titles and others. You will learn how to do all of that and more in Chapter 4.

Chapter 4

Magazine Markets

Now that you've organized your writing business and set your goals, it's time to take a look at the broader publishing marketplace you will be entering. There are thousands upon thousands of magazines with readers of all kinds around the world, and it's important that you understand not just which magazines you intend to work for, but why—and how you can use some titles to help you land even more work at others.

The Universe of Magazines

Most people who set out to become magazine writers think about seeing their byline and work appear in the pages of consumer magazines. These are publications such as *AARP The Magazine*, *Field & Stream*, and *Runner's World*, magazines that are written for a specific audience of consumers and that generally have well-known titles appearing on bookstore shelves all across the United States.

What a lot of writers don't know is that consumer titles are merely the best-known *type* of magazines, just as Earth is the best-known planet in our solar system. The universe of magazines is far bigger than just consumer magazines, and it includes everything from trade and academic magazines to technical titles and online publications.

All of these magazines need articles to fill their pages, and many of them accept queries from writers who are not staff members. As a magazine writer, you should consider the entire universe of magazines when deciding how best to sell your story ideas. It just plain makes sense: The more places you have to sell your work, the better chance you have of fulfilling the writing goals you defined for yourself in Chapter 3. This is true whether you want to write about women's fashion trends, hot-rod automobile restoration, or the sport of pole vaulting.

The best way to understand the entire universe of magazines is by breaking it down into broad categories and then looking at the kinds of writing that magazines in those categories tend to publish. Since most writers tend to want to work for consumer magazines, that's where you should start your exploration of the marketplace.

Consumer Titles

Consumer magazines, as mentioned earlier in this chapter, are titles written for specific audiences. Consumer magazines rely on their circulation of loyal readers to sell advertising, which companies buy because they want to reach those specific readers. A company that sells saddles, for instance, will want to buy advertising in *Horse Illustrated* because that magazine reaches consumers who need to buy saddles. The editors of *Horse Illustrated*, then, are looking to buy articles from you that will help them to keep their audience of readers, and in turn their advertising clients.

Magazines that fall into the consumer category come in all subjects, styles, and circulations, and their pay rates vary accordingly. Some pay writers as little as ten cents per word for an article, while others pay as much as $5 per word. In general, the highest-paying consumer titles tend to have the biggest circulations and best-known names, which means they also tend to have the most competition among writers looking to win assignments.

To give you an idea of just how widely varied the consumer-title segment of the magazine universe is, take a look at the following sample of topics and some of the consumer magazines that cover them:

- **Animals:** *ASPCA Animal Watch, Dog Fancy, Miniature Donkey Talk*
- **Art and architecture:** *American Artist, Architectural Digest, ArtNews*
- **Automotive:** *Car and Driver, Hot Rod Magazine, Petersen's Custom Classic Trucks*
- **Business/finance:** *Forbes, Hispanic Business, Rochester Business Journal*
- **Child care:** *Catholic Parent, Family Digest, Working Mother Magazine*
- **Entertainment:** *Dance Spirit, Home Theater, MovieMaker Magazine*
- **General interest:** *The Atlantic Monthly, Parade, Reader's Digest*
- **Health/fitness:** *Climbing, Muscle & Fitness, Prevention*
- **Juvenile:** *American Girl, Boys' Life, Highlights for Children*
- **Music:** *American Songwriter Magazine, Modern Drummer, Rolling Stone*
- **Politics:** *The Economist, U.S. News & World Report, World Policy Journal*
- **Religion:** *Bible Advocate, Christianity Today, Jewish Frontier*
- **Sports:** *Bowhunter, Cruising World, Inside Kung-Fu*

The list is long, to be sure, but it represents only some of the topics that consumer magazines cover, and only a fraction of the actual number of consumer magazine titles for which you might be able to write. It probably doesn't even include many of the titles you initially thought of when you considered a given topic. Sports, for instance, usually makes writers think of the consumer magazine *Sports Illustrated*. Yet there are countless others that need story ideas from writers like you every day.

There is also an entire segment of the consumer magazine market comprised of regional magazines. This segment includes titles like the following:

- *Alabama Living*
- *Cape Cod Life*
- *Florida Monthly Magazine*
- *Kentucky Monthly*
- *Mississippi Magazine*
- *Time Out New York*
- *Wisconsin Trails*

That list could go on and on as well, with multiple titles in each one of the fifty states, not to mention regional and international titles, too, such as *Blue Ridge Country*, which covers lifestyle along the mountain range that spans several states.

The point, of course, is that simply because you are a reader, you probably know more about consumer magazines than any other types of magazines. Most people read consumer magazines from the time they are young. At the same time, though, you most likely do not know just how big the actual segment of the consumer magazine industry is. That's something you need to learn as you enter the business of magazine writing.

QUESTION?

Where can you find a list of magazines that accept writing submissions?
Writer's Market is an annually updated book, more than 1,000 pages long, that lists book publishers, consumer magazines, trade magazines, and more. It is a trusted resource that most magazine writers keep on their bookshelf, right next to their dictionary.

Even more, though, you need to learn that this large marketplace of consumer magazines is only one among several segments of the entire magazine universe. Trade magazines are another segment, with plenty of titles you can pitch on all different kinds of story subjects, as well.

Trade Titles

Trade magazines, sometimes called trade journals or professional journals, often pay writers as well as consumer magazines do. But because trade titles don't have the massive public presence that consumer titles command, they are often easier to break into with story queries. In other words, they're a terrific place for new magazine writers to try to land their first assignments.

The point of trade magazines is to reach people working in a given field. The articles may be oriented around the lifestyles, business trends, or professional demands that those people face, but they are all centered on the field or industry itself.

A single issue of a banking trade magazine, for instance, may include a profile of a prominent banker, a story about trends in high-interest loans, and a feature about security issues that tellers face regarding robberies. All of these stories are slanted from different angles, but they have the common theme of banking running through them.

ESSENTIAL

If you want to write for a trade magazine, you need to be either an expert in the field the magazine covers or a good reporter who can delve deeply into the subject matter through interviews with industry experts. Trade magazine readers know their stuff, and they want down-and-dirty details more than cursory overviews in their stories.

Just as consumer magazines offer readers a wide range of topics in myriad ways, trade journals produce stories about a wide range of professions in all different styles. Here's a look at a handful of the topics that trade magazines cover, along with a sampling of titles from each topic area:

- **Aviation:** *Aircraft Maintenance Technology, Cabin Crew Safety, Professional Pilot*
- **Beauty:** *Cosmetics, Massage Magazine, NailPro*
- **Business:** *Contract Management, Executive Update, Portable Restroom Operator*
- **Construction:** *Automated Builder, Hard Hat News, Underground Construction*
- **Education:** *EarlyChildhood News, Teacher Magazine, Tech Directions*
- **Entertainment:** *BoxOffice Magazine, Dance Teacher, Southern Theatre*
- **Farming:** *American Fruit Grower, Onion World, Angus Beef Bulletin*
- **Finance:** *Banking Strategies, Mortgage Banking, On Wall Street*
- **Information Systems:** *Desktop Engineering, Game Developer, Journal of Information Ethics*
- **Journalism:** *American Journalism Review, Poets & Writers Magazine, Writer's Digest*
- **Machinery:** *The Fabricator, Practical Welding Today, Stamping Journal*
- **Medical:** *Continuing Care, Medical Economics, Podiatry Management*
- **Travel:** *Cruise Industry News, Motor Coach East, Vacation Industry Review*

As with the consumer magazine segment of the marketplace, you can see that the trade magazine segment is incredibly varied by topic, and even more widely varied when you drill down to specific magazine titles. Unless you are a doctor, for instance, you probably imagined that there were medical magazines out there, but not necessarily on the precision level that *Podiatry Management* might provide to the business of foot care.

The point, again, is that as a magazine writer, you need to expand your understanding of the magazine marketplace so that you will make good on every opportunity you have to sell your work. These opportunities extend even beyond the consumer and trade titles to the world of academic magazines.

Academic Titles

Academic magazines, sometimes called scholarly journals, are typically found in libraries, universities, and colleges. Some experts and students do subscribe to scholarly journals—doctors, for instance, use them to keep up on the latest trends in treatment, peer-reviewed studies, and pharmaceutical trials—but for the most part academic magazines are used as research tools. This is what sets them apart from trade magazines. While the trade titles typically have serious content, their tone is not quite as serious as that of academic titles.

For this reason, you usually need to be an expert in an academic magazine's field in order to land a writing assignment from an editor. For instance, some writers who start out writing medical stories for general-interest consumer magazines find that they need far deeper knowledge to write stories on the same topics for academic titles. Some writers even go back to school for a master's degree in their chosen field of writing, say, getting a degree in biochemistry so they can land more work writing for academic magazines that doctors read.

A look at the following sample of academic titles will give you an instant understanding of just how precise your knowledge must be to land work as a writer:

- *American Journal of Mathematics*
- *British Journal of Middle Eastern Studies*
- *Ecological Applications*
- *Ethnomusicology*
- *Harvard Studies in Classical Philology*
- *International Migration Review*
- *Japanese Language and Literature*
- *Journal of Applied Probability*
- *Journal of Computational and Graphical Statistics*
- *Systematic Botany*
- *The Journal of Blacks in Higher Education*
- *Yearbook for Traditional Music*

The readers who look to these kinds of magazines for information expect deep knowledge and expert insights, and as such the editors who make assignments are looking for writers who can provide more than just nifty nouns and verbs. You of course need to know your subject matter no matter what kind of magazine you work for, but when writing for a scholarly journal, you need to know it as well as the experts in the field itself. The same is true of pieces you may write for technical titles.

Technical Titles

Technical magazines are similar to academic titles in that they are read by experts in a chosen field. However, the content of technical titles is more about practical applications than it is about academic theories. Where an engineer may look to a scholarly journal for statistical information about how bridge building affects waterfront populations, that same engineer would look to a technical title for information about how to build the actual bridge using the newest construction methods.

Again, you're looking at a highly knowledgeable readership, and as such you will need to be an expert yourself in order to land writing assignments from technical magazines. As with the other segments of the magazine marketplace discussed so far, a look at a handful of the titles in the segment will quickly help to make this point clear:

- *Automotive Design and Production*
- *Biotechnology Progress*
- *Ceramic Bulletin*
- *Communications Convergence*
- *Defense News*
- *Drug Discovery & Development*
- *Electronic Publishing*
- *Medical Device & Diagnostic Industry*
- *Robotics World*
- *Scientific Computing*
- *Test & Measurement World*

Often, people who write for technical magazines are professionals within their fields. A top-name architect, for instance, may agree to write an article for an architectural technical title that explores the pros and cons of designing with a new form of building material in mind.

This again means that you as a writer must also be an expert on the subject matter if you hope to land an assignment from this type of magazine. If you have expertise in a complex industry and can offer information in a user-friendly format, then you have an excellent chance of breaking into these types of titles.

Online Titles

More and more magazines are launching every day without a print component. They exist entirely in cyberspace, generating all of their subscriptions and advertising revenue online. While they may look different from traditional magazines, their essence is the same: They need good writers and strong stories to keep their readers interested.

ALERT!

When writing for an online magazine, you not only have to know your subject matter, but you also have to be able to write in a shorter, blurb-friendly style as opposed to longer, feature-length pieces. People who read online want to see more than page after page of text. They want to point and click among various stories and topics.

Online titles span the various segments of the print-magazine industry, with some online titles being for consumers and others being trade-oriented or even technical magazines. What they all have in common, though, is that they need writers who can offer content in the format that Internet readers prefer: typically shorter sections of stories that link to other sections of the same story or even to additional stories produced by other writers.

Online-Only Magazines

It can sometimes be easier to break into writing for online-only magazines than into print magazines, for the simple reason that there is typically less competition. A lot of writers—particularly older, established, print-magazine writers—don't want anything to do with online titles. This opens the door for new magazine writers like you to gain some experience, albeit sometimes in return for a lower paycheck than you might find at a printed magazine.

Online Versions of Print Magazines

On the other hand, many printed magazines also have separate online versions with unique content—as do some television news channels, entertainment programs, and the like. Again, this means ever more opportunity for you to break into the field of writing and either stick with online titles or transition into working for the printed titles with which those online magazines are affiliated.

National Credibility

The prestigious National Magazine Awards recently added a category called "General Excellence Online," giving full credibility to the writers who are working in cyberspace. Its category definition is broad, perhaps because it needs to encompass the ever-changing world of online content. The award currently recognizes print magazine Internet sites as well as online-only magazines and Weblogs that have a significant amount of original content. A recent list of finalists included these online publication titles:

- National Geographic Online
- Beliefnet.com (spiritual)
- CNET.com (technology products)
- Men.Style.com
- Newsweek.com

Other online magazines include *Slate*, which has covered news, events, politics, and culture for the past ten years. Its longevity is proof that online magazines are here to stay. When you add its content to the widely varied subject matter of the online titles cited by the National Magazine Awards, you can see that there are plenty of topics being covered for online readers. As with all the other segments of the broader magazine universe, this means ever more opportunities for you, the writer, to sell your work.

Competing Titles

Now that you understand the broader universe of magazines, you may be tempted to think that you can write for every magazine that covers a subject you find interesting. For instance, if you are interested in boating but have no expertise in professional boatbuilding, you may decide that you want to write for the consumer titles *Power & Motoryacht*, *Yachting*, *Boating*, and *Motorboating*, but forgo pitching your articles to technical titles such as *Professional BoatBuilder*.

In reality, though, you likely would not succeed—because magazines within certain segments of the industry are constantly competing with one another for subscribers and advertisers. *Power & Motoryacht* competes with *Yachting* just the same way that *Motorboating* competes with *Boating*. The salespeople from these magazines tell their advertisers that they have the "best writers in the business," which means that if you're writing for one of these monthly titles, you aren't likely to be welcomed into the fold by its competitors.

FACT

Among consumer titles that have enthusiast specialties, such as needlepoint or horse racing, industry-specific advertising can account for more than 90 percent of the magazine's income. These magazines need every competitive edge they can get, including a unique stable of writers that is "better" than that of their competitors.

Who Competes with Whom

The issue of competing titles affects all different kinds of magazines, and in some circles it is more pronounced than others. Many weekly magazines, for instance, will buy stories from writers who work for their competitors—simply because they have to produce far more stories than do monthly magazines, and as such they need all the good article ideas they can get. Technical and academic titles, too, will often allow you to write for competing magazines because there are so few experts who know some subjects well enough to satisfy those readers. Even some consumer magazines won't mind if you write for their competition, though it depends on the magazine and the editors in every specific case.

What Competition Means to You

In general, you need to be aware of which titles compete with which other titles—especially in the consumer magazine segment—because once you end up getting a few bylines in one magazine, you may be shutting yourself out of writing for another. Your query to *Gourmet*, for instance, may be met with a response along the lines of, "Great idea, but we see you write all the time for *Bon Appetit*. If you will end your relationship with that magazine, we may consider giving you a chance at writing for ours."

This certainly will not happen in every case, but it's an element of the magazine-writing business that you need to take seriously because it will affect your chances of getting published and, in the end, reaching your writing business goals.

Creating Your Stable of Titles

Many successful magazine writers get around the problem of competing titles by organizing their own, personal stable of complementary titles. This allows them to research a topic once or become an expert in a few different subjects, but write about their ideas several different times from several different angles, thus boosting their bottom line by selling multiple stories.

You can see how this philosophy works by looking at the example of boating magazines in the previous section. Let's say you become an expert at covering the design of new yachts. You may become a regular writer who covers new-yacht launches for *Power & Motoryacht*, but who at the same time is able to rewrite and sell different angles of your stories—say, profiles of the yachts' owners—to a luxury lifestyle magazine such as *Robb Report*. And if you travel to boating destinations to do your reporting on these new yachts, you also might be able to come up with a good story pitch for a magazine like *Travel & Leisure*.

Those three magazines, then, would become part of your personal stable of titles, or the titles where you can put different spins on your work to sell it in different ways. Having a personal stable of titles makes you much more likely to earn a higher income, since you can report once and sell three or four times, instead of starting from scratch with new ideas and reporting work for every story idea you sell.

If you have dreams of becoming a six-figure freelancer, then you should think hard about what titles you can bring into your personal stable. Most of the top-earning magazine writers go back to the same titles again and again with their ideas, always re-slanting and refining pieces they've been paid to write for other titles in the past.

In many cases, you won't even have to look too far to find titles that complement your chosen titles nicely. With more and more corporations gobbling up more and more magazines these days, your editor at one magazine can often put you directly in touch with an editor at a complementary magazine—simply because they all sometimes work for the same parent company.

Using Corporate Consolidation to Your Benefit

Take a look at just a handful of the magazine titles that the Hearst Corporation owns:

- *Cosmopolitan*
- *Country Living*

- *Popular Mechanics*
- *SmartMoney*
- *Town & Country*

These five titles represent very different audiences, but their editors all report to the same parent company at the end of the business day. What this means to you, as a writer, is that if your editor at *Country Living* really likes a piece you write about the latest home-entertainment technology in country homes, then you may be able to get that editor to connect you with a colleague at *Popular Mechanics*, where you could re-slant your reporting for a feature about the science behind those newfangled entertainment systems. You do the reporting once, but you sell two stories. That's just smart business.

QUESTION?

Is it professional to ask your editor to put in a good word for you with another editor at a different magazine?
Absolutely, as long as the two magazines are not direct competitors. Getting a reference from an editor is just like getting a reference from any other colleague.

It all boils down to using corporate consolidation to your benefit as a magazine writer. Editors at one magazine certainly don't know every other editor at every other magazine that's part of the same corporation. Nevertheless, they definitely have more credibility with those other editors than you do, especially if you are just starting out in the magazine-writing business. One phone call from an editor who likes you at one magazine may be all it takes to land you a first assignment with another magazine. You can continue to build on your relationships with other magazines from there.

Remember Your Goals

If your goal as a magazine writer is to sell one or two stories a year, then this kind of networking may be more effort than you need to make. After all, you have no need to build up a huge Rolodex of editors if you only want to sell stories about your pet Fluffy to *Cat Fancy* now and again.

However, if you're looking to generate a steady group of editors who will listen to your story pitches, then there is no easier way to start than by using word-of-mouth recommendations to your advantage within a particular parent company's stable of titles. You might even be able to build your personal stable of unique, complementary titles while receiving paychecks from the same parent company again and again.

Make Your Connections

It all starts with your understanding of the overall magazine marketplace, which leads naturally to the next step of how you connect with that marketplace. Whether you already have the attention of the editors you want to pitch or you're starting from scratch with an editor who's never heard your name, you will need to send your ideas in the form of professionally written query letters—the format in which magazine writers submit pitches to editors every day.

Before you send those queries out, make sure you read Chapter 5. It explains where your query letters are likely to land, why you should follow standard industry formatting, the main messages you need to convey, and more.

Chapter 5

Query Letters

Writing successful query letters is as much of an art as it is a science. Your own talents as a writer will shine through in a great query letter, but they should do so in a regularly accepted industry format that gives the editor every piece of information she needs to quickly make her decision about your story idea. How can you write pitches that get accepted? What beginner mistakes must you avoid? That's what this chapter is all about.

The Editor's Crowded Desktop

Every successful magazine writer knows that writing great query letters is in many ways the heart of the job. The link between good ideas and paid writing assignments is the well-written query letter that grabs an editor's attention and refuses to let go.

Most magazine writers spend a good deal of time crafting their query letters. A lot of writers will spend a day writing queries only to "stick them in a drawer" for a night or two, then take them out, read them closely, and decide whether or not they are actually worth sending to editors. That's how important query letters are. Just as you have a process for writing great articles, you should have a process for writing great query letters.

FACT

Even the most seasoned magazine writers send query letters to their editors. Yes, they may be shortened versions of the real thing after the writer and editor have developed a longstanding relationship, but all writers earn their livings by pitching stories. If you stop sending queries, then you will stop earning an income.

Why do query letters have to be so fabulous? Because editors are bombarded with them the same way that Yankee Stadium is pelted with Jason Giambi's home-run hits: repeatedly and without fail. Receiving query letters is a certainty part of every editor's day. For some editors at the biggest, most prestigious magazines, though, receiving *dozens* of query letters is a part of every single day's work.

No matter how careful you are in your wording, no matter how great your story idea, your query letter will end up in the pre-existing and ever-growing stack on the editor's desk. You need to make sure it stands out by grabbing the editor's attention, keeping the editor's attention, and making the editor want to take a chance on your story.

And you must do all of that within a single page, and within the widely accepted format that allows editors to scan query letters quickly.

How Queries Are Formatted

At their most basic, query letters are, well, letters. They are letters that ask the question: Would you like to buy my story idea?

When you are writing a query letter, you are acting as a salesman. Your product is your story idea, and you want the editor to buy it instead of all the other story ideas stuffed into query letters on her desk. Even more important, you want the editor to see the value in buying your story idea *quickly*. With all of those other query letters piling up on her desk, an editor's slipping your letter back in the pile to "think it over" is often just another way of rejecting your idea.

One of the easiest ways to turn an editor off is by going against the standard, one-page format that writers have for years used in query letters. At its core, the format goes like this:

- Spectacularly written and compelling lead
- One or two paragraphs that support the lead and explain how the story would progress
- Your qualifications to write the story
- Your contact information, including telephone and e-mail

It all sounds very simple, but it's not. In fact, if a query letter were to be compared with anything else in sales, it would have to be the "elevator pitch" that so many businesspeople practice endlessly. It's the two-minute mini-speech that they can make about their product during the course of an elevator ride with a potential client. Your query letter is just like that, except you don't have the benefit of having your editor held captive in an elevator. You have to make your quick pitch in the face of myriad distractions and other sales pitches just sitting there, waiting to be read—and you have to get your pitch absolutely right, from the first word to the last.

Inside Query Components

A query letter usually includes a lead, supporting paragraphs, your qualifications, and your contact information. Take a closer look at the components of the query letter, and you'll see why each one is just as important as the next.

The Lead

Just as with articles that you write, your query letters need to capture the reader's attention right out of the gate. Only in this case, you have to remember that the reader is an editor—a person who has read far more stories than the average person and who requires far better writing and information to get excited at all.

Put yourself into the editor's job for a minute, and you'll see just how this comes to pass. Go to a bookstore, pick up a magazine that you don't usually buy for fun, and force yourself to read every word of every story in it. Then, close the magazine and start over from the beginning. When you get to the end, close the magazine and start again, reading the entire publication a third time.

Just when you think your brain is about to burst from boredom, pick up your own query letter and read the first sentence—which, if it's any good, will likely serve as the first sentence of your completed article.

You'll quickly see that for editors, your "must-read" lead is simply something else that they must read in the course of their day, which typically includes reading the same stories again and again, combing them for mistakes. This is not reading for fun, nor is it reading to get excited. As much as an editor may love her job, reading your query letter is just like reading everything else. It's work.

QUESTION?

Do editors prefer to receive query letters via snail mail or e-mail?
It depends on the editor. You can look in writing guides or even call the editor's assistant to ask what a particular editor prefers, but even if it's e-mail, use the same short format as written letters. Never, ever send an attachment. They get ignored as possible viruses.

So how do you write a compelling lead that will get the editor's attention? You start by using your writing skills—yes, those things that made you want to become a magazine writer in the first place. Right out of the envelope, you want that editor's eyes glued to your words.

Consider the following two query letter leads for a travel-magazine article, and decide for yourself which one is more likely to get an editor's attention.

The Generic Lead:

> "I am writing to propose a travel story about a hike that I took through Jamaica's Blue Mountains. It is a beautiful and rugged place where only the best hikers will be comfortable, because the peaks are so high and full of grandeur."

The Action Lead:

> "'Are you sure we're going the right way?' Tiffany calls. She's been on these trails before. Her first outburst of concern fuels the visions I've been harboring between heaving breaths for the past hour, of being the first flabby white woman to drop dead in the lush, hidden heart of Jamaica's Blue Mountains."

It's not even close, right? The first lead sounds like something you would write to your mother, while the second lead sounds like something that just may be the start of a story that actually deserves to get printed in a travel magazine.

What makes the second example so much stronger? It includes just three short sentences, but in those sentences you've communicated to the editor that your article will have characters, that there will be dialogue, that you actually visited the place, and that you have an interesting way of putting words and sentences together.

That's what a great lead does: It communicates on several levels through terrific writing. A great lead also makes an editor want to keep reading, to learn more about why she should choose your story to put into her magazine. That's where your supporting paragraphs take over.

Supporting Paragraphs

You can usually fit anywhere from one to three supporting paragraphs in a one-page query letter, depending on the length of the paragraphs. The shorter, the better, but the point of this section of your query letter is to establish that there is a lot of meat to your story idea—that it's more than just a clever lead followed by a bunch of nonsense that will make magazine readers give up and turn the page.

Supporting paragraphs can include examples of sources you intend to interview, of research you have already done, of facts and figures that make your story worth telling, or of anything else that you think will help sell your idea to the editor. In the case of the Jamaica action lead, you might have opened the supporting paragraph section of your letter by explaining that your death on the trail would have been horribly bad timing, given that the area is just now opening itself up for greater amounts of tourism that readers might enjoy.

ALERT!

Don't waste your time writing your entire article and sending it along with your query letter for the editor's consideration. Rarely will an editor pick up a story and put it into his magazine as-is. More often than not, editors want you to present them with an idea that they can help you shape into the format and tone their magazine requires.

Your supporting paragraphs should be just as well written as your lead. Moreover, they should be as informative as possible, even if sometimes that information comes at the expense of your writing style. Remember, you're a salesman here, not just a writer. You need to do more than leave the editor thinking, "That writer has an interesting way with words." You need to close the deal on a sale and get the editor to believe you are the right person to tell the story.

Your Qualifications

After your supporting paragraphs, you should take another short paragraph to explain why you are qualified to write the story you are proposing.

This can be a simple as saying, "I was the first writer invited to experience hiking along these Jamaican trails with local guides, and I can therefore tell a story that the world has never before heard." Or it can be more substantial, almost like a mini-resume: "I am a seasoned travel writer whose work has appeared in *Conde Nast Traveler, Travel & Leisure,* and the 'Escapes' section of the *New York Times.*"

FACT

Never lie about your qualifications in a query letter. Some writers say they have written for publications where their work has never appeared, with the notion that this "experience" will help land an assignment. More often than not, it only lands their reputation at the bottom of a heap from which there is no rescue.

No matter what qualifies you to write the particular story you are pitching, your continued goal is to make that sale. At this point, you should have the editor practically eager to pick up the phone and call you—which is where your contact information comes in.

Your Contact Information

The last part of your query letter should be a line that tells the editor how to reach you. Even if your contact information is at the top of your letterhead, you should include an ending paragraph of one or two sentences that tells the editor when the best time of day is to reach you, and which method of communication you prefer. You may consider enclosing a self-addressed, stamped envelope if you're using snail mail instead of e-mail, although nowadays, many editors prefer to respond by e-mail no matter how the query was sent.

If you are just breaking into magazine writing and have a day job where you cannot talk on the telephone about your story ideas, then you should tell the editor that the best ways of contacting you are during the evenings at your home or via e-mail any time of day. What you want to avoid is having that editor call you at work, where you will have to speak cryptically to avoid being overheard and will likely leave a terrible first impression on the editor—not at all ideal for your first attempted sale to any magazine.

Once you have finished crafting your query letter, do like the experienced magazine writers do and "stick it in a drawer" for a few days before sending it. Only after a few days' time can you take a second look at it with fresh eyes, at which point you will be able to determine whether you've included all the important sections and made the two key points that all query letters must make.

If you want editors to contact you via e-mail, then make sure you have a professional-sounding address. *HotBabe900@excite.com* may have worked for you in the past, but it's not what you want the editor of *Scientific American* to see in your query letter's contact line. Instead, try something like *JaneSmith@aol.com* or *ProWriter@comcast.net*.

Two Points You Must Make

Even if you have done a letter-perfect job of including all the pertinent sections of the standard query letter, your story may get rejected. Sometimes this will be because your idea just wasn't right for the magazine you pitched. Sometimes it will be because the magazine already has a story in the works that is quite similar to the idea you are suggesting.

Many times, though, you will get rejected if you fail to communicate the two most important things an editor wants to hear: that your story idea is great, and that there is nobody in the world but you who can write it.

It's a Great Story Idea

It can be tough to make an editor understand just how terrific your story idea is, especially since you can't very well gush out a sentence like, "This is a great story idea!" The key to communicating this fact in your query letter is using your lead and supporting paragraphs to tell the editor something he doesn't already know, and to say it in a way that he hasn't heard before.

One helpful tool in this challenging task is basic knowledge of the publication that you are pitching. If you know, for instance, that a travel magazine has not covered the island of Jamaica in more than a year, then your supporting paragraphs might include something like this: "*Traveler Overseas* has done many great stories in the past year, but never before have its readers been invited into the mysterious land of Jamaica's Blue Mountains." With a sentence like this, you are not only telling the editor that you have a great story idea, you're clueing him in that it's one his readers will be excited about because it offers them new information about an intriguing place.

ALERT!

If you have written a story for a competing magazine that is similar to the piece you are pitching in your query letter, don't mention the competing magazine piece. Even if it ran in one of the best-known titles in the world, you don't want your editor to feel that you are recycling "hand-me-downs," even if you're putting an entirely new spin on your reporting.

You Are the Person to Write It

You would be surprised how many query letters pitch essentially the same story ideas to the same editors. The average travel magazine editor, for instance, receives countless queries that read: "I've always liked the Caribbean and would be interested in writing a travel story for your readers." The writer has no qualifications beyond a desire to see the Caribbean. That's not making a good case for landing the writing assignment.

When you are outlining your qualifications to be the story's writer, be sure that you don't just tell the editor that you are *able* to produce the finished product. What you want to do, instead, is leave the editor with the understanding that nobody in the world except for you can write this story.

In some cases, your personal qualifications will be a function of the story. After all, if you're the only person ever to come out of hiking in Jamaica's Blue Mountains in one piece, then you are certainly the only person who can tell the story of that experience. Other types of stories are harder to pin down, though, such as how-to stories that anyone with general expertise may be able to write. The same is true of profile features that anyone with good interviewing skills could pull off.

There's no denying that a handful of unscrupulous editors steal magazine writers' ideas from query letters and give them to staff members to write free of charge. This is unethical and certainly uncommon at most legitimate magazines, but you can protect yourself against it by pitching stories that you, and only you, are qualified to write.

Should your idea fall into the latter category, simply do your best to tell the editor why you should be the one to tell the particular story. Sometimes, your best bet is simply to write something like, "I think my idea is perfect for your travel magazine, which is why I am pitching it to you first." In other words, if all you have on your side is timing and flattery, you have to use them to the best advantage possible.

Helpful Suggestions

There are a couple of other things you can note in your query letter to help increase your chances of actually landing an assignment. These things include the availability of accompanying artwork and suggestions for cover blurbs that the editor might run to promote your piece.

Where these items go in your query letter's structure is a function of how important they are to telling your story. But if you have them to offer, you need to let the editor know it. Some editors—especially at titles that rely heavily on newsstand sales—believe a sizzling cover blurb is more important than the actual story idea itself. Other editors may go for your idea because of the accompanying artwork, especially if your idea needs visuals from a place where it will be expensive for the magazine to send a photographer.

Artwork

If you have accompanying artwork available to go with your story idea, you must let the editor know what format the artwork is in and who owns the rights to it.

Sometimes, artwork is available in a tangible format such as 35-millimeter slides. More and more often, though, artwork is transferred to magazines digitally, and most magazines have standards of quality that allow them to use some but not all of the images they receive. As a general rule, if you have digital artwork available to accompany your story, define the quality of the images in your query letter. Something like this should suffice: "My images are 300 dpi resolution at 6 inches wide by 4 inches deep." This tells the editor how big the photos might run before the quality will be compromised.

Copyright information is also key when pitching artwork along with a story idea in a query letter. If you took the photos and own the rights to sell them, then you should say so, just like that. If you have handout photos from a travel company or marketing director, then you need to tell the editor in no uncertain terms that you are passing along art that came from a general source (thus alerting the editor that other magazines may have the same images in hand at the same time).

ALERT!

Even if you own the rights to a photograph you took of another person, many magazines will insist that you provide them with a "model release form." These forms are signed by the person whose photo you shot, and they give the magazine an extra layer of protection against being sued by the person for using their likeness in print.

One last word about offering your photos along with your story idea: Make clear in your query letter whether you are pitching your story idea and pictures as a package deal, or whether you will want to be compensated with an additional fee for your photography. In many cases, editors will try to acquire the story and photographs together, but at the same rate for which you would usually be paid for just the story.

If that's okay with you, no problem. But if you want to be paid for the additional content you are providing (as many writers do), then you should make your intentions clear in your query letter.

Cover Blurbs

Offering editors cover blurbs—the words that promote stories on a magazine's cover—along with your story idea is a terrific way to get their attention, especially if the magazine is heavily geared toward newsstand sales. In fact, some women's-magazine writers say they put their suggested cover blurbs right in the lead of their query letters, thus getting the editor to immediately envision how the blurb will look on the magazine's cover. These writers also know that many editors have to discuss cover blurbs in story meetings with their own bosses, and that editors appreciate writers who make their jobs easier by coming up with the cover blurbs themselves. This is a terrific psychological tidbit, one that you can use to your advantage no matter what topic you are pitching.

Beginner Mistakes to Avoid

There are a handful of mistakes that beginning writers tend to make when writing query letters. Any one of them can sink an otherwise perfect chance at landing a magazine-writing assignment. Here's a look at how you can avoid making the most common beginner mistakes in your own query letters.

Spell the Editor's Name Correctly

You would be shocked to learn how many magazine writers send letters to editors without verifying the correct spelling of the editor's name. Even a name as normal-sounding as Alex Smith can be spelled as uniquely as Alex Smyth. And how do you know if Alex is short for Alexander or Alexis? A letter that you address to Mr. Alex Smith might actually need to be addressed to Ms. Alex Smyth.

Never, ever, ever send off a query letter without verifying the spelling of the editor's name. If you can't find the name on the magazine's masthead, then call the editorial office directly and get the receptionist to spell the name for you. After all, if you can't even spell the editor's name correctly, why should she believe that you will get your facts right in a full-length article?

Enclose a SASE

This, of course, is a moot point if you are sending your query letter via e-mail, but editors who prefer to receive queries through snail mail also usually prefer to respond that way. They will not, however, take the time to go dig an envelope out of the magazine's supply closet, address it to you, and then find a stamp for it in order to give you a response.

If the editor likes your story idea, he'll probably e-mail or call you. However, if you're going to get rejected—or if you are sending materials that you want sent back to you after the editor reads them—then you must include a self-addressed, stamped envelope.

Pitch Stories, Not Topics

A lot of beginning magazine writers make the mistake of pitching topics in their query letters instead of actual stories. Consider the difference:

- "I would like to write a story about Jamaica."
- "I would like to write a story about a hike that I took through a previously mysterious section of Jamaica's Blue Mountains."

The first idea is for a topic, and it's not a story at all. It could be about anything, and it fails to give the editor a clear picture of what you actually want to write. By contrast, the second idea is quite specific about the actual story you hope to share with the magazine's readers. This is what editors want: as much information as possible about the idea you are trying to sell them.

Be Patient

There's nothing more annoying to an editor than a writer who sends a query letter, then follows up a day later with an e-mail that asks, "Did you get my query letter?"

Of course the editor received your letter. He put it into the stack of letters he received that morning, and he will get around to opening it just as soon as he has a free minute. It may be later that day, or it may be later next week. "My goodness," he's probably thinking. "If this writer can't wait a single day to hear back from me, she must be very needy. That doesn't sound like somebody I'd like to work with."

Most editors have no problem with your following up a few weeks after sending a query letter, just to check in and ensure it was received. But don't be a squeaky wheel about getting feedback too soon. Remember: You're selling yourself as much as you're selling your fabulous story idea.

Chapter 6

Cementing Your Base

After your query letters start landing you assignments, you will want to begin thinking about cementing your base—so that you can receive assignments from the same magazines again and again. There is no better way to do this than by getting your name onto a few mastheads, and perhaps even specializing in a field. You can also make yourself the writer of choice at some magazines by doing projects on a barter basis once in awhile and by networking constantly.

Getting on Mastheads

Any successful magazine writer will tell you that she has a few top clients—a few editors who consistently seek out her story ideas and even offer her features that editors conceive in-house. The value in such a relationship is that you, the magazine writer, have a relatively stable source of income. The very existence of the relationship means that you get to spend less time sending out query letters and more time actually writing magazine articles.

Most good writers seek to cement this kind of relationship by getting their name onto the magazine's masthead. The writer may be called a contributing editor, an editor-at-large, or even something more specific such as fabrics editor at a fashion magazine. The title you receive usually isn't the most important thing, though. What really matters is the fact that you will have promoted yourself from the ranks of "writers" to the level of "regular colleague."

FACT

It is a common misperception that all the people named on a magazine's masthead are staff members. In reality, many magazines have only a skeleton crew of full-time workers while most of their writers—and even some of their editors—are independent contractors.

Being a Go-To Writer

The difference is substantial, and something that you should not take lightly. Being a magazine's go-to writer, or writer of choice, means that you will be considered first for assignments. Some editors will even brainstorm story assignments with your skills in mind, crafting ideas that play to your talents. This is a boon for you both creatively and financially. You'll be getting more of the work you like, which translates into a happier existence, and you'll be getting more work in general, which translates into better pay.

How do you go about getting on a magazine's masthead? It truly depends on the magazine. Some editors are willing to make better deals than others, while other editors are bound by whatever details their corporate parent companies will allow them to suggest to you.

Following Accepted Protocols

You can ask to be put onto a magazine's masthead, but in some situations, this may be considered out of line. For instance, if you've written just one article for a magazine, it's probably not within the bounds of good behavior to ask your editor for a monthly column and a seat at the annual editorial-meeting table.

On the other hand, if you've written a half-dozen good articles for a magazine and are already functioning as the de facto "in the field" editor on certain topics or for certain sections, it doesn't hurt to ask your editor what the possibility might be of your name being added to the masthead. In some cases, the editor will even make the offer to you before you ask about the possibility at all.

Typical Masthead Deals

When you think about getting your name on a magazine's masthead, your first reaction might be to consider the prestige. You will officially be more recognizable and, hopefully, more valuable to that magazine than the other writers out there sending in query letters to the same set of editors. Well done, and excitement deserved!

However, when making the actual deal to put your name onto a masthead, you also have to stay cool and think in terms of business. The magazine obviously feels it has a reason to put your name on the masthead—perhaps you are well known in the field and can help to generate advertising revenue—and you need to make sure that you are compensated for allowing the magazine to get more mileage out of its relationship with you.

ESSENTIAL

If a magazine editor asks to include your name on the publication's masthead, don't yell "Yippee!" and celebrate. Instead, ask the editor what you will receive in return for allowing the magazine to use your name. Recognize the fact that in many cases, you will be helping to make the magazine more money and thus should be compensated accordingly.

Typical masthead deals include allowing the magazine to use your name in exchange for receiving a certain amount of work or pay. The magazine could promise you a set number of article assignments a year, or a monthly retainer, or a combination of both. It also might promise to include you at important editorial meetings where stories are brainstormed, or it might agree to pay your way to trade shows if you're an expert writing about a given industry. In some cases, you will even be offered reimbursed membership dues for magazine writers' organizations or for groups related to the topics you cover.

All of this sounds wonderful at first blush, but you have to remember that the magazine will want something in return for its largesse. Most often, editors will offer you these guaranteed assignments and benefits in exchange for your promising not to write for any of their competitors.

ALERT!

Usually, when your name is put onto a magazine's masthead, the deal includes a provision that prevents you from writing articles for that magazine's competitors. Be sure you take into account any work opportunities you will lose when deciding whether a magazine is offering you enough benefits to join its masthead.

Sometimes, agreeing not to write for a magazine's competitors is no problem at all. You may not be writing for them anyway, so you will have lost nothing by taking the masthead deal.

Weighing Your Options

In other cases, though, you will have to carefully weigh what income you will lose from other magazines—as well as the relationships you may be forced to give up with those other magazines' editors. If you find yourself in a situation where the risks outweigh the benefits, you may want to turn the masthead deal down and try to continue working for the magazine on a regular, query-letter-by-query-letter basis. Your goal is to continue getting as many article assignments as possible, but you want to do so in a way that allows you to control "Brand You"—your byline and the reputation that goes with it.

Controlling "Brand You"

Sometimes, magazines will put your name on their masthead without asking your permission—in some cases, after just one article. Many writers get excited when they see this, but the truth is that the practice is something about which you should be at least a bit concerned.

Remember: In most cases, magazines want your name on their masthead so that they can make more money. Advertising salespeople walk around with a copy of the magazine in hand, telling their clients, "Look, we have the best writers in the business! You should buy more ads with us!" This means that your name, "Brand You," is being used to increase sales for the magazine. You should be compensated for that with more than an editor's explanation about how "all writers get their name on the masthead."

New magazines, in particular, tend to put every writer's name on their masthead without asking permission, simply as a way of establishing credibility for the startup magazine itself. Again, though, if you think about this from a business perspective, it means the magazine is building its own reputation on the back of yours. That's something for which you should be compensated, through either a monthly retainer, a promise of steady work, or something else that satisfies your needs.

QUESTION?

Do magazine editors always ask permission before using a writer's name on a masthead?
No. In fact, some magazines ask writers to sign contracts that give the publication the full right to use the writer's name and likeness however, wherever, and whenever the magazine chooses—without asking the writer's permission, even if it's years after a story is written.

The main point to remember about getting onto magazine mastheads is that it's usually a good thing in terms of cementing your workload base, as long as you make your deals smartly. And, once you've landed on a masthead or two, you may even begin to think about further stabilizing your income by specializing in a field.

Should You Specialize?

This is a question that has dogged magazine writers for years. Some successful writers swear that they would never earn a decent living if they had failed to specialize, while other writers insist that specializing in one or two fields does nothing but close doors to countless other magazines for which you might like to someday write.

Which camp is correct? Probably both. As all writers are different, there are various paths to success that depend in large part on every individual writer's skills. However, in terms of the business of magazine writing, there are definite pros and cons to specializing that can be taken as general rules.

The Pros

The main reason many writers choose to specialize in a given field is to make themselves into "expert writers." When you're an expert writer, it means that not only will you be able to find work within your main genre of magazines, but also that any time any other magazine even touches on your topic, it will likely turn to you to write its stories as well.

A good example of how this works is with writers who specialize in movie reviews. The main market for this kind of writing may be newspapers, entertainment magazines, or even movie-focused Web sites. A movie-review writer may be able to land on a few of these media mastheads and develop a steady stream of work, a tidy little career in a specialized corner of the writing industry.

However, that's not where the work will end. A new movie about race-cars, for instance, may prompt that writer to do an article for a car magazine. A new movie about global warming may land the writer an assignment in an environmental magazine. A new movie about relationships may get the writer an assignment in a women's magazine. And, in many cases, the editors of those other magazines will seek out the writer, instead of the other way around, because the writer will be the acknowledged expert in the field.

Specializing in a field also makes you more likely to garner work that is ancillary to your magazine-writing income, such as technical editing, proofreading, and even public relations copywriting. It is not uncommon for expert writers to be approached by editors and even advertisers with offers of payment for simply "looking something over" to ensure its accuracy. This is not magazine writing per se, but it is valuable extra work because it will add to both your bottom line and to your reputation as an expert in your field.

If you decide to specialize in a field, be sure it is not one that is already crowded and, thus, highly competitive. There are a lot of writers out there who know about health issues, for instance, while writers specializing in environmental sciences are fewer and farther between. Expertise in the latter should get you more work with less effort.

The Cons

For many writers, the main downside to specializing in a field is the constant writing about that one given area. You may love food when you decide to specialize as a restaurant-review writer, but after your 5,000th article about the difference between linguine and macaroni, you may decide that specializing is a little bit, well, boring.

Basically, when you decide to specialize, you are often trading creative wandering for income stability. You are saying that you would rather ensure a steady stream of work from one area of expertise than follow your creative juices wherever they may lead you.

Specializing does not preclude you from continuing to send query letters wherever you wish, of course. At the same time, it usually does lead to enough work that you may find yourself so busy taking on assignments that you can't or won't make time to send out queries in other areas.

Is it smart to specialize in a topic where you will be the only expert, even if you don't like the topic?
Usually, no. When you decide to specialize in a topic, it should be one that you love. You will be writing about it, hopefully, for decades to come. All the money in the world isn't worth spending that much time on a topic you dislike.

If you find yourself lucky enough to become an expert writer on a topic that you really love, then specializing is often a very good way to go. Writers who fall into this category typically end up on the mastheads of the best magazines in their chosen area of expertise, and the writers become "hot properties" for other magazines should they ever decide to take their byline elsewhere. This is another form of income stability, something to be taken with due seriousness if you intend to make magazine writing your long-term career.

Working for Promotion or Barter

Ensuring that you have a steady stream of work from your favorite magazines sometimes goes beyond sending query letters and receiving story assignments. The editorial department is only one section within the magazine as a whole, and other departments—including marketing and advertising—often need content written for various uses.

In some cases, you can use this to your advantage by making deals that will cement your relationship with the magazine while at the same time giving you other benefits. You can offer to write content for other departments within the magazine in exchange for other things that you might need (instead of your regular paycheck).

FACT

At many magazines, writers are able to pick up extra work by writing advertorial and custom-publishing pieces in addition to editorial articles. If you offer to help out for free or for barter on one of these pieces and do a good job, then you may be first in line for similar paid assignments when they become available.

Trading Services

For example, let's say that you are currently receiving three story assignments each year from a magazine editor. The editor mentions that the in-house staff is overworked because the marketing department needs a dozen advertorial pieces (advertisements promoting the interests or opinions of corporate sponsors) written in the next two weeks. You offer to help write a few of the advertorials not for pay, but for something else that you need—say, some office supplies, an airline ticket booked through the magazine's travel service, or a free classified advertisement.

In some cases, the editor will not only take you up on your offer but will remember your generosity when it comes time to make actual story assignments later. You may lose a few dollars in the short run, but you'll have gained at least some form of compensation for your work and, more important, your editor's gratitude. Sometimes, you can even trade your one-time services for guaranteed future assignments—if you trust the magazine and believe the future work will actually materialize.

QUESTION?

Should you work for free on a one-time deal in exchange for more assignments in the future?
Probably not at first. If you have a longstanding relationship with a magazine's editor, then perhaps this is a nice way of saying "thank you" for years of business. But in general, you cannot depend on future assignments as payment for past work.

These kinds of deals also may work for you after your magazine-writing career is more established, such as if you write a book. You can look to trade your writing services for a comparable "payment" in free advertising for your masterpiece, and you will have laid the groundwork for such a deal by having worked successfully with the magazine on a similar trade or barter in the past.

Trading Your Time

Another good way to use trade and barter to your advantage is by offering to trade a certain number of work hours each month for a monthly stipend. You can make yourself available not just to the editorial department, but to all departments at the magazine. In this way you become a "Johnny on the Spot" who, in exchange for twenty or thirty hours of monthly service as needed, will receive a monthly stipend that's commensurate with the magazine's pay rates.

This type of trade will guarantee you a certain income month after month, even if editorial story assignments suddenly dry up. Deals like this also will help you to network throughout the magazine and beyond—another key to cementing your base.

The Importance of Networking

You may have a spectacular relationship with your editor, but editors do leave and go to other magazines. It's not a question of whether it will happen to you, but when. You have to ask yourself as far in advance as possible: How can I ensure my continuing relationship with the publication even if my editor resigns?

This is where networking comes in. The only way you can be certain that you will keep a magazine as a regular client is by doing good work that more than one person sees. Your own editor is, of course, your main contact, but if you know another editor or two, then you will be in a much better position for the long term.

It's paramount that you work directly with your editor and respect his authority in all matters. Networking does not mean "going around" your designated contact at a magazine. Instead, your goal should be to make additional contacts that complement your relationship with your editor.

If you know those editors as well as a few people in the marketing and sales departments, then you will be in even better shape. If you know all of those people plus a few of the magazine's key advertising clients, that's possibly all the networking that you will ever need to remain a magazine's go-to writer of choice.

Making Contacts

How can you make these contacts? The easiest way is by making yourself available for as many different kinds of assignments as possible. Let's say you write the television column for a technology magazine, but you also have some expertise in computers. It's a simple matter of a phone call to ask your television-column editor whether he can put you in touch with the magazine's computer-column editor so that you can pitch a few story ideas. Do a good job, and you'll have two editors on your side. Learn something about cell phones, and maybe you can pitch that editor, as well, to further expand your contacts within the magazine.

The same idea applies to working with a magazine's marketing and advertising departments, too. Most editors will have no problem with passing along key telephone numbers to you if you tell them that you are looking to land some more work by writing advertorials and marketing materials. You're already a friend of the magazine, after all, so you should be able to help out the other departments while meeting your goals for your own increased income.

Here are a few kinds of other work you can offer to do as a way of networking with various departments at a magazine:

- Proofreading
- Writing advertorials
- Writing custom publishing materials
- Writing PowerPoint presentations
- Fact checking

Working on advertorials and custom publishing materials (advertising materials that are geared toward a particular interest or consumer group) has a built-in networking benefit, as well. If you're writing an advertorial about one of the magazine's key advertisers, then you will have to work with that advertiser's marketing department to some extent—thus allowing you an opportunity to network with the point people at that company. This gives you a new level of sources through which to work when brainstorming editorial story ideas. You'll likely be in a position to hear about new products and services before any other writers, and thus you can be first to pitch story ideas about those products and services to your editors.

E ALERT!

Taking on public relations work for a magazine's advertiser is a good way to earn extra income, but be careful that your writing for the advertiser does not create an editorial conflict of interest. In most cases, you cannot be both a product's promoter and its editorial reviewer. Always keep your relationship with the magazine's editor as your top priority.

And so, while this kind of networking will help you cement your base by being a magazine's go-to writer, it also will help you expand your base to make the magazine's advertisers your clients, too. This is just plain smart, because it gives you additional income while making you even more valuable to the magazine itself.

Think about it from a business perspective. If a magazine's key advertisers respect you as a writer, they're going to say so to your editors, who will often be more likely to give you additional assignments as a result. It's a win-win situation, which is the best kind of business relationship you can have. It's the kind of relationship that not only cements the magazine as one of your repeat clients, it cements you as one of the magazine's go-to contributors.

Chapter 7

Assignment Letters

There are two key forms that you will likely deal with after landing a magazine-writing assignment. The first is an assignment letter, and the second is a contract. You'll learn about contracts in Chapter 8, but first it's important that you understand the importance of assignment letters. Some magazines offer lengthy assignment letters, others don't offer them at all, and still others fall somewhere in the middle. You need to know how to deal with each of these situations to protect yourself legally and financially.

What Is an Assignment Letter?

Assignment letters are just what they sound like: letters that outline your magazine-writing assignment. That's the simple answer, at least. The real answer is a bit more complicated.

The Evolution of the Assignment

Magazine assignments used to be made on a handshake and a smile. As you learned in Chapter 1, writers and editors used to discuss an idea, a deadline, and a fee, and then walk away with what amounted to a verbal contract for the writing assignment. Few people called it that at the time; most people said, "We have a deal" instead of "We have a contract." But for legal purposes, the deal was, indeed, a verbal contract.

Sometimes, a magazine editor will be responsible for sending you an assignment letter and a contract, or a combined version. In other cases, your assigning editor will send you the letter, while the magazine's managing editor will send you a separate contract. It's up to you to ensure that you receive all the paperwork you need to protect yourself.

Nowadays, with the ever-increasing reliance on attorneys to straighten out misunderstandings, businesspeople of all stripes pay much closer attention to contracts whether they're written or verbal. Professional magazine writers are no different, and they know that assignment letters are a form of legal agreement. Magazines don't call them contracts, but in fact, they in many ways are (or at least they are evidence of intent to form a legal agreement). This is why it is important that you take assignment letters seriously and understand what they should include.

Typical Contents

You will learn the specifics of what assignment letters should include later in this chapter, but for now, you simply need to know the difference between what magazines typically call assignment letters versus what they typically call contracts. In general, the difference amounts to the following:

- An assignment letter outlines what you are being hired to write, when your story is due, and how much you will be paid.
- A contract outlines who owns the rights to your work, describes what will happen if there is a problem with your story, and defines your legal relationship with the magazine.

In many cases, magazine-writing contracts will say that assignment letters are incorporated as part of one, overall legal agreement. Sometimes, the contract and the assignment letter will even be part of the same form. In other cases, you will receive a separate assignment letter and contract from the same editor, or the two different forms from two different editors. In still other cases, you will receive no contract at all and an assignment letter that is little more than a two-line e-mail.

None of these arrangements is necessarily any better than the next; it's just that different magazines have different organizational structures and, thus, different ways of getting paperwork to their writers. Practically speaking, though, it puts the burden on you to make sure you receive a proper assignment letter—or at least the key elements of one—so that you can protect your legal and financial interests.

Why You Should Insist on Them

You should insist on assignment letters for the basic reason that if you are going to do work, you deserve to get paid. An assignment letter—even in the absence of a contract—serves as legal proof that a magazine hired you to do a job and promised you compensation in return.

There are many reasons you should retain written proof of this arrangement. Sometimes you will need a copy of your assignment letter to straighten out a misunderstanding, while at other times you will need the paperwork to ensure that less-than-reputable editors make good on what they have promised you.

Does an e-mail count as an assignment letter?
Sometimes, yes. When an editor sends instructions to you via e-mail instead of on company letterhead, you should retain a printed copy of the e-mail in your records, alongside the magazine's writing contract, if there is one.

Interoffice Miscommunication

As with most offices, magazine editorial departments have communication problems from time to time. One editor thinks another editor is handling something when, in reality, it's not getting done at all. This is basic miscommunication. It's nothing sinister, but all the same you don't want it getting in the way of your getting paid for the articles that you write.

Let's say, for instance, that your regular editor sends you an assignment letter but fails to send a copy of it to the magazine's managing editor. The managing editor, who probably is responsible for making sure you get paid, has no written record of the amount to which you and your regular editor agreed. Thus, when you file your article on time and as assigned, you may have to offer the managing editor proof of your arrangement with your regular editor.

This sort of thing happens all the time, say, when one of the editors involved goes on vacation. Will the problem likely get straightened out on its own, even if you don't have a copy of your assignment letter? Sure—but perhaps not in time for you to pay your rent.

New Editors

Most magazines' editorial staffs are constantly changing. Editors come and go, with new editors stepping into a sea of agreements and assignments left behind by their predecessors. You want to make sure that you will still have the work you were promised even if the person who promised it is no longer with the magazine.

When you find yourself with a new editor, it can be immensely helpful to simply offer that editor copies of the assignment letters you already have received. The conversation might start something like this: "I've been working with the other editor for several years now, and these are the assignments I'm currently writing. I thought you might like to have records of them, so that you'll know what's coming from me even if there is no record of the paperwork on your end." In one shot, then, you will have introduced yourself, made clear that you are already working on the assigned articles, and presented yourself as someone seeking to be helpful to the new editor in charge. Not a bad way to begin a relationship at all.

Money Matters

Questions about payment crop up all the time at magazines, and an assignment letter can help to answer them quickly. As you learned earlier in this chapter, an assignment letter, even in the form of an e-mail, is written proof of a magazine editor's intent to hire you for a job. If that letter or e-mail states that you will be paid $700 for the job, then you have written proof of the contracted payment amount.

Some magazines pay "on acceptance" of your article, while others pay "on publication." When possible, insist on written acknowledgment that you will be paid "on acceptance," which is the day you complete your assignment. Otherwise, you may write an article in January and fail to get paid until the magazine decides to print it the following December.

You can easily surmise when this kind of written proof will be invaluable, such as when there is a disagreement with the accounts payable department. Again, the problem may be a simple misunderstanding, but at the end of the day, you want to make sure you get paid.

Deadlines and Kill Fees

Sometimes, a contract or assignment letter will state that if you miss your deadline, then you will not be paid the full amount for the article. Instead, you will sometimes be entitled to a "kill fee." Technically, this is the amount a magazine pays you if it "kills" your assignment, but it can also be the amount you may be entitled to if you fail to file your story on time.

FACT

Most magazine editors will give you an opportunity to file at least one revised version of your article before imposing a kill fee. Your revision usually does not have to be filed before your original article's deadline, but you may receive a new deadline that you have to meet for the revised article.

The easiest way to prove that you have made your deadline, of course, is to have a written copy of that deadline in your files—your assignment letter. That way, if an editor tells you that you will be receiving a kill fee instead of your full compensation even though you submitted your story exactly when the editor wanted it, then you can point to the assignment letter as proof that you made your deadline and demand your payment in full.

Requests for Revisions

One of your obligations when you write a magazine article is to assist your editor with revision requests. It's rare for an editor to receive a story—even from longtime, highly successful writers—and put it directly into the magazine's pages without at least asking a few questions or wanting a few changes to the copy.

There is a difference, though, between editors who ask for revisions to a story and editors who ask for an entirely *different* story after you fulfill the original assignment. If you fulfill the original assignment as stated in the editor's assignment letter, then all you should have to do before publication is assist with revisions. You should not have to write an entirely new story from a wholly different angle, unless the editor intends to pay you a second story fee.

If you find yourself working with an editor who seems to constantly change her instructions about what your story should include, then you need to refer to your assignment letter and point out that you have already completed the job as it was assigned. In some cases, the editor may force you to take a kill fee instead of being paid in full for your work. Unfair, certainly, but it's usually a far better financial option than spending weeks or even months revising a story countless times for an indecisive editor.

ALERT!

Some editors, often those who are new to the business, will ask you for a story about apples and then decide—after you've written it—that they really want a story about oranges. This is bad assigning on the editor's part, and it does not constitute a reasonable request for revisions. Your assignment letter will help you prove that you met the editor's original request.

What Assignment Letters Should Include

Now that you understand just how important assignment letters can be in different situations, it's time to take a look at everything they should include. Different editors handle the assigning process in different ways, but whether you receive an e-mail or a three-page document on company letterhead, you should look for the following things in your assignment letter:

- The date the assignment is being made
- The working title of the assignment
- The word count for the story
- The general outline and/or suggested content of the story
- The names of any specific sources your editor wants you to contact
- Your deadline
- Instructions on where and how to file your story
- The payment amount and terms
- The kill fee

Breaking It Down

If you receive your assignment letter via e-mail, then the date will be time-stamped on the file and the working title will likely be in the subject line. Again, a more formal approach is better for your purposes, but even this most basic kind of written information will be helpful to you should a problem arise later.

Most editors consider a story's requested word count to be a guideline, not an exact number that you are expected to hit. If your assignment is, for example, supposed to be a 1,200-word story, you should do as most successful magazine writers do and file anywhere from 1,200 to 1,300 words, thus giving the editor a bit extra to work with but not so much extra that the editor has to spend hours editing your piece to fit the allotted space.

FACT

It is common practice among magazine writers to file about 10 percent more copy than an assignment letter requests. Editors typically appreciate the "room to edit," and adding 100 words to a 1,000-word piece is usually not very time consuming for the writer. Do note, though, that filing less than a requested word count is frowned upon.

The Content Section

The section of the assignment letter that outlines the actual story will be key to your records if your editor begins to request rewrites that are far more complex than standard revisions. If you have any questions at all about what the story should contain, or about the tone or structure it should take, then you should ask those questions in writing and then staple your editor's written response (i.e., a printed-out e-mail) to your assignment letter for clarification purposes.

A typical content section of an assignment letter for a parenting magazine might read something like this: "As we discussed on the telephone, your profile feature will be about Donald Trump, one of the most successful real-estate moguls in American history. You will interview Mr. Trump and his wife at their Florida residence and focus your interview not on

Mr. Trump's business practices, but instead on the couple's experience as new parents. Your feature should include details about their day-to-day schedules as they relate to the new baby, and should offer insights that other parents might find helpful for balancing their own work and home-life needs."

Note how this description clearly states that you should *not* focus your story on Mr. Trump's business practices. This is the kind of detail that will help you give the editor exactly what she wants, and that also will help you defend your choices should unreasonable revisions be requested.

You can change the focus of your story after receiving an assignment letter, but only with permission from your editor. If you stumble upon something that you think will make a better angle, then you should contact your editor and ask whether changing the story's focus is warranted. If possible, get a revised assignment letter.

Your Deadline

Your deadline is just that, a deadline. Not a guideline, not a sort-of-when-it's-due date, but a deadline. If you miss it and the editor wants to hold you to it, then you can be paid a kill fee with no questions asked about the content of your story itself.

Most successful magazine writers don't just make their deadlines; they beat them. Filing a story a few days in advance is an excellent way to get on an editor's good side, especially if you send your story with a note that reads, "I know this piece isn't due until Friday, but it's a holiday weekend coming up, and I thought you might enjoy having a few extra days to consider any revisions you might want."

Whether you meet or beat your deadlines, be sure you note them the day that you receive your assignment letter. For longer assignments or cover features, you may have several deadlines, including one for a first draft and another for a final draft. These simply allow the editor to see that you are making progress on your reporting and writing, so that the magazine is not left in the lurch when expecting a major centerpiece feature from you.

Filing Instructions

Also be sure to look closely at the section of your assignment letter that tells you how and where to file your story after you complete your assignment. Of course you will need to send a copy to your editor, usually via e-mail. In some cases, though, you also will need to send a copy of your story to a managing editor or an executive editor.

FACT

Most magazine editors want writers to submit their articles via e-mail as Microsoft Word documents. However, some magazines request special formatting, including margins and spacing that are different from the software's default settings. Pay close attention to these requests in your assignment letter, and ask for help if you need it.

When you are instructed to send your story to a second editor, it usually means that your assigning editor handles the words that go into the magazine, and a managing editor or executive editor processes invoices and works with the accounts payable department. That second editor likely needs a copy of your story to trigger the payment system so that you can get paid. If you fail to send the copy, your story may appear in print before your payment request even gets put into the accounting system.

Payment Details

Your payment amount is just what it sounds like, and it should be written as a dollar figure in your assignment letter. In the same section of the letter, you should find the payment terms, which include notations about whether you will be paid for your work on acceptance or on publication.

As previously stated, "on acceptance" is a better deal for you as a writer because you will be paid as soon as you complete the job. If you agree to be paid "upon publication," the magazine can hold your story as long as it chooses, sometimes more than a year, without advancing you a single penny.

If your assignment letter does not include your editor's contact information, then be sure to ask for it at the time the assignment is made. That way, you will have no problems down the line if you are filing close to deadline and have last-minute questions.

When Your Editor Won't Write One

Sometimes, an editor will tell you that he doesn't like assignment letters. No matter how politely you ask for one, he simply won't give it to you. Some editors just prefer to work out the details of a story in a conversation either in person or over the telephone, and that's the end of that.

Now, there's nothing wrong with a long, detailed conversation about an upcoming magazine-writing assignment. You can ask questions and even propose angles and leads, just to make sure you and your editor are thinking about the story in the same manner. Most writers actually prefer working through story ideas this way, in anticipation of notes from the conversation being turned into an assignment letter eventually.

However, there is a problem with your failing to receive any written assignment letter at all, even after the most detailed conversation in the world. As you have learned throughout this chapter, an assignment letter is a key resource and tool should problems arise with the editor later.

Taking the Initiative

What can you do if you run into an editor who just refuses to write you an assignment letter?

The easiest and least-confrontational path is to send the editor an e-mail in which *you* outline the assignment for *him*. It could read something like this: "Thank you for your time on the phone today. I would like to make sure we're on the same page about my article, '101 Ways to Train a Ferret.' My piece will have a general introduction followed by 101 bulleted items featuring ferret-training tricks and methods. I will quote several professional ferret trainers throughout the piece as well as rely on my personal expertise training my own ferret, named Floyd. The total word count will be 5,000, and I will file the story by June 15, 2008. My fee will be $3,500, payable upon the article's acceptance. The kill fee will be 30 percent of that $3,500 amount if my story is not accepted."

Wait for your editor to reply with his agreement of your assessment, or with notes about any changes he would like to see in your description of the story, and then print out your original e-mail attached to his reply. You've got your written assignment letter for your files, albeit with an extra step on your part.

Following Up

If the editor refuses to reply to your e-mail, then you can send a follow-up note a few days later. Do not call, which invites a verbal instruction instead of a written one. Rely on e-mail instead, telling the editor that you would like to get to work on the story assignment immediately but that you are awaiting his reply to your e-mail just to make sure you are doing everything the way he wants it done. Usually, this will be enough of a nudge to get even the most anti-assignment–letter editor out there to reply to you in kind.

ESSENTIAL

While it is important that you get the written information you need before beginning a magazine-writing assignment, it is paramount that you ask for it politely. Be honest with your editor about your desire to have a proper assignment letter, but do not take a hostile tone. Your relationship with the editor is key to getting future assignments.

Assessing Your Risk

Sadly, there will be times when an editor simply will not reply. For whatever reason, the editor will not want the assignment's details to be in writing. If you find yourself in this situation, then you must decide whether you want to risk doing all the work of the assignment without even a basic written promise of compensation.

Should this situation arise with an editor you know well and have worked with many times before—say, a last-minute piece she calls you about and needs first thing the next morning—then you may want to go ahead and do the work. After all, you will have a good history of working with the editor and, hopefully, a good record of being paid on time.

However, if you end up in this situation with an editor or a magazine that is new to you, then you definitely should think twice about taking the assignment at all. More than a few writers tell horror stories about completing 2,000- or 3,000-word articles for magazines that later refuse to pay them, and it can be a long, frustrating battle to get a magazine to make good when you don't have a written assignment letter as legal proof of your deal. These kinds of problems can occur with startup magazines and long-standing titles alike. If you're working with an editor or a magazine for the first time, be especially wary about working without an assignment letter.

Additional Concerns

The same thing goes for dealing with contracts, which are more complex today than they have ever before been in the history of magazine writing. Chapter 8 continues this discussion of protecting your legal and financial rights. There you'll take a look at some of the clauses you are likely to find in the contracts that accompany your assignment letters, and you'll find some suggestions for modifying typical clauses to make the contracts you sign more writer-friendly in general.

Chapter 8

Negotiating and Signing Contracts

The contracts that editors ask magazine writers to sign today are more complex than ever before in the history of publishing. Writers are being asked to shoulder more risks and to give away more rights, usually without being offered additional pay. You don't need to be a Harvard-trained lawyer to protect your financial and legal interests, but before you sign anything, you do need to have a basic understanding of how magazine-writing contracts work.

Contracts 101

At their most basic level, magazine-writing contracts are about the owner-ship of rights. When you put pen to paper, or start tapping away at your keyboard, you are not just writing a story; you are creating content that, according to United States law, you automatically own. The law protects newly created works through the legal mechanism known as copyright. You need not register the words you write in order to possess copyright. It is automatically assumed the minute you create new content.

ALERT!

You do not have to register your stories with the United States Copy-right Office in order to possess copyright, but registration does afford you additional rights should someone steal your work. Look for more detailed information about copyright in Chapter 10.

This means that, by default, you own the rights to the stories you create as soon as you create them. And, if you want to sell your stories to maga-zines, you need to give the magazines the legal right to publish your copy-righted work.

If a magazine simply took your story from your computer's hard drive and printed it for the world to read, the action would be a form of theft. You have to give the magazine permission to publish your copyrighted work. Contracts make this possible. They are the written permission to publish that magazines require.

Historically, contracts allowed magazines to publish a writer's story once. After the magazine published the story, the ownership of the story reverted to the writer, who was free to sell the story again, in part or in whole, to who-ever would buy it.

Today, magazines often demand far more rights, sometimes for the entire copyright throughout eternity. The difference from previous contracts is massive, especially considering that writers often are paid no more for the entire copyright than they were paid for one-time use permissions.

First North American Serial Rights

First North American serial rights are the traditional standard in publishing. When you sell these rights to your story, you are giving a magazine the right to print your work first in North America, before any other serial publication (a.k.a. magazine).

FACT

If a magazine fails to send you a contract before publishing your work, then legally, your arrangement with the magazine is understood to be for first North American serial rights. A magazine without a signed contract that transfers copyright cannot successfully claim that it owns your story outright.

When you assign first North American serial rights to a magazine, you are basically saying that the magazine can be the first to print the story, but that it will then give you back the right to publish the same exact story however, wherever, and whenever you choose. This is the best possible deal for a magazine writer to make. It means that you not only get paid for having your story published, but that can sell the story again later for additional income.

Time Limits

Sometimes, magazine contracts will assign a time limit to the purchase of first North American serial rights. A typical contract clause may read like this: "The first North American serial rights shall be considered exclusive until the last day of the month in which the article is published in the magazine, or until one year from the date the magazine receives the completed manuscript, whichever occurs first."

This means the magazine has a year to publish your story, and if it fails to do so before a year passes, you can sell your story elsewhere—even if the magazine still intends to publish it. This time frame also guarantees you the right to use the story however you'd like the month after the story appears in print, even if that month comes before a year has passed.

The Upshot

Both of these contract stipulations are good. They set a limit on the amount of time the magazine can "sit" on its right to publish, thus guaranteeing that you will be able to re-use your work before it becomes too old and stale to sell elsewhere. These are the sorts of deals that professional magazine writers seek out.

Work-for-Hire and Hybrid Contracts

If a contract does not deal exclusively with first North American serial rights, it will probably be either a work-for-hire contract or some combination of first North American serial rights and work-for-hire. Work-for-hire contracts, sometimes known as all-rights contracts, are far less friendly to writers than first North American serial rights deals. Unfortunately, they are also becoming far more common.

Work-for-Hire Contracts

Work-for-hire contracts stipulate that the story you are writing is a work the magazine is hiring you to create, as opposed to a work that you are creating and "lending" to the magazine. The difference is important because it involves the ultimate ownership of copyright. When you sign a work-for-hire contract, you are essentially agreeing that the magazine—not you—will own the story's copyright from the minute you send in your manuscript.

Practically speaking, this means extra potential income for the magazine and less potential income for you. Here's why. If you own the rights to your article, then you can sell it several times—or at least use your reporting to craft several similar stories for multiple publications. If the magazine owns the rights to your article, then you can never sell it again. You write the piece and then have to move on to reporting and writing a new piece if you want to receive any additional income. That's more work by you for the same amount or even less pay over time.

The magazine, on the other hand, can use the story as many times as it wishes. It can repackage it as custom-published brochures and sell it to advertisers after already having printed it for subscribers. Some magazines repackage stories into anthologies and make more money from them in bookstores. The Internet is an ever-growing source of revenue, too, which a magazine can easily capitalize on if it owns all the rights to your story—and never has to share the wealth that the story generates over the long term.

QUESTION?

Why would any writer sign a work-for-hire agreement that gives away total copyright to a story?

To earn a paycheck. More and more magazines are insisting that writers sign these agreements. If a writer won't sign—even a longtime, well-known writer—the magazine looks to work with someone else who will. Work for hire is becoming a cold, hard fact of the magazine-writing business.

For these many reasons, professional magazine writers often refuse to sign work-for-hire contracts. Refusal does come with consequences; in some cases, writers end up never again working for some magazines. However, some writers say their refusal to sign is akin to taking a moral and ethical stand. They believe magazines are hindering their ability to earn a living, and they believe magazines—or, more accurately, the corporations that own them—are acting not out of fair business practice but out of pure greed.

Hybrid Contracts

Sometimes, you will receive a contract from a magazine that intermingles the language of first North American serial rights and work-for-hire deals. An editor may explain to you that even though the work-for-hire language is in there, the magazine really is buying only first-publishing rights, but that those rights come with a few added usage options for the magazine.

Don't be fooled. If a contract is not strictly for first North American serial rights, then you are giving away something else that likely is of financial value. You may not understand your pocketbook loss at the time you make the deal, but you likely will see the lost opportunities over time, as the magazine finds new ways to re-use your story to generate earnings.

Scary Clauses to Consider

Whether a magazine's contract is for first North American serial rights or a work-for-hire deal, it often will include other clauses that have less to do with copyright and more to do with legal issues. You need to take these very seriously, as they can have implications for you long after your story is published.

The culture of lawsuits in the United States has made many magazines leery of carrying the risks that go along with publishing (odd, since that is their chosen business). In many cases, magazines are trying to push the risks associated with publishing onto their writers, usually for no additional compensation.

This risk-management shuffle will most often come to your attention as part of your writing contract. Not every magazine asks writers to sign clauses like those described in the following sections, but enough magazines do that it's important you understand exactly the position you are putting yourself into by signing.

Indemnification

Indemnification clauses deal with the question of who will pay the attorneys' fees if someone files a lawsuit against the magazine because of a story you wrote. If a magazine-writing contract includes an indemnification clause, the magazine is usually insisting that you pay your legal bills in addition to the magazine's legal bills in the event of a court action.

A contract's indemnification clause takes effect the minute a lawsuit is filed against the magazine. The lawsuit could be frivolous and completely without merit, yet you will still be responsible for defending yourself and the magazine in court.

How an Indemnification Clause Reads

A typical indemnification clause reads like this: "The author will indemnify publisher against, and hold publisher harmless from, any and all losses, costs, and expenses (including attorneys' fees) incurred by publisher with regard to author's work." Notice that the clause states nothing about whether a legal action is valid or not. It only states that you, the writer, will pay for everything should anyone file a lawsuit against the magazine, for any reason, in response to your work.

Arguments For and Against

Now, a lot of writers feel that demanding this kind of financial commitment from them is ridiculous—especially in exchange for a mere $500 or $1,000 magazine-writing assignment. Considering that legal costs can quickly run into the tens and hundreds of thousands of dollars, that's quite a big risk for a writer to take for a single job.

On the other hand, many editors argue that if a writer does something that triggers a court action, the writer should be the one to deal with the consequences. Magazines usually have lawyers on retainer to protect their staff members, but those protections usually do not extend to writers who create articles on a freelance basis.

The Main Point

The practical upshot of the argument is that you, the magazine writer, need to be cautious about signing contracts that contain indemnification clauses. If you work as an S-corp or a limited liability corporation (as discussed in Chapter 3), you should have some protections that may keep your personal assets intact in the face of a lawsuit (check with your attorney about your personal situation). On the other hand, if you work simply as an individual, signing contracts with your personal social security number, then you may find yourself—and your life savings—wholly on the line should things go wrong after your story appears in print.

If a magazine will not let you cross out an indemnification clause in a contract, you can at least ask to insert the words "by judgment sustained." This means that you agree to pay all legal expenses—but only if a court rules in the plaintiff's favor against you and/or the magazine. It's at least some protection, if not an ideal solution.

Third-Party Promises

Another clause that has begun cropping up in magazine-writing contracts is the third-party promise. This clause goes hand-in-hand with the indemnification clause in that it basically promises the magazine that your work will not infringe upon the rights of anyone who might later file a lawsuit.

How the Third-Party Promise Clause Reads

A typical third-party promise clause reads like this: "The author agrees that the work will not violate or infringe upon the copyright or other intellectual property rights of any third person or entity, and that the work will not violate any agreements made by any third person or entity."

Arguments For and Against

From the magazine's standpoint, this clause means that you are agreeing that what you write won't step illegally on anybody else's toes. At its most commonly understood level, this type of clause deals with plagiarism. You are promising the magazine—as well you should—that you have not violated any other writer's copyright by using content without permission.

FACT

Plagiarism is one of the biggest offenses a magazine writer can commit. You will not only lose your paycheck for a particular assignment, but you will often suffer irreparable harm to your reputation throughout the magazine industry. Just don't do it.

There are other implications to third-party clauses, though, and some writers believe they are drastically unfair. Consider this example, first cited in Chapter 3: You quote a company's marketing director about the production of a new kind of adhesive fastener, only to find out later that the scientist who invented the fastener did not give the marketing director permission to take the news public.

Knowing Where You Stand

Now, you have to ask yourself, is there any way you could have known that a marketing director—a person whose job it is to work with writers like you—had stolen the details of his own product's creation before making them public? Of course there's no way for you to know every single detail of every single deal that your sources make with other people. There's not even a way for you to know which other people your sources talk to in general.

And yet, a third-party clause makes you promise that you do know such things, that you are omnipotent, that "the work will not violate any agreements made by any third person or entity."

This is sticky stuff at best, meant to protect the magazine further in the case of a lawsuit. Ideally, you will be able to cross third-party clauses out of any contracts you sign. If you can't cross them out, then you should at least add the words "to the best of the author's knowledge." That is a much fairer representation of where you stand after a good-faith effort to do your job professionally.

Using Your Likeness

Some magazine-writing contracts include clauses that give the magazine "the right to use your name, likeness, and work, or any portion thereof, in conjunction with the promotion of the magazine or any affiliated publications including, but not limited to, promotions for upcoming issues that will include the work, circulation solicitations, advertisements for the magazine, and year-end reviews and anthologies of the magazine."

Now, a lot of those uses of your name and photograph may seem perfectly legitimate to you, but notice the short phrase in the middle: "including, but not limited to." What this phrase tells you is that the magazine is taking the right to use your name and photograph however it wants, whenever it wants, for all time.

Your byline is your calling card in the magazine-writing business. You want to ensure that your name and likeness are used only with your permission and only by publications that are reputable. Do not give away unrestricted rights to your name and likeness, even to a magazine you work with frequently.

Consider a case in which you sign a contract with one of these clauses, only to find out later that the publisher uses unscrupulous business practices that make you look bad with your editorial sources. Even if you disassociate yourself from the magazine and refuse to ever write stories for it again, the magazine has written permission from you to continue using your name and likeness as it sees fit, in perpetuity. Whenever possible, avoid signing such clauses. It's important that you protect your reputation as a writer.

Research Ownership

Here's a clause that could cost you a lot of money: "Author agrees not to permit anyone else to publish or use the work or any portion thereof, including any background information, research, or other materials developed in conjunction with the work, for any purposes."

Basically, what you're agreeing to if you sign this clause is that you will not use any of your reporting—whether or not it is actually published—for any reason, ever. This means that if you interview fifteen sources over the course of three weeks, and the magazine agrees to publish just one portion of one interview, that you can never use the rest of your research to create other stories for other magazines.

The magazine's thinking is that it wants to keep anything even similar to your story out of the hands of its competitors. But from your standpoint as a writer, this means doing an awful lot of work that never receives compensation. Whenever possible, strike this clause from your magazine-writing contracts.

Previous Contract Revisions

Magazines that you work for more than once may eventually send you a contract that begins by stating something like this: "This agreement supersedes all past and future agreements."

The explanation from the magazine will be that it has begun using a new form of contract, and it wants you to sign it just as all the other writers are being asked to sign it.

From your perspective, though, what this line in a contract does is nullify all previous contracts you have signed, thus forcing you to re-negotiate the rights to everything you've ever written for the magazine in the past.

QUESTION?

Are "all past and future" clauses necessarily bad?
No. If you can negotiate a better deal with the contract on your desk, and then ensure that it applies to all previous contracts you have signed with a magazine, then you will actually come out ahead. It can be hard to keep track of such details, though, so be cautious.

Pay close attention to the changes the new contract requests. In particular, be sure that before you sign such a clause, you are not giving back rights to the magazine that you retained for yourself in previous agreements. At the least, be sure to ask for compensation if the magazine is taking something new from you, even if it's on a story you completed long ago.

Credit Clauses

Once in a while, a magazine contract will include a clause that reads like so: "You agree to ensure that the magazine will receive suitable credit such as 'First published in *Our Magazine* in 2007' upon the exercise of any of the rights retained by you in the work."

This clause may seem innocuous at first glance, but again, don't be fooled. You want to retain your rights so that you can re-use your reporting and writing to sell more stories. What magazine is going to publish a story if it has to give credit to another magazine in the process? Strike this clause whenever possible. It effectively eliminates the value of any rights you are retaining.

How to Negotiate Effectively

Rights issues and scary clauses are a fact of the magazine-writing business. If you want to succeed in publishing your work, then you need to know how to negotiate contracts just as effectively as you write articles. The main thing to remember is that you do not have to accept any magazine's contract, ever. You are making a business deal, and if the terms of that deal are too stiff to bear, you can walk away.

Having said that, the reality of publishing nowadays means that you will often have to negotiate for the best deal you can get if you want to get published at all. The following sections describe some ideas to help you succeed, or at least to tone down the magazine's most unreasonable demands.

"The Other Contract"

A lot of magazines have two different contracts, one for new writers—full of demands—and another for long-time writers who refuse to sign the more demanding deals. Sometimes, if you are handed a work-for-hire contract, you can simply ask for the first North American serial rights contract. It just may exist. Problem solved.

Making Your Case

Even this superficial introduction to contractual issues may give you a better understanding of the clauses in the paperwork than your editors have. Many editors simply pass along contracts that they receive from their magazine's legal department. They often don't even know what the contracts demand. If you explain to them calmly and professionally why you have a problem with certain clauses, the editor will sometimes become your advocate and help you to negotiate fairer terms.

Expanded Usage

If a magazine insists on retaining exclusive rights to your work, as opposed to first-use rights, then you can bet the publication intends to use your work in multiple ways. Do your best to figure out what these expanded uses are. Does the magazine intend to reprint your article for sale to advertisers? To publish it on a Web site?

When you know how your story might be used, you can say very politely to your editor, "You're going to use my story in the magazine, but then also run it on the Web, where you're generating tens of thousands of dollars in advertising revenue. I'm not ever going to get a cut of that extra income, so I think you should bump up my pay a bit right now, on the front end." A good number of magazines will cough up at least an extra few hundred bucks in the face of this argument, so it's well worth making.

Limited Exclusivity

Should a magazine insist on forcing you to sign a work-for-hire contract, you might be able to negotiate a non-exclusivity clause into it. This means that you are, in fact, giving the magazine exclusive rights to do whatever it wants with your story forever, and in any media, but that after a certain time period, you also get the right to use the story.

You can often accomplish this by simply adding a time limit to the clause that defines the magazine's publication rights: "Author grants magazine the exclusive right to publish the article in any issue of the magazine before it is published in any other form by any other party. *For one year after publication* in magazine, the magazine has the exclusive right to publish or reprint the article in any other media."

The short, italicized addition to the clause means that after a year has passed, the magazine no longer has exclusive rights to your work. This means that you can sell your story again, in part or in whole, however you like.

When to Walk Away

Sometimes, a magazine's editor will not negotiate a proposed contract at all. This is not a personal vendetta against you or writers in general. Rather, it is sometimes magazine policy, and the editor has no choice.

Always, always, always try to negotiate a better contract for yourself. You may fail more often than you succeed, but every legal protection and copyright that you retain is a victory for you in the long run.

Should you sign, or walk away? The answer truly depends on the situation. Writers in desperate need of paychecks sign onerous contracts every day. Some writers who dream all their lives of writing for a certain magazine will sign whatever contract they must in order to see their byline in print. Still other writers—successful professionals—simply make judgment calls about how likely their articles are to incite lawsuits and then sign away rights accordingly to land good-paying assignments. Only you can determine when you should walk away from a contract, based solely on your personal level of comfort with the deal.

When to Use an Attorney or Agent

In some cases, you can put a businessperson—an attorney or literary agent—in between you and the magazine, to act as your business representative. Usually, this happens with brand-name writers and long cover features in prestigious publications, but you too can find a middleman to handle negotiations if you're willing to pay the (often steep) price.

One thing attorneys can help with is the purchase of errors-and-omissions insurance. These policies can offer you at least some protection should you be forced to sign indemnity clauses and third-party promises, but the policies are expensive, usually at least several thousand dollars a year. Because of their cost, the policies are not a viable option for most beginning magazine writers.

In most cases, simply using what you have learned in this chapter will protect you fairly well from the most insidious contract clauses. If you can afford an agent or an attorney, that's all the better for your cause, but don't feel that you must hire a middleman in order to negotiate a fair deal from most magazines. Stick up for yourself, and make the best agreement you can with every story you sell. Nine times out of ten, everything will work out just fine.

Chapter 9

Juggling Multiple Assignments

Now that you're landing assignments and signing contracts left and right, you need to look at the big picture of how you're going to get all of your work done. Being a magazine writer means being your own boss, which includes setting deadlines, treating all of your clients appropriately, and shifting priorities when necessary. This chapter will help you learn how to meet your commitments—a task that can be much harder than it sounds.

A Successful Magazine Writer's Day

It's hard to define what a "typical" magazine writer's day is like from minute to minute because most writers have their own systems for getting things done. Some writers do their best work well before sunrise, so they wake around 4 a.m., work until noon, and give themselves the rest of the day to relax and perhaps catch up on paperwork. Other writers prefer to sleep in, starting their days around lunchtime and working well into the night, long after editors in most time zones have gone home for the day.

Still, no matter what hour-by-hour schedule magazine writers keep, most successful writers in the business accomplish the same things during the course of their day. These tasks include everything from writing new query letters to invoicing clients, but in most cases the bulk of a writer's day is filled with, well, writing.

ESSENTIAL

It doesn't matter what time of day you write, but you must be available to your editors—at least by cell phone—during normal business hours. Keep in mind that all of the magazines you query will not be in your own time zone, and allow a few hours on either side of the nine-to-five period for phone calls.

If you break down the actual writing that most professionals do in a single workday, you see that some days are a juggling act, while other days are more like a long-distance marathon.

Juggling Acts

The days that feel like juggling acts to professional magazine writers are the days when there are multiple deadlines to be met. As the old saying goes, "When it rains, it pours." Never does this feel so true as when five queries get accepted and are all due to different editors on the same exact day.

On a day with multiple deadlines, you may spend various amounts of time writing a combination of editorial items, such as:

- A 1,000-word article for Magazine A
- A 200-word blurb for Magazine B
- A more fully fleshed-out query for Magazine C
- An author's biography (about yourself) for Magazine D
- A 500-word column for Magazine E

That would be a productive day, to be sure, but it's definitely a typical day in the life of many successful magazine writers. The challenges with this kind of assignment juggling are multifold, including having to switch gears from writing long paragraphs to short blurbs. You also have to go back and forth between individual magazines' styles and tones as you write different items for different editors. If you're used to working on one project at a time, for one boss with one set of standards, this is a pace that might take some getting used to.

Long-Distance Marathons

At other times, you will find yourself spending hour after hour writing one thing for one magazine's editor. Perhaps it will be a 2,500-word feature, or even a 5,000-word cover article. Sometimes, crafting these kinds of pieces will require several days' worth of your time in a row, making the writing process feel like a long-distance marathon.

It can be difficult to find the psychological stamina for writing such articles, especially if you're used to shorter assignments. Keeping your focus and making steady progress might require some mental adjustments.

Structuring Time

With these varying workload demands, successful magazine writers often find themselves structuring their time with as much care as they might structure an article.

When working on longer pieces, it's important to maintain your focus. A quick trip to the refrigerator or the mailbox can be the beginning of a string of distractions that will prevent you from making your deadline. Stay mentally sharp, get the job done, and you'll win more plum jobs in the long run.

You, too, will have to do this when you find yourself with a stack of successful query letters. You will have to set aside blocks of hours, if not days, to devote to certain projects. You will have to know your own pace, and you will need to be realistic about your tendency to daydream so that you can build in enough additional time to complete all of your work to the satisfaction of more than one editor. And you will have to do it all while ensuring that every single one of your editors feels as though she is your *only* editor.

Every Client Is Your Only Client

Any good businessperson will tell you that getting a customer is only the beginning. Keeping the customer is the really tricky thing, and it is what will pay off in the biggest dividends over the long haul.

The writing business is no different. Your editors, and the magazines they create, are your customers. After you've landed your customers with terrific query letters, you need to work on keeping them so that you can garner more and more assignments. You can do this the same way most other businesspeople do: by making each one of your clients feel as though he is truly special.

How many editors might a successful magazine writer have?
A professional writer has at least a dozen, sometimes with a few coming from a single magazine. A writer who expands her magazine writing into books and marketing materials will have even more editors, perhaps twenty or thirty over the course of a year's work.

Different Clients, Different Needs

Now, editors are people, and all people have different personalities. What you have to do for one editor to make her feel special is likely to be different from what you have to do for another editor to get the same result.

For instance, some editors feel as though they're your favorite client if you simply answer the phone whenever they call. In their minds, they may have a vision of you sitting in your home office, waiting by the headset, eager to talk to them and only them. (Well, maybe it's not that extreme, but they will feel much more important than they do with their writers who make them leave voice messages during working hours.)

FACT

Making an editor feel that you are always at the ready when he needs you is a surefire way to keep him as a long-term client. A lot of times, editors have last-minute assignments to parcel out. If they know they can reach you easily during working hours, they are likely to call you first for those jobs.

Other editors require more attention if you want to make them feel as though they are your only client. This can include anything from daily e-mail exchanges to friendly weekly calls to sending holiday cards in December.

These actions, on your part, are more assertive than responsive (like answering the phone would be), but some editors enjoy the idea that you are reaching out to them consistently. It makes them feel as though they are always at the front of your mind, like they are your most important contact out there in the magazine universe. This sense will carry over to all of their interactions with you, including reading your query letters. They will feel as though you got an idea for a great story and didn't even think about giving it to any other magazine.

Tips and Techniques

There are many ways to make every one of your editors feel as though he or she is your only editor—like you are always working with them in mind even if you have no currently pending assignments. Sometimes, you actually will be doing this, while at other times you will simply be working on maintaining your relationships. Both are key to keeping your go-to writer status while working for multiple titles.

Here are some tried-and-true techniques that successful magazine writers use to make editors feel special:

- E-mailing a copy of a timely news story with a note that reads, "I saw this and thought that we could spin it into a good angle for the magazine."
- Calling or e-mailing with interesting news or gossip about the industry the magazine covers
- Referring to the magazine's audience as "our readers" in all your correspondence with an editor
- Remembering your editors' birthdays, children's names, and other significant personal information
- Dropping in for lunch from time to time, if only to catch up and brainstorm future story ideas

These may sound like small potatoes in the grand scheme of things, but every little bit helps.

Setting Your Own Deadlines

Of course, all those "special feelings" won't get you very far if you don't get your work done, too. Juggling editors and assignments also includes juggling deadlines—and since none of your editors will know what the other ones are doing, it will be up to you to ensure that you don't get overloaded with too much or too little work at once.

E ALERT!

Many new magazine writers understand how to juggle assignments when too many come in simultaneously, but you also must remember to spread deadlines out so that there will always be work on your desk. Making sure that your deadlines are properly spaced will also ensure that your paychecks arrive with some degree of regularity.

Sometimes, you won't have a choice about your deadlines. There are drop-dead dates in every publishing schedule, and if an editor wants your story to run in a particular issue of a magazine, then your deadline will have to conform to the pre-existing publishing schedule. You will be in a take-it-or-leave-it situation when it comes to accepting the assignment, no matter what other work you may already have agreed to complete.

In a lot of cases, though, you will find that editors have some leeway in the deadlines they can give you—which, in turn, can allow you to in effect set your own deadline schedule. This is key to being a successful magazine writer because you can space out your deadlines for various assignments and allow yourself enough time to give each story your very best effort.

QUESTION?

How much time do editors usually have between your deadline to them and their deadline to the printing press?
It depends on the magazine. Sometimes magazines work months in advance of on-sale dates, while in other cases the editors will be getting your stories at the actual last minute.

You just have to be savvy enough to know which editors you can ask for more leeway, as opposed to the editors who always work up to the last minute and don't have deadline flexibility built into their schedules.

When You Have a Choice

It should be pretty easy for you to figure out which editors have flexible deadlines after your first or second assignments for various magazines. You never want to miss a deadline, of course, but your first conversation with an editor about deadlines will likely be a good indication of whether there is any room for due-date negotiations.

Some editors actually appreciate your honesty when negotiating deadlines. If you tell them up front that you have a busy week ahead and will need a few extra days to complete your assignment, they will be spared any surprises when your story comes in those extra few days later than originally planned. That gives them the ability to adjust their own schedules accordingly.

If you realize that you are going to miss a deadline, contact your editor immediately—hopefully, at least a few days before the due date. You should never, ever wait until the day a story is due to tell your editor that it will be late. It's unprofessional and shows that you can't balance your own workload.

When you have a choice of deadlines, space your work out and always give yourself a few extra days to allow completed stories to "sit" before you turn them in. If you finish a story, put it away, and then go back and look at it a day or two later, you will almost always find mistakes you can correct or improvements you can make. Having the extra time to "self-edit" while still meeting your deadline will save your editor work and make him more likely to hire you again in the future.

If You're Overloaded

All of those beautifully crafted query letters may just land you more work than you can handle at once. This embarrassment of riches may sound like a good thing, but in reality it can be incredibly stressful.

Three editors each waiting on the same afternoon for three different full-length features is an awful lot of pressure for any writer of any experience level. It's called overload, and you have to know how to handle it.

The easiest way for you to avoid assignment overload is to begin working on stories well before they are due, at least a week in advance. That way, you will never face a blank computer screen on a deadline day when you have several editors expecting multiple articles about different topics.

If you find yourself in assignment overload, the first thing you should do is make an honest assessment of your situation. You may be the type of person who can pull an all-nighter and crank out every last word you need to before your deadlines hit. On the other hand, you may be the type of person who can handle only one story at a time, perhaps two stories a day, tops. Only you know which description suits you best, and thus how you are likely to fare at a crunch time.

All-night writers can get the job done, of course, but if you're one of those, you should remember to allow some time off the following day or two, if only to recharge the creative juices. If you're one of the slower writers who simply won't be able to finish on time, then you should immediately contact the editors whose deadlines you're going to miss. They may be upset—rightfully so—but better that they know as soon as you do, early in the day, instead of at 4:59 P.M. when they're getting ready to fire you altogether.

If you must call an editor to renegotiate a deadline on the day a story is due, offer to have the work done as soon as possible—ideally, the next day. Do not call your editor and say the work isn't done on time. Look to the future and set a new deadline that you will be certain to make.

Some writers avoid deadline overload by noting the due dates for their articles on a month-view calendar. This is a great visual aid because you can literally see the assignments "stacking up" as you list them on the same date. More than three magazine deadlines on one day is probably a sign that overload is in the offing. You'll be able to tell editors at the time the assignment comes in that you already have two other deadlines on the day they suggest, and then you can offer a new deadline that fits better into your schedule.

Keeping Updated To-Do Lists

Another technique that many writers use for avoiding deadline overload is keeping updated to-do lists. These are similar to the grocery lists you may keep on your kitchen refrigerator, reminding you of things you need to pick up at the store. In the case of to-do lists for writing, the information starts out in your computer.

Start by creating a Word document that you can save on your desktop or in another location that you visit every day. The idea here is not to make a to-do list that you update from time to time, but instead to create a list that will be a daily, almost constant reminder of the work that needs your attention first.

FACT

If you don't have a file location on your computer that you look at every day, then you can print out your to-do list as a Word document and keep it on top of your physical desk, crossing out items as you go and then updating your electronic file once or twice a week.

There are a couple of options for organizing your to-do list. One option is not necessarily better than the next; you simply need to determine which method fits with your particular writing style and schedule.

Listing Assignments by Date

Listing assignments by date can be helpful, even if you already note assignments on the dates they are due on your calendar. Why? Because while the calendar notations will help you ensure that you don't get yourself into a deadline crunch, the to-do list will help you prioritize the work you need to do on any single day.

Here's how a to-do list might look if organized by date:

- "Women Who Love Carbs," for *Glamour*, 2,000 words, due 7/6
- "Yard Work That Burns Calories," for *More*, 750 words, due 7/15
- Requested, researched query about fad diets for *Redbook*, due 8/1
- "10 Best Butts in Show Business," 100 words per profile, for *In Style*, due 8/17
- "Raising a Daughter with a Good Body Image," for *Parenting*, 2,000 words, due 9/1

Notice that there isn't much detail in each line. The listings are just the basics, reminders of sorts that will keep you focused on the assignment you have due next. You will be able to update this kind of list easily—simply deleting the line at the top when you finish the work—and you can refer to your assignment letters for specific details about the actual assignments themselves.

Listing Assignments by Publication

Some writers prefer to keep their deadline dates organized by using their calendar, while at the same time keeping a to-do list that helps them see the overall scope of the work they have promised to various magazines at once. Again, this is no better or worse than any other method. It's just a different technique that may work better for you—especially if you typically work for only a few magazines but have several assignments pending with each at any given time.

A to-do list organized by publication might look something like this:

- *Car and Driver*: Review of new Mazda, review of new Honda, blurb on hydrogen engine research
- *Road and Track*: Feature about Route 66 restoration, self-profile and photo for contributors page
- *Consumer Reports*: Story about pricing on hybrid cars, queries for upcoming story-planning meeting, blurb about new car-cleaning product

Having a solid understanding of the total workload you have already accepted is just as important as knowing which stories are due first. This is because when good last-minute opportunities arise, you want to be able to jump at them.

Making Time for Valuable Last-Minute Work

Magazines are fluid entities. Their page counts vary from month to month in keeping with the amount of advertising that gets sold. Editors usually have a good idea, based on previous years' ad sales, of how many editorial pages will be needed for any given issue. But from time to time, an issue will shrink or grow at the last minute—and the editor will have to rush to cut or add additional articles to the editorial mix.

QUESTION?

Do editors keep stories in reserve to fill in last-minute holes?
Many editors do, and most call such stories "evergreens." The name refers to the fact that the stories never go stale because they have no timeliness hook, like evergreen trees that keep their good looks throughout the seasons. This makes them ideal for filling last-minute editorial holes.

This is the time when you may get a frantic phone call from an editor with whom you have worked before—and you want to be ready to respond, to keep your go-to writer status. Knowing what work is already on your plate, and what you have coming up, will be key to deciding on a moment's notice how you can best squeeze in another assignment.

Answering the Call

Ideally, you will be able to respond to your editor's last-minute request during that initial conversation, after a quick glance at your calendar and your to-do list.

However, if you're already up to your eyeballs in assignments, you may need a few hours to try to shuffle some other deadlines around. There's no harm in this as long as you are honest with your other editors.

Shuffling Things Around

Simply call the one who is most likely to negotiate a new deadline with you, tell her that there's a last-minute writing opportunity you'd like to take, and ask whether you can please move back your deadline on her story by a day or two. Most of the time, you'll be able to keep all the work you have and squeeze in the new story assignment—again keeping all your clients happy.

Having Resources Ready

The easiest way to ensure that you can answer last-minute calls from desperate editors is by having your resources ready. Think for a minute about what your resources might include as a professional magazine writer:

- Past articles you have written
- Notebooks full of research from previous assignments
- Transcripts of previous interviews
- Materials handed out to you on press trips
- Bookmarked Web sites

All of these things can be incredibly helpful to you in completing a last-minute assignment quickly—if, that is, you know where everything is at the actual moment you realize you need it.

Time Is Money

Having your resources ready—your files neatly organized, your notes labeled and dated, your handout artwork alongside important press releases—will be key to helping you juggle assignments effectively. The less time you have to spend looking for resources to complete an assignment, the more time you will have to actually write stories, and thus the more stories you can agree to take on.

Knowledge Is Power

Knowing what you have on hand will also help you to determine whether you should take on a last-minute job at all. If you know you don't have all the information you'll need to satisfy an editor's last-minute request, then you can estimate the amount of time that will be required to actually get the job done.

Fitting that necessary amount of time into your existing schedule then becomes a simple question of the hours in the day. If you know your editor needs the last-minute story in the next five hours, but that it will take you seven hours to complete the research to write it, then you will know not to waste your editor's time by accepting the job. Most editors appreciate this level of honesty.

Chapter 10

Copyrighting Your Work

As you learned in Chapter 8, a copyright automatically protects your writing the minute you create a story. However, there are additional—and potentially important—protections you can garner if you take the time to register your work with the U.S. Copyright Office. The process is relatively inexpensive and can be quite simple if you know how it works before filling out your first set of forms.

Copyright Basics

A copyright is a legal protection for writers who produce what the government calls "original works of authorship." Magazine articles certainly fit into this category, as do screenplays, books, and even musical arrangements.

You can copyright your articles whether they are published or not, as your copyright begins the minute a work takes "fixed form." In the case of magazine articles, this usually means that copyright begins when you create a Word document and use the "save" key function on your computer.

The protection of copyright prevents most other uses of your work without your express, written permission, but there are exceptions. For instance, if your story is an idea that you have not yet written down, then it is not protected by copyright because it is not in a fixed form. And, even if your work is in a fixed form, others may be able to use parts of it without your permission.

FACT

The "fair use" doctrine is an exception to copyright law. Basically, it allows other people to use small portions of your copyrighted work within their own creations, such as quoting a paragraph from a book that you wrote. Another exception is any work you do for the government. This is usually placed automatically in the public domain.

The Copyright Symbol

When the 1976 Copyright Act became law, it required the use of the copyright symbol for protected works. That symbol is a C inside of a circle, most often shown like this: ©.

Today, the use of the copyright symbol is no longer required to establish that a copyright is in effect, though some writers still use the symbol if only to make clear that they understand the value of their work and will not stand for copyright infringements. You will learn in this chapter how making this understanding clear can be beneficial later on, if your copyright is violated.

How Long Copyright Lasts

Any magazine article that you write today will be protected by copyright from the time that you create the work until seventy years after your death—unless you assign the copyright to someone else, such as an heir, or sell all your rights to the work to a publisher. If you coauthor a magazine article, the copyright will last until seventy years after the last surviving author's death, or until there is a similar transfer of copyright to a third party.

Copyright lasts longer on articles you write under work-for-hire contracts. In those cases, the copyright lasts ninety-five years after initial publication, or 120 years from the article's creation, whichever time period is shorter. Again, though, because you will have signed a work-for-hire contract, the copyright will not be yours. It will belong to the magazine that hired you to write the article.

QUESTION?

Can you get your copyright back after you give it away or sell it to a third party?
Yes, but only during certain windows of time and after following specific notification guidelines. Usually, you will need the help of an attorney who specializes in copyright and trademark law.

Changes in Copyright Law

From time to time, the U.S. government enacts changes to copyright law. You can keep abreast of important changes that may affect you by reading notices from professional writers' organizations such as the National Writers Union or the American Society of Journalists and Authors, or by reading the *Federal Register*, which is published daily by the National Archives and Records Administration. You can find links to the Federal Register at the official Web site of the U.S. Copyright Office at *www.copyright.gov*.

Why Bother to Register?

The first question most magazine writers ask regarding copyright is this: "If the articles that I write are automatically protected by copyright from the minute that I create them, then why should I bother to fill out forms and pay the government a fee to actually register my work?"

The short answer is that if you don't want to, you don't have to. Your work will still be protected to a large extent. The longer answer is that if you take the time to register your work, you will enjoy additional legal and possibly financial advantages in the years to come, whether your copyright is ever violated or not.

Your Rights to Sell

As you learned in Chapter 8, when you give a magazine the right to publish your work, you are essentially loaning them the use of your copyright. This is why copyright is most important to magazine writers—it allows you to earn a profit from the words that you put down on the page. There are other things that a copyright allows you to do, though, and as time goes by you may find it important to have legally nailed these things down:

- To translate your work into a foreign language
- To convert your work for another use (such as using an article as the basis for a motion picture)
- To prepare a derivative work, such as incorporating your article into an anthology

Again, copyright is not an end-all, be-all, but the protections it does provide are essential to helping you to earn a living as a magazine writer. After you create a work, you own it for a certain amount of time before it goes into the public domain. This is, quite frankly, your time to use what you've created to earn a buck, and to allow your heirs to continue collecting until the copyright runs out. Making sure you have protected all your options, including the option to defend yourself fully against copyright infringements and to demand appropriate compensation, is a valuable tool in continuing your own personal magazine-writing business.

Your Rights to Sue

If someone violates your copyright, you can file an injunction or a lawsuit whether you have registered your copyright or not. Your failure to register your work with the U.S. Copyright Office does not, in any way, take away your right to pursue legal action against a violator.

However, if you took the time to register your copyright within ninety days of publication, or at least before the copyright infringement occurred, you can qualify for statutory damages in addition to actual damages. This makes it much more likely that you will actually be financially compensated for the theft of your copyrighted work. In some instances it makes it more likely that an attorney will agree to take on your case in the first place.

E ALERT!

Proving actual damages—the amount of money lost by a violation of your copyright—is a difficult task. This is why you want to register your copyrighted work. If you do, then you will be eligible for statutory damages, which require proof only that your copyright has been violated, not that you have actually lost future income.

Statutory damages can range from $750 to $30,000 per copyright infringement, and they can go into the low six figures if a judge rules that someone willfully violated your copyright (that is, that the person didn't make an honest mistake but instead simply ignored your copyright symbol or statement of "all rights reserved").

Again, statutory damages are available *only* to writers who register their works with the U.S. Copyright Office, making the actual registration fee a worthwhile investment in protecting your future rights.

All of the above should make it clear to you that if you take the business of magazine writing seriously, then you should protect yourself by registering your articles' copyrights. The good news is that the process is relatively simple. You can, in most cases, find everything you need online.

Finding Forms Online

The official Web site of the U.S. Copyright Office, *www.copyright.gov*, includes an easy-to-use toolbar across the top of its home page. One of the links is labeled "Forms." This is where you should find everything you need to register your work, including a schedule of applicable fees.

QUESTION?

What does it cost to register a copyright?
The U.S. Copyright Office raised the registration fee for Form TX (which covers most magazine articles) from $30 to $45 starting on July 1, 2006. The office asked for the increase in order to cover what it called general rising expenses.

When you click on the "Forms" link, you will be directed to a list of all the forms that are available as downloadable PDFs. All of these forms are viewable with Adobe Acrobat Reader, and you can print them out if you would like to send them in via snail mail. "Literary Works" is the first batch of forms you will be able to choose among, and the form most often used by magazine writers, Form TX, is at the top of that list. Click on the link, and the form you need should open on your computer screen.

Form TX

Form TX is only two pages long, which makes it easy to follow and fill out. It asks for information such as the following:

- The title of your work
- The name of the magazine in which it was first published (if published at all)
- The year you created the work
- Your name and contact information

All of these items are easily understandable, even if you're registering a work for the first time. There is no need to worry that you will need expert assistance when filling out Form TX, though there is an online version of the form available with line-by-line instructions, should you want to follow them.

Short Form TX

There is also a Short Form TX that you can use if you are the sole author of the work and the work does not contain a substantial amount of material that has "been previously published or is in the public domain." In most cases, a magazine article will fall into this category, and you will be able to file Short Form TX, which is only one page long. However, if you intend to also file Form GR/CP (see below), you will have to revert to using the two-page Form TX.

Form GR/CP

An additional form, called GR/CP, is also in this section of the U.S. Copyright Office's Web site. It can be filed as an addendum to Form TX, allowing you to submit a group of works at once instead of filling out multiple copies of Form TX.

This is the form that most professional writers use to register their works, and usually they do so on a quarterly basis. It's easier to register several articles at once, and—as you will see—it can be quite cost effective as well.

The Benefits of Filing Quarterly

There are three main benefits to filing your forms on a quarterly basis with the U.S. Copyright Office: You will be more likely to remember to actually file, you will save money on mandatory filing fees, and you will file within the time limits required for demanding statutory damages if necessary in the future.

Most professional magazine writers are required to send in quarterly income-tax payments to the Internal Revenue Service. You can use these quarterly dates as a reminder that it's also time to file your copyright registrations for all of the articles you've written in the past three months.

Remembering to File

Remember that calendar you put together in Chapter 9, to keep track of all your writing assignment due dates and avoid deadline overload? Well, that calendar is also a terrific place to make notes about the quarterly dates when your income-tax payments are due—and when you can file your copyright registrations as well.

After a few quarterly cycles during your first year as a magazine writer, submitting your forms every quarter to the U.S. Copyright Office along with your tax payments to the IRS will simply become an old habit. And that's just perfect for making sure you actually file the forms amid all your other writing activities.

Saving Money

As you read earlier in this chapter, you can file form GR/CP as an addendum to Form TX, thus registering multiple articles at one time. The good news is not just that this saves you paperwork, but also that it saves you money. Lots and lots of money.

The fee for filing Form TX is $45, but there is no additional charge for filing Form GR/CP as an addendum—and listing as many other eligible articles as you would like to register at the same time. This makes the quarterly filing process quite cost-effective, especially if you have a particularly prolific few months in a row of work.

So, let's say you have ten articles that appeared in print in the previous quarter. You can register ten versions of Form TX, and pay $45 apiece, for a total of $450, or you can register one Form TX with the Form GR/CP addendum, thus paying only the original $45 fee and saving yourself $405 overall.

Saving those dollars obviously makes a great deal of sense, as they will add up substantially over the life of your magazine-writing career. If you write forty articles a year for five years and file individual forms, you'll pay a total of $9,000. If you group the articles quarterly for those five years, you'll pay a total of $900. The difference is $8,100 over five years—more than enough to upgrade your laptop with all of the newest software to keep your magazine-writing career booming.

Meeting Time Limits

Again, it bears repeating that filing for copyright protection on a timely basis will preserve your right to demand statutory damages should your copyright ever be infringed. By filing quarterly, you will always meet the deadline that the government imposes. And you will be happy that you did should the day come when your copyright is violated.

If Your Copyright Is Violated

Anger is the emotion that most writers feel—strongly, and rightly so—when they realize one of their copyrights has been violated. To see your work under another person's byline in a magazine article or on a magazine's Web site can be utterly infuriating. Equally as enraging is seeing an article that you sold to a magazine for first North American serial rights being reprinted time and time again without your permission or any additional compensation coming your way. You're also likely to be livid if you see one of your magazine articles lifted and posted on a third party's Web site.

Remember, your writing is how you make your living. If someone violates your copyright by using your work without your permission, then they are stealing from you, plain and simple.

ESSENTIAL

If you intend to accuse a publication of violating your copyright, it is important that you retain a copy of the evidence. Should your work be posted on a Web site, print out a hard copy of the page. If your work is printed in a magazine, keep a copy of the total issue for future legal uses.

The first thing you should do after collecting evidence of the copyright violation is calm down. Take a few deep breaths and realize that copyright violations happen literally every day to writers working for all kinds of magazines. Does it stink that it happened to you? Of course. But you have options for resolving the situation. You need to think like a businessperson instead of a wounded creator in order to get your due in the most professional manner possible.

Option One: Making Nice

Your first option for trying to resolve the theft of your work is to assume that the person who used your work made an honest mistake. It's hard to imagine this happening in the case of a legitimate magazine stealing a story outright. On the other hand, it's easy to understand how an intern creating a charity newsletter might lift your article reviewing a "fun run" and copy it into the newsletter out of simple enthusiasm at seeing the charity's name being put into print.

Magazine editors talk to one another not just about writers' abilities but also about their temperaments. Trying to resolve problems—even large ones like copyright theft, no matter how angry you are—in a calm, professional manner will work in your favor over the long run of your magazine-writing career.

The routes you can take to make nice in situations like these depend on whether the copyright violation occurred online or in print. Certain laws protect you in one form of media but not necessarily in others.

Violations on the Web

If your work is posted online without your permission, then you can invoke the Digital Millennium Copyright Act, usually referred to as the DMCA. It became law in October 1998 and implements two World Intellectual Property Organization treaties.

The DMCA does a lot of things, but for your purposes as a magazine writer, you'll want to know that it has a provision known as "notice and takedown." Basically, this provision means that if you find your work online illegally, you can notify the person who posted it and demand that it be taken off the Internet immediately, without question.

Nine times out of ten, the offender will not want a hassle and will remove your work from his Web site immediately. If he does not, then you have lost nothing legally. You still retain all your rights to try to make nice in other ways or to take legal action and attempt to collect actual and statutory damages.

Violations in Print

A good way to handle a potentially accidental copyright infringement when the violation is in print is to contact the offending publication and ask for the editor in chief (or for the marketing director of the company or organization, if that is the type of publication that lifted your work). When you get the top person from the offending publication on the telephone, you can calmly explain that his publication printed your copyrighted work without your permission. In many cases, that statement alone will be enough to trigger a profuse apology and offer of compensation. You can, at that point, ask for a payment amount that you believe is fair—say, the same amount you were paid to write the story in the first place—and end the matter when the person promises to pay you in full.

If the person balks or goes silent, then it is appropriate for you to explain—again, calmly—that violation of a registered copyright can carry stiff financial penalties, sometimes rising into the low six figures for willful violations. Most people get the message at this point and realize that simply paying you the original story's fee is a darn good deal. This is a good scenario because you get fairly compensated, they don't get sued, and your reputation for being a professional remains intact.

Option Two: Making Them Pay

Unfortunately, not all of the people who violate your copyright will want to take the high road and settle the problem amicably. This is especially true if the violator has deeper pockets than you do. He may realize that you don't have the wherewithal to file an actual lawsuit, and he therefore will continue to flout your legal rights, assuming that he is facing no real danger except your ire.

What does it cost to hire an attorney with expertise in copyright violations?
Hundreds of dollars an hour, easy. And that amount does not include additional court fees, document copying and transfers, and other costs that can quickly add up into the tens or even hundreds of thousands of dollars.

These are the kinds of people you *should* sue, not only because they need to learn a lesson about making nice when they're in the wrong, but also because if they're playing a nasty game of hardball with you, then there probably are other writers out there who have experienced the same outcome. You will have "fellow witnesses," so to speak. Mounds of evidence that, together, will be far more effective in halting the perpetrator and making him repent than anything you can produce all alone.

The question then becomes, "How do I bring a person like that to his knees?" You'll need the help of a well-trained professional.

Getting Help

Finding a good attorney—no matter what your situation—is never an easy task. In the case of copyright infringement, you will have the added requirement of finding a good attorney who has a degree of specialty in copyright and trademark law. Sometimes, these kinds of lawyers refer to themselves as "first amendment attorneys." Other times, you will see the word "copyright" or "trademark" listed among their specialties.

FACT

Some professional writers' associations keep copyright-knowledgeable attorneys on a retainer, to help members with legal problems that can be resolved fairly quickly. Your membership in a writers' group may therefore be your easiest path toward finding a reputable attorney to battle a copyright infringement.

Depending on how big the city is where you live, you may be able to find a copyright-and-trademark attorney in your local telephone directory. If you find nothing in the phone book, you can check with your local bar association for recommendations. Go to the American Bar Association's Web site, *www.abanet.org,* click on the "public resources" link on the home page's left-hand side, and then click on "lawyer referral services" under the heading "Get Legal Help." A map of the United States will open, allowing you to click on the state where you live and search for reputable referrals with the proper expertise.

Moving On

When all is said and done—whether you file and win a huge lawsuit or simply settle for having the offending material returned to you—the most important thing you can do after a copyright infringement is move on. This can be hard, especially if you have to battle in court against someone who stole from you without remorse, but moving on is paramount to the future success of your magazine-writing career. As mentioned earlier in this chapter, the matter of your professional reputation is as much at stake as the value of your copyright. Editors talk to one another, and nobody wants to take a chance and work with a writer who is known as being prone to file lawsuits frivolously.

Once you have settled your complaint and resolved your copyright-infringement issue, you can get back to the business of, well, running your business. You can even tout your victory in a press release, if that's appropriate, as part of your continuing plan to market yourself. There's absolutely nothing wrong with redeeming your reputation after a long battle, especially if it's out in the open and being watched by the editors with whom you hope to continue working.

Chapter 11

Marketing Yourself

Being a successful magazine writer has as much to do with marketing skills as it does with grammar skills. You may be able to write beautiful articles, but you will never be given the chance if you can't get your name and ideas in front of assigning editors. This chapter will help you understand the competition you face for assignments and will give you the tools you need to become recognized in your area of expertise.

It's a Race to Win Work

Every spring, in the middle of downtown Manhattan (the magazine publishing center of the world), the American Society of Journalists and Authors holds its annual three-day writers' conference. The main event of the long weekend is a keynote luncheon speaker—usually a bestselling author or award-winning writer—who steps up to a podium in the ballroom at the Grand Hyatt New York and addresses a literal sea of professional and would-be magazine writers.

While the speaker's words are often interesting, it's the audience that usually makes more of an impact on beginning magazine writers. The simple act of seeing hundreds upon hundreds of writers packed into a banquet hall, all of them looking for ideas about becoming better at their craft and garnering more work, makes a powerful statement about the high level of competition that exists in the magazine-writing business.

FACT

There are more than 100 college-level schools and departments of journalism and mass communications in the United States. The sheer number of graduation ceremonies means that there are literally thousands of aspiring magazine writers entering the workforce—and becoming your competition for assignments—every single year.

For every story out there that has a chance of being published, there are countless professionals looking for the chance to do the actual writing. You may be surprised to learn that many editors receive query letters regularly for the exact same story ideas from multiple writers. Especially in magazines that deal with topics such as dieting, fashion, and beauty, queries for similar stories come in from different writers almost every day.

Lots and lots and lots of people want to land magazine-writing jobs. The competition is downright brutal.

You Are One in a Million

You may believe that you are special, with one-in-a-million writing talent. In the harsh reality of the magazine-writing business, however, you really are one among—well, if not a million, then certainly one of thousands of writers seeking to land assignments.

This can be awfully hard to accept, because writing is such a creative enterprise. When you concoct a sentence or craft a paragraph, you will often feel that your thoughts and your way of expressing them are unique. The sad truth is that more often than not, your work will be just the latest in a long line of similar prose to cross magazine editors' desks. Many aspiring writers have likely come before you, offering similar ideas written in similar styles.

ESSENTIAL

Many people with a gift for writing are "creative types" who feel that their talent is all they need to win work in the magazine-writing business. You would be wise to disabuse yourself of this notion immediately. To succeed, you have to be a great writer and a great marketer of your ideas and skills.

You need to accept the fact that there is serious competition out there for magazine-writing jobs. It's the classic conundrum of art versus commerce. You need to make sure you don't skew your attitude too far toward the artistic end of the spectrum, which is where most writers naturally start out.

Art Coexisting with Commerce

The art-versus-commerce debate has gone on for centuries, with artists from Claude Monet to Eminem trying to balance what they wanted to create against what they could sell to the world. Magazine writing is no different. Crafting beautiful articles is most definitely an art—but one that exists in the greater realm of commerce. Magazines are, after all, products intended to be sold. That makes you, the writer, a producer of commerce as much as a creator of art.

E ALERT!

The phrase "starving artist" is based in fact. Many a writer has held to her ideas in the face of criticism from assigning editors. This usually does not result in the romantic Hollywood ending of the writer being discovered as a triumphant genius. Most often, it results in the writer having no assignments, and thus no money to buy food.

The point of understanding your competition is accepting that you have lots of it. Period. You need to get over yourself and get on with the business of marketing yourself—in a way that will land you assignments and chances to prove your abilities to editors and readers alike.

The Challenge of Self-Promotion

As hard as it can be to accept the level of competition in the magazine-writing business, it can be even more difficult to take on the task of self-promotion. Many writers are, by their nature, passive types who prefer to sit at their computers and type than to get out into the world and trumpet their accomplishments.

If you're a typical writer, you're probably not shy about asking questions in interviews, but you probably are shy about promoting the good interviews you've done. That's better left to the salesman, editors, and marketers who promote the magazines, right? You shouldn't talk about yourself. Your job is to get your sources to talk, so that you can create great articles.

QUESTION?

Why do so many writers have a hard time promoting themselves?
Because as a writer, you are taught to let your subjects come through in your work. Heralding your own accomplishments is the antithesis of this. Marketing yourself forces you not only to stand in the spotlight for a change, but to brag when you have the audience's attention.

That kind of attitude is the main challenge of self-promotion that most writers face. You understand by now that writing is a business, and you probably instinctually understand that all businesses rely heavily on marketing to get their messages out. What you need to wrap your brain around is the idea that when you are seeking to land assignments, you are a company selling a product—a writer selling stories. You need to come to terms with the idea that there's nothing wrong with marketing yourself and your work to the editors you hope to interest.

Nobody likes a braggart or a nag, so you need to market yourself to editors in ways that are a bit more subtle than screaming through a bullhorn. Do think about marketing yourself all the time, but don't become so obsessed with marketing that you fall in love with your own image and annoy potential clients in the process.

There are plenty of ways to market yourself that will come easily to you, even if you're among the shyest of writers. You may even have begun doing some of the following things on your own—without realizing that you can take your efforts to another level by thinking about them in terms of self-promotion.

Query Letters and Introductory E-mails

You learned a lot about the general use of query letters in Chapter 5, but one thing you probably did not think too much about was the idea that your query letter is often your first contact with a given magazine's editor. It's worth a second thought, because it means that query letters can also be gateways to self-promotion opportunities.

Changing a Loss to a Win

Most writers, when their query letters are declined, feel at least some sense of rejection. The difference between beginning writers and professional writers in this sense is that the beginners tend to wallow in self-pity, while the pros immediately follow up on the lost job opportunity and try to win work with a second attempt.

FACT

The vast majority of magazine writers receive far more rejections than acceptances to their query letters. Having a query letter turned down is not a cause for slumping under your bed sheets and eating a half-gallon of ice cream. It's a simple fact of the magazine-writing business, and you need to learn to quickly overcome your disappointments.

How? By e-mailing or calling the editor who rejected the query and asking politely for suggestions on how to better meet the magazine's needs next time. It's a cheap and easy way to market yourself as someone who goes the extra mile, who doesn't blanch at the first sign of trouble, and who truly wants to land an assignment and help make the magazine great in the process. There is a danger in taking this tack, though: You don't want to seem needy or annoying. If an editor doesn't want to discuss her decision, then you must respect that choice.

On the other hand, a single, polite note or telephone inquiry can often pay off with big dividends. Even if your idea for an article was a poor fit for the editor's current needs, she may be looking to fill some other editorial hole down the line. Asking a basic question—"Is there another way I might be able to help you? Something else you need written for an upcoming issue?"—could put you in the right place at the right time for landing a gig.

ALERT!

Usually, it's better to follow up with editors via e-mail instead of on the telephone, where they may feel "pounced upon" with little time to think. Unless you know that an editor prefers to speak with writers on the phone, follow up your query letters with e-mails that give editors a chance to reconsider your skills at their leisure.

You can use a similar philosophy to contact editors even if you don't have a specific story idea to pitch in a query letter. Many professional writers send out introductory letters or e-mails to editors with whom they hope to work, following the same self-marketing notion that getting your name out there is often the best first step you can take.

Simple Introductions

An introductory letter or e-mail is just what it sounds like: a way of introducing yourself to an editor. It's not the same as a query letter, which proposes a specific article idea. Instead, an introductory e-mail or letter is a sort of alert for the editor who receives it, a way of notifying the editor that you are out there in the world, that you are looking for work, and that you believe you would be a good fit with his readers.

Even though introductory e-mails seem more casual than formal query letters, you should put the same amount of work into writing them. Know the publication that you are contacting, and offer a general sense of why your background is a good match for writing assignments that will appeal to the magazine's target audience.

A good introductory e-mail should be addressed to the appropriate editor—with his or her name spelled correctly—just as a query letter would be. However, instead of progressing into an actual story idea, the body of the introductory e-mail might read something like this: "In reading through the most recent edition of *Mature Years* magazine, I noticed that you ran several profiles of people who were newly retired and looking to the Christian faith for help with their changing lifestyles. I am a professional magazine writer who volunteers with several groups that cater to this same demographic at my regional church. I'd love to speak with you about your future editorial needs and about how my volunteer work could translate into articles for *Mature Years*."

With a short note like this, you will have conveyed that you read the editor's magazine, that you have access to sources appropriate for his audience, and that you are interested in brainstorming actual queries that will be on target for the magazine's future needs. That's a whole lot of good stuff in a short, easy-to-read, attention-grabbing space.

Entering Writing Contests

When you think about writing contests, you probably imagine the opportunity to win a plaque or even a bit of cash. This line of thinking is a good start, but you also need to take it to the next level and understand how writing contests can be a terrific platform for self-promotion.

Some writing contests are legitimate, while others are not. Tip-offs to rip-offs include having to pay exorbitant entry fees in exchange for small prizes or no prizes, or being offered a chance to win an editorial evaluation instead of an actual prize. Be sure to research the group running any contest before submitting your entry fee and materials.

The Judges

For starters, all writing contests have judges—and those judges are often editors who make assignments at the magazines where they work. To be a writing contest judge, the editor is essentially agreeing to read all of the articles put before him. If yours is in the pile, then the editor will read it—and get to know your skills and style in the process.

Now, there's usually no way to tell which editors will be judging which categories of which contests, so this method of self-promotion is not about cornering an editor who has been rejecting your query letters for months on end. Instead, think of entering writing contests as a way to get your work in front of editors whom you may otherwise have no way of knowing. And, if your work is good, you will be getting it in front of the editors not as "one in a sea of queries," but as "the best among the field of competition."

Free Press

Even better, should your work actually be the best among the field of competition, you will receive free press through the organization that runs the writing contest. These groups usually highlight winning contest entries on their Web sites and in news releases that are sent to huge databases of industry professionals and news organizations—people you would have to spend weeks contacting if you tried to promote your fabulous writing skills on your own.

FACT

The free press that you can receive by winning a writing contest is terrific because it is specific to you and your work, but it comes from a third party. The organization conducting the contest will usually send out press releases that tout your achievement, making the group act like a de facto marketing agent on your behalf.

The upshot is that you should enter as many writing contests as you can. And as long as the contests are legitimate, don't grumble about the entry fees. Think of them as marketing expenses (and remember to list them as a potential tax write-off for your accountant to consider).

Being Active in Writers' Groups

Another terrific way to promote yourself and your work is by becoming active in professional writers' organizations. These can be small or large, targeted to your particular area of expertise or toward writing in general. The American Medical Writers Association, for instance, would be ideal if you want to write only about diabetes, while the National Writers Union might be a better choice if you intend to cover a broad spectrum of topics in your magazine-writing assignments.

Go Beyond the Basics

Simply joining the writers' groups that are appropriate to your area of expertise is a good first step, but to really turn your membership into a self-promotional opportunity, you need to take the additional step of becoming active in the groups themselves.

QUESTION?

Why is being active in writers' groups so important?
There are two reasons. First, because volunteering for committees and tasks will help you to make connections by getting to know other writers. Second, because listing your service on your resume demonstrates a level of professionalism and commitment to the business that many other writers lack.

Smile and Say Hello—To Everyone

The more active you are in a writers' association, the more connections you will make and the more networking you will be able to do—without feeling like you are "self-promoting" at all. The very act of introducing yourself is a form of marketing: "Hi, I'm Janet Thompson. I write about cigars and fine wines." You never know how the person sitting at the committee table next to you will react. Ideally, it would be by saying something like, "Do you know Tom Johnson over at *Wine Spectator*? He's a good friend of mine. I'd be happy to introduce you."

These are the kinds of connections you will not make if you simply join a group and send in your membership fee year after year. You must take the step of offering to help with something—anything—that the organization needs. You'll be surprised how much name recognition, how many contacts, and how much future business you can win by volunteering your time.

Attending Industry Conferences

The same philosophy applies to attending industry conferences, which include trade shows and other events where the people and businesses that you write about will be present. In the case of the writer whose expertise includes fine wines, for instance, it would be a good idea to attend an event such as the Boston Wine Expo, where more than 450 wineries offer just shy of 2,000 wines for consumers to taste.

Not only are trade shows like this one full of possible story ideas, they're also usually crawling with magazine editors who are looking for story ideas themselves. And trade shows are a facet of virtually every industry out there, so no matter what you want to write about, you can probably find a trade show to attend.

Always look your best when attending a trade show. You never know whom you'll bump into, and you very well could meet the editor of a magazine you've been pitching for quite some time. You want to make the best impression you can— that of a professional journalist taking his job of covering an industry seriously.

You also can use trade shows as a way to get yourself more connected to the industry about which you would like to write. You can introduce yourself to marketing directors from the companies that have displays, hand out your business card, and ask to be put on their mailing lists. That way, you'll have an edge over other writers when new products are introduced in the years to come. If you work hard enough and get to know enough people, you may even gain an edge in information over magazine staff members. That will make you invaluable when it comes time for editorial planning sessions.

Joining Magazine Staff Meetings

If you get to the point with a magazine that you are doing repeat assignments on a regular basis, then there is no harm in asking your editor whether you could attend an in-house editorial planning session. Most magazines hold these sessions on an annual, monthly, or even weekly basis (depending on the magazine's frequency of publication), and the purpose of the meetings is to lay out a general schedule of articles the magazine will produce for upcoming issues.

Being in the room when these discussions take place gives you a huge advantage over writers who are "present" only in the form of their query letters. And as you know by now, in such a highly competitive marketplace, getting every advantage you can is important to landing assignments.

QUESTION?

What is appropriate behavior at a magazine staff meeting?
Having a positive attitude throughout the story-brainstorming process is paramount. If you've been offered a seat with the inner circle, you must try to help improve all the story ideas being discussed, not just the ideas for stories that you will be paid to write.

If you do get the chance to attend a magazine's editorial planning session, be sure to use the word "we" more than the word "you." If you quip, "I think you need to do a story about solar energy," it sounds much different than if you remark, "I think we need to do a story about solar energy." The "we" reinforces the notion that you are part of the magazine's core team, which is self-promotion in and of itself. You're implying that you're an indispensable business and creative partner, which is exactly what you want to be.

Creating a Web Site

More and more magazine writers are creating their own Web sites as a way to market their work and abilities. Some Web sites are a simple, single page that offers a writer's resume and contact information, while other Web sites are full-on Flash graphics productions that let you search through a writer's past articles to get a better grasp of their style and expertise. The simpler sites are less expensive and usually fully effective—and sometimes you can even build them yourself.

FACT

Creating your own Web site is not just a great marketing tool, it's also a money saver. If you post your resume and clips online, then you will not have to pay to mail printed versions when editors request them. Those postage and copying savings can add up to hundreds or thousands of dollars annually, depending on how many queries you send.

Hiring a Pro

You can hire a professional Web-site designer to create a high-bandwidth, graphics-heavy Web site for you if you think you need it. One good way to tell whether this might be a good investment is to look at the Web sites of other writers in your field. If you see that they are investing heavily in their self-promotion online, then you might want to consider at least matching their offerings in terms of content and style.

Building It Yourself

If you have basic design skills and a decent grip on using programs like Microsoft Publisher, then you can skip the professional's fee and build a Web site yourself. Once you learn how the basic design programs work, you can use templates to give your site a cohesive look that will be on par with many other writers' sites. For many writers with basic computer skills, this can be done over the course of a week.

If all you want to do is post a resume and a few clips, you can even look at other writers' sites and copy their formatting—but not their color schemes and design templates. Again, the idea is to market yourself as unique in the field. You don't want your site to look exactly like anybody else's.

Chapter 12

Making Time to Improve Your Craft

One of the most challenging things about being a magazine writer is balancing your time. It can be hard finding enough hours in the day to write query letters, report and do interviews, network with editors, and complete your assignments—so hard, in fact, that you can quickly become lost in the business side of your work. It's important to take a step back once in a while and pay attention to the creative side of your work, too.

Remember, You Love to Write

Invoices, sales pitches, copyright forms, contracts—all of these important magazine-writing job duties can weigh you down psychologically if you find yourself focusing on them day in and day out. That's unfortunate for obvious reasons, but it's even more so because a frustrated writer is usually a bad writer. You can't very well sell articles to magazines if your verb and adjective choices outright stink.

You need to make sure that you not only keep your wits about you when managing your writing business, but that you also remember why you got into the business in the first place: because you love to write. Scheduling days into your calendar when you will have nothing to do but write is a good way to make sure your creative juices keep flowing.

Every Minute Counts

You can really get into a writing groove by turning off your telephone, shutting down your e-mail, and focusing—if only for a few hours—on whatever article you happen to be writing. Even if you can't set aside an entire day just to write, you can at least set aside part of a day to focus on the craft you love.

QUESTION?

Is it smart to turn off your telephone and e-mail when editors might be trying to reach you?
Of course not. You need to be available to your clients. However, if you're not on deadline and aren't expecting any editors' calls, then there's nothing wrong with giving yourself at least a few hours of uninterrupted writing time.

It's surprising how much more fun magazine writing can be when you give yourself the time to focus on an assignment without any distractions. This is especially true for assignments about topics that truly interest you. It's also a good idea for assignments where you have tons of great research and interview notes that you need to pare down to meet your required word count. The more interesting an assignment is, the better your article has the potential to be—potential that you might not even realize if you're trying to write various paragraphs in between phone calls to accounts-payable departments and the U.S. Copyright Office.

Words to Live By

If you find that you're the type of person who gets too wrapped up in the business end of magazine writing, then you should consider placing reminders all around your work space to help you remember why you love to write in the first place. Lots of writers jot down meaningful quotations or even just beautifully crafted sentences that they come across while reading for pleasure. Print out a few of your favorites and place them strategically on your desk, in places where they won't get lost or be shoved out of view. This is a terrific way to help you remember that when the business tasks are done, you get to go back to the fun of creating memorable sentences of your own.

Sticky notes are terrific supplies for magazine writers to keep handy. You can use them not just to mark important parts of your notes and files but also to keep some of the quotes and phrases that inspire you tacked onto or nearby your computer screen.

Taking a peek at these inspirational quotes from time to time should help inspire you not just to write but to write *well*. After all, they wouldn't be such memorable phrases if they were poorly constructed, right?

Reading for Fun

As every teacher in every writing school around the world will tell you, one of the best ways to improve your own writing is to read other people's work. It can be hard, after sifting through nouns and adverbs at your computer all day, to do anything other than plop down on the couch and watch a mindless television reality show, but it will benefit you greatly if you can get into the habit of reading at least a magazine or even a few chapters of a book before bedtime every night.

You don't have to read anything that deals with your day-to-day research and writing—heck, you can re-read *The Devil Wears Prada* fifteen times if that's what helps you relax at the end of the workday—but you should make an effort to read something just for fun on a daily basis.

FACT

Reading other writers' work is a terrific way to break out of any monotonous writing patterns into which you may have fallen. Simply seeing word choices that differ from your own vocabulary is a great way to perk up the creative-writing muscles in your brain. The stimulation is instantaneous, just part of the experience of reading for fun.

If you enjoy reading magazines, that's terrific, but don't limit yourself to reading only the publications for which you work (or aspire to work). Half the fun of reading is discovering new ideas, new voices, and new ways of putting words down onto the page.

Fiction Is Your Friend

A lot of magazine writers shy away from reading fiction. It's a gut reaction of sorts, one that likely stems from the fact that magazine writers earn their money by writing nonfiction. After you spend hours upon hours collecting quotes and doing research for magazines that cover everything from bicycle technology to online postage systems—as if those topics were as important as peace on Earth itself—you can find yourself feeling that fiction is a little, well, hokey. The truth is that reading fiction can be a wonderful break from reality, as well as a fabulous way of helping the writer in you learn new techniques for developing characters and incorporating dialogue into your work.

As a nonfiction magazine writer, you never want to invent dialogue or characters in your articles. You'll be fired and, likely, blackballed for years. However, you can use some of the same techniques that fiction writers do to enhance the quotes and descriptions of real people you interview for your stories.

Paying attention to the way good fiction writers pattern their paragraphs, and the sentences within them, will certainly help you to make your own nonfiction writing livelier. Even better, you'll probably notice the rhythm of whatever you're reading without even having to try. It's sort of like learning by osmosis, with the added bonus of getting to read an interesting story along the way.

Reading fiction will also help you to see how good writers develop characters over the course of a piece—by leaving little clues, like bread-crumbs, for the reader to follow page after page. You can use a similar technique when writing narrative nonfiction articles for magazines, and your articles—while fully factual—will take on the tone of a great mystery or romance novel.

Ideas Are Everywhere

Reading for fun is also the easiest way to keep up with who the hottest writers are at any given time. Picking up a copy of *Time* or *Newsweek*, or a book from *The New York Times* bestseller list, will give you a good idea of what mainstream America is reading and thus talking about. This will not only keep you interested, it will help spark ideas for spin-off stories that you might be able to sell yourself.

Keep a notepad and pen handy at all times. You never know when a book or article you're reading will spark an idea for a related nonfiction article that you can sell, and you'll want to write the idea down so that you can promptly forget about it and go back to reading for fun.

That's not to say that you should read these types of things for fun if they don't interest you. Remember, the point is to recharge your creative juices, not to feel as though you're trapped in some energy-sapping study group. But if you find keeping up with national trends of interest, there's no reason you can't get your relaxation fix while at the same time allowing terrific story ideas of your own to percolate in the back of your mind.

Attending Writers' Conferences

Another terrific way to improve as a writer is to attend writers' conferences. You'll find yourself surrounded by other people hoping to be just as creative and successful as you want to be. You can not only learn from them, you can also build friendships that will help you throughout your career.

There are countless writers' conferences around the world, and you could make a career out of attending them. (Some people do, and end up putting themselves right out of business, like perpetual graduate students who never stop studying long enough to get a job and pay their tuition bills.) No particular conference is necessarily better than the next, but they all offer different angles from which to approach the craft of writing.

You should look for conferences being held by groups that seem to target the kind of writing you want to do. Usually, conferences are a mixed bag of seminars and speeches that may or may not appeal to you. If you can't find at least two interesting seminars or workshops every day of a conference, then you should probably look to attend a different conference.

Some examples of popular writers' conferences include:

- **American Society of Journalists and Authors Conference, New York:** Nonfiction
- **Bread Loaf Writers Conference, Vermont:** Fiction, poetry, and nonfiction
- **Chicago Writers & Editors/One-on-One, Illinois:** Nonfiction
- **Institute for Travel Writing and Photography, Florida:** Nonfiction and photography
- **Maui Writers Conference, Hawaii:** Fiction, nonfiction, and screenwriting

As you can see, some conferences are purely for nonfiction writers (the Chicago and New York events are further targeted toward magazine writing instead of books), while other conferences include different disciplines such as fiction writing and screenwriting. Depending on your long-term goals for your writing career, you may choose to attend different types of conferences in any given year, or you might prefer to focus on attending the same conference every year or two as you build friendships and networking opportunities.

Attending Without Attending

In some cases, you can get a lot of the information from a writers' conference without even attending it. More and more conference organizers are making the audio of presentations available on CD after the conferences end, which means that you can order only those sessions you care to hear and listen to them in the comfort of your own home.

You may save a few bucks by skipping a conference fee and instead ordering the audio of a few key sessions, but keep in mind that what you hear on the tape is not all of the information available at writers' conferences. Networking with fellow writers between sessions can give you just as many ideas for improving your craft as listening to a speaker.

The downside to purchasing the audio of a conference is similar to the downside of reading only nonfiction in your area of expertise. You're essentially setting yourself up to hear just a handful of select voices instead of a cacophony from which you might be able to draw interesting new lessons on how to be a better writer.

Making the Most of the Trip

When you do attend writers' conferences, be sure to make the most of the trip by creating your own "events" in between the ones scheduled by the conference organizers. Most writers' conferences take place over long weekends, usually Fridays through Sundays. That means that if you can fly in a day early or stay a day late, you'll have entire workdays free to visit with editors from nearby magazines. If you're attending a conference in a publishing hub such as New York City or Chicago, then you can make an awful lot of face-to-face appointments with editors you already work for or just hope to get to know.

QUESTION?

Can you expect an editor you don't know to see you in person?
Yes—as long as you don't request too much time. While an editor you already work with might want to have lunch while you're in town, an editor you haven't yet queried may be willing to meet you at his office for only a few minutes. That's still a literal foot in the door.

Also do your best to make dinner reservations with fellow writers whom you may know from e-mail but have never met in person. Sit back, have a few drinks, and talk in general about your writing career. You never know what kind of mutual connections you can make, or what kind of terrific magazine-writing lessons you can learn based on your fellow writers' experiences.

Creative-Writing Exercises

As you now know, there are a lot of skills that go into being a great magazine writer. But at the heart of all of them is usually a passion for writing itself. There's no better way to rejuvenate and enhance that passion than by setting aside time to do some creative-writing exercises.

While magazine writing is a creative enterprise, the term "creative writing" refers to a specific style of crafting words into sentences, paragraphs, and stories. When you're working on a creative-writing exercise, you should be more focused on the way words interact on the page than you might otherwise be on things like word count, punctuation, and even grammar.

The idea is to set yourself free from the daily constraints of writing 1,000- or 1,200-word magazine features and instead let your writing instincts carry you as far as you care to go, on any subject that pops into your mind.

FACT

The Web site *www.creativewritingprompts.com* offers more than 200 prompts that will get you started on creative-writing exercises. If you allow yourself the time to do one exercise each week, then you'll be able to use this free writing resource for four full years of your career.

Doing creative writing exercises is sort of like taking a walk in the park as opposed to setting a treadmill's timer to maximize your walk's physical impact. When you're doing writing exercises, you should let your mind wander a bit off track, just to see where you—and your writing skills—might end up. You can do this in many ways, but two of the most common ideas are to focus on a detail or to focus on your imagination.

Focus on a Detail

When you focus on a detail for a creative-writing exercise, you shut out everything else around you and try to find new and interesting ways to describe an object you know all too well. The idea here is to do stream-of-consciousness writing—just letting the words flow out of you and onto the page, regardless of whether they make sense or not. You will be training your senses of observation more than anything, helping yourself to better gather information in the future so that you will have better material to work with when writing articles.

ESSENTIAL

You must put aside your notions of grammar, sentence structure, spelling, and punctuation when you attempt a stream-of-consciousness writing exercise. Forget everything you know about "cleaning up copy" and instead just let the words flow out of your mind, like water from a high-pressure faucet.

Starting this kind of exercise is easy: Choose an object on which to focus, and just start writing. The object can be as complex as your car or as simple as the blade of grass growing outside your garage. The point is to write about that one object, and nothing else, for as long as you can, or for an allotted amount of time that you give yourself (say, anywhere from ten to thirty minutes).

You'll soon learn that if you focus on any one thing long enough, you can find many interesting things to write about it. The task itself will be fun exercise for your brain, but the skills you get from doing the task will continue to benefit you throughout your magazine-writing career.

FACT

Many talented magazine writers focus on details when crafting leads to complex articles. The bigger the idea or concept that you are writing about, the more simplified your lead needs to be to draw the reader in. Writing about a single blade of grass, for instance, could be an interesting opening to an article about pesticides and golf courses.

Focus on Imagination

You can also use stream-of-consciousness writing exercises to jog your imagination. This is obviously most helpful to writers of fiction, but nonfiction magazine writers who do these kinds of exercises tend to find them helpful in terms of broadening their capacity to come up with new and interesting article ideas.

One prompt from the site *www.creativewritingprompts.com* is a good example of this type of exercise: "Use the first line of any nursery rhyme to tell a story." You can certainly imagine any kind of story you want with this exercise, but in letting your ideas flow onto the page, you in many cases will see patterns and ideas that you may have subconsciously been working on all along. If nothing else, you may come up with an interesting turn of phrase that you can tuck away and use later to make one of your magazine articles really sing.

Word Limits

Some creative-writing exercises are not done in stream-of-consciousness style but instead with word limits. These types of exercises are terrific for writers who want to improve their conciseness, particularly for leads and nut grafs.

Again, here's an example from *www.creativewritingprompts.com*: "In 200 words, describe a hot day." Now, there are plenty of writers out there who could go on for 2,000 or even 20,000 words about a hot day. If you're one of them, then perhaps learning how to pare back your work to essential words and phrases will be a more helpful creative-writing exercise.

Is it harder to write long pieces or short ones?
Most magazine writers say that it is far more difficult to "write short." Creative-writing exercises that limit you in terms of word count are an excellent tool to help you craft tighter leads and nut grafs later on in your full-length stories and query letters.

Adding to Your Skills

Sometimes, improving as a magazine writer comes from learning additional skills. Your words, after all, are not the only things in the magazine's pages. There are headlines, pull quotes, photographs, captions, and more. Each of these magazine-article elements adds to the reader's understanding of your words, and each can add to your understanding of how to craft great stories as well.

The Power of Photography

Pictures are often the most dramatic element on magazine pages. Readers respond almost viscerally to images, while they have to take time to read and think about words before they can form an emotional response. What does this mean for you as a writer? In many cases, your words will be cut to make room for bigger and better photographs with captions. If you want to write the best story in a magazine, then it has to be written tightly *and* in a way that complements the images chosen to run with it.

Even if you don't intend to ever take photographs to go with your articles, you can practice crafting pieces that work alongside visuals by assigning yourself a topic and then not just writing about it, but also photographing it. This exercise will help you to understand that sometimes, images really do convey information better. It will also help you see that you should save the precious word count you have for information that can't be told through accompanying pictures.

ESSENTIAL

Whenever possible, ask your editor to show you a laid-out version of your article, complete with photographs and caption spaces. In many cases, you can use information that you had to cut out of your story to create powerful captions that readers will remember—essentially, ministories pegged to specific images that go along with your text.

This can be as simple as creating a story titled "My New Niece, Heather." Snap a few different digital shots of Heather playing, sleeping, and eating, and then write a story to go with them. You'll soon find that instead of spending an entire paragraph describing Heather's adorable smile, you can instead show a photograph of her smiling and write about the toy or activity that makes her so happy.

What you'll learn in the end of this exercise is that you can be an even better writer if you learn to envision the entire story package, not just the words themselves. Editors will love you for it!

Practice Makes Perfect

If you do decide that you have a knack for photography, keep practicing. High-resolution digital cameras are coming down in price enough that many writers are buying them and using them to submit images along with their articles. In most cases, writers receive additional compensation when they offer editors photographs along with stories. Taking pictures is a nice way to earn an extra few dollars while still researching a single article.

Why do editors like writers who can also take pictures?
You save them time and money. They don't have to hire a separate photographer, and they know your photos will match your story. There will be no miscommunication between separate writers and photographers who turn in words and pictures that fail to work together on the page.

You'll learn more about adding photography to your magazine-writing career in Chapter 19. For now, think of taking pictures as being similar to the other creative-writing exercises discussed in this chapter. Simply trying to envision how your words will end up looking on the page will give you new and exciting ideas about how you can write them, or how you can suggest to an editor that they be packaged.

Reviving Your Commitment to Downtime

A lot of the ideas discussed in this chapter for practicing the craft of writing are great fun to undertake, but they do require your time—something you will no doubt feel incredibly short on as you get your magazine-writing business up and running. And, truth be told, there's no reason to start out on a creative-writing exercise if you're just plain exhausted. You won't get very much done, you'll likely get frustrated, and you may lose sight of how much you love writing in the first place.

This is the time when the best way to practice your craft is to take a break from it. As with anything, when you obsess constantly about how to become a better magazine writer, you may end up driving yourself loony-tunes. Sometimes, the only way to improve at something is to let it go out of your mind for a while, to completely disengage from the process and give your brain time to relax and recharge.

If you're the type of person who tends to get caught up in things, you are likely to forget about your very real need for downtime. One way to solve this problem is by purchasing season tickets—for a baseball team, an opera house, whatever—that will force you to take breaks at regular intervals and focus on something other than writing.

After a day or two of doing no writing at all, you may not yet be ready to get back to work full-time, but you will likely find yourself more interested in the idea of taking on a creative-writing exercise or shooting a few photographs with story ideas in mind.

Remember that re-establishing this kind of self-motivation is a worthwhile goal in and of itself. It will almost always lead you back down the path toward being a better, more focused writer.

Chapter 13

Expanding Your Base

You may get to a point in your magazine-writing career where you want to branch out and do more than just continue working for the same handful of magazines again and again. It's important that you have a base of clients, of course, but you may decide eventually that you want to expand upon that base. How do you expand smartly and make more money in the process? That's what this chapter is all about.

Should You Grow Your Business?

By the time you get to the point that you're thinking about expanding your magazine-writing business, you will need to have established a firm base. There's no better way to sink yourself over the long haul than to try to expand too quickly, before you have a regular set of clients to count on for assignments and income.

The first thing you need to do before deciding how you *can* grow your business is to decide whether you *should* grow your business. The main question you need to answer is whether attempting to grow your business will hurt your chance of keeping good clients that you already have. If the answer is yes, then you should definitely think twice before launching yourself into new areas of work.

E ALERT!

The idea of making more money is a powerful lure, but you have to keep your base happy if you want to stay in business for the long haul. If you already have four magazines giving you regular assignments, don't accept a one-time-only job from a new client—no matter how well-paying—that will force you to forgo your regular work.

You also need to realistically assess whether or not you can physically handle an expansion of your business. For magazine writers, more business typically means more writing—and with more writing can come things like repetitive strain injury and carpal tunnel syndrome, very painful injuries to your wrist muscles and nerves caused by spending too many hours sitting at a keyboard.

If you're already working ten-hour days for six days each week, then you may not be in the best position to expand into new markets that will require you to do a lot more work for not a lot more pay. Yes, it's good to expand your business in ways that will let you work less while earning more, but you need to make a point of finding those kinds of jobs before you set out to expand in the first place.

Be Realistic

One of the hardest things for anyone in any profession to do is make a realistic assessment of their current situation. You need to do this as a magazine writer because you can't figure out where you're going if you don't know exactly where you're starting. Ask yourself a few key questions before you decide you're ready to expand:

- Are you willing to work more hours than you're working now?
- Is your desire to expand based on wanting to make more money, or to write for different kinds of magazines?
- Are you able to keep the good clients you have while working with new clients, too?
- Are you willing to drop your lower-paying clients if you find new, regular clients who pay better?

These are the kinds of questions that will help you see, very realistically, where you stand and how much risk you want to take by trying to expand.

The answers to these questions will also help you determine your goals for expansion: to make more money, to write for different magazines, to broaden your client list in general, to replace a low-paying client with a higher-paying one. Having taken the time to assess your situation in these terms can be incredibly helpful when you actually define your expansion goals and set out to achieve them.

Think Smarter, Not Harder

In a lot of cases, you won't have to do very much extra work at all in order to expand your magazine-writing business. Many top-dollar freelance writers earn their livings by thinking smarter about the work they're already doing instead of setting out to work harder for an ever-growing list of clients. How do they do it? They start by repurposing the content they already own.

Repurposing What You Already Own

Repurposing content is a fancy way of saying "rewriting stories." If you remember, in the very beginning of Chapter 1, you learned about the idea that magazine writers are content providers. Repurposing the content that you've already created is simply a way of providing that content to more than one client at a time. Report once, sell multiple times. It's a formula for financial success and, in many cases, business expansion.

If you intend to use repurposed content to expand your magazine-writing business, you need to make sure you keep detailed notes about all your interviews and story research. You will need all the extra information you can get when it comes time to rewrite an article, and your new editors may want fact-checking information that your previous editors did not.

Opening New Doors

The idea behind repurposing content is that you can use what you know from one part of the magazine-writing universe to open doors at additional titles. Let's say that you're an expert on the climate of the Arctic and that you write frequently for environmental magazines about things like icebergs, polar bears, and global warming. You probably have accumulated thousands of pages of independent research and interview notes on the subject matter, and you've written countless articles for all of the major magazines in your field.

When you decide to repurpose that content, you are essentially saying that you want to rewrite your stories using all the same (or perhaps slightly updated) Arctic environmental information so that it will appeal to a different readership. Some examples of ideas might include:

- An article about polar bears for a children's magazine
- An article about polar bears for a wildlife magazine

- An article about the best cruises you can take to see icebergs for a travel magazine
- An article about the science behind the icebergs on popular tours for a travel magazine
- An article about how global warming has affected local fishing economies, for a fishing magazine or local Alaskan magazine

The idea here is that you already have (in your head, or in your notes) most of the information required to write these articles. You simply have to rewrite it and package it in a way that fits with the new magazines' formats.

How Much Revising Is Enough?

Sometimes, you won't have to revise your articles at all. A magazine editor may read your work in another publication and decide that it would be great to use all or part of it in his own magazine. In that case, you would sell him a straight reprint and be done with it. The only finger you'd have to lift to earn a second paycheck for the same story is the finger that presses the "send" button on your e-mail with the Word document attached.

FACT

"Reprint" is the term used for an article that is sold more than once without any substantial changes to its content. A "revise" is an article that is sold more than once, but with enough changes made to the content that it is essentially a new work. A derivative work, yes, but a new work overall.

In other cases, and perhaps more commonly, you will have to make at least some revisions to an article before you can sell it a second time. Some editors want total rewrites or even new pieces based on what you wrote previously, while other editors are happy to print slightly modified articles that have new leads or structures more in keeping with their own magazine's tone. It will be up to you and the new magazine's editor to decide how many changes you need to make in the copy in order to sell the repurposed content, and you will need to keep in mind the contract that you originally signed when you created the article in the first place.

Remember What You Sign

In Chapter 8, you learned the difference between first North American serial rights and work-for-hire contracts. When you decide you want to repurpose content that you wrote for another magazine, you enter the legal terrain for which those different types of contracts are designed.

QUESTION?

Who can sue you if you resell an article whose rights you don't own?
Both the magazine in which the article first appeared, and the second magazine you sold it to as original content. If you signed a work-for-hire contract, the first magazine owns the story. It can sue you—and the second magazine—for copyright infringement, and the second magazine can sue you to recover its expenses.

If you signed a first North American serial rights agreement when you originally wrote the article, then you should be able to resell it without making any changes to it (assuming the second magazine's editor doesn't mind running the same exact copy as the first magazine). However, in many cases the second magazine will ask you to sign a new contract that promises the content you are delivering is original. This means that you may be able to use your original article as the basis for a story in the second magazine, but you will have to rewrite it and perhaps add new information to it in order to comply with the second magazine's contract.

FACT

Because reporting a story is often more time-consuming than actually writing it, many writers choose to completely revise every article they repurpose for a second sale. This allows them to put the article into the new magazine's preferred tone and style and also to avoid any possible confusion about who owns the rights to the copy.

All of this actually sounds more complicated than it really is. Think of the example given earlier in this chapter, about a magazine writer whose expertise includes polar bears in the Arctic. If that writer can sell stories about polar bears to adult and children's wildlife magazines, then he can probably outline them and structure them in exactly the same way. He'll just have to use shorter sentences and more visual references for the children's version, something he can do by writing the adult version and then revising it instead of writing an entirely new article.

What Should They Pay?

When you repurpose content, you often can expect to be paid full price, just as if you were writing an entirely new article. This is the case when you do enough revisions that the piece is essentially a unique creation, even if it's all based on previous reporting and research. You should earn what you would if you set out to write the article anew, even as much as a couple of dollars per word.

If the editor specifically buys a reprint of an article that does not require revisions, then you should expect to receive less pay. The particular amount will depend upon the magazine's budget for reprints, but usually, an article that is 1,000 or 1,200 words long won't bring in much more than about $500 in reprint fees.

Still, that reprint fee is $500 that you didn't have before, and it's money you didn't have to do any new work to earn. Not a bad deal if you can get it.

Entering New Markets

Another way to grow your writing business is by entering new markets. This is usually a lot more work than repurposing the content you already own, but it's definitely the way to go if you realize you're spending an awful lot of time writing about things that really don't interest you.

Remember to keep your business-expansion goals in mind when entering new markets. If you want to sell an article or two outside of your regular area of expertise, that's fine, but you'll need to keep your regular clients happy along the way. If you want to totally shift markets—say, from oceanography to high fashion—you can drop your old clients as you get new ones.

Specializing by Accident

Some writers find themselves ready to expand their business after they specialize by accident. It just sort of happens organically. You write what you think will be a one-time article for one magazine, say about drug use, and then another magazine hires you to write a similar story on the same topic because they liked the first one so much. Before you know it, you're accepting assignments from multiple magazines for articles about drug use, and you've accidentally become a recognized specialist in the field.

Now, maybe you find drug use to be the most boring topic on the planet, and you've just been accepting those assignments all along because, hey, you're trying to earn a living here, and this is the work that's coming the easiest to you. That's perfectly legitimate, but it's also a key reason that you might wake up one morning and decide that you need to grow your writing business into new and different markets.

Maintaining Multiple Markets

No matter why you decide to enter a new magazine-writing market, you need to realize that you in many ways will be starting over completely. You will have no reputation with these new editors, whereas editors of magazines whose topics you cover regularly might recognize your byline. You will be back at square one in terms of sending query letters and getting those first precious assignments, and you need to be prepared for the inevitable rejection letters that are bound to come your way.

Once you do start landing assignments in a new corner of the magazine-writing universe, you'll face the additional challenge of having to maintain a reputation in more than one area at once. This can be a major hurdle all on its own, especially if you are entering markets that are keen on up-to-the-minute breaking news.

When you decide to branch out into new markets, remember to use your contacts from writers' groups and other networking associations. Your friends may know editors who can help you switch into a new genre with the advantage of a personal recommendation to get your foot in the door.

On the other hand, if your markets are complementary—say, parenting magazines and children's magazines—then you may have an easier time maintaining a strong reputation in both at once. Again, your goals for expanding your business will help you determine which path is best for you, but why do things the hard way if there's an easier route you can take to the same amount of income?

Copywriting

That same philosophy of doing less to earn more holds true for the area of copywriting, which is another possible avenue you can take as you expand your magazine-writing business. Copywriters are people hired to work with a magazine's advertisers to create content for readers. This content can be advertorial features that appear along regular editorial features in the magazine's pages, or it can be other things such as promotional pamphlets that get sent out to readers along with their monthly magazine subscription.

Copywriting is not the same as the copyrighting that you learned about in Chapter 10. When you are a copywriter, you are not spending all day filing copyright forms to protect ownership of an article. Instead, a copywriter is a person who writes promotional material for magazines, including advertisements and advertorial features.

In most cases, the work that copywriters do does not receive a byline. This actually plays to your advantage if you are already writing for a magazine's editorial department and want to expand your business by doing some copywriting for its advertising department. You will already know the magazine's tone and style, and you can easily produce whatever is needed without hurting your editorial reputation for objectivity among the magazine's readers.

Conflicts of Interest

The thing to watch out for with copywriting is that you do not create a conflict of interest. You and your editors at various magazines can determine where the ethical line should be drawn on a case-by-case basis. In general, however, you do not want to put yourself in a position where you have to write both editorial and advertorial features about the same companies or products.

Be careful when accepting copywriting jobs that come from advertisers in your key clients' magazines. You may get a fat paycheck for writing catalog information for an advertiser whom you regularly cover editorially, but when the magazine needs an objective writer to cover that company again later on, you may not land the assignment.

You may be able to keep it straight in your mind which copy the advertiser is paying for and which is being created solely for readers, but the advertiser surely will want the same amount of influence over all pieces you write. This creates a level of confusion that is unnecessary, and it puts you into an untenable position in terms of credibility with both the advertiser and the magazine's readers down the line.

Big(ger) Paychecks

Why take the chance? In terms of expanding your business, the answer is money. Writing advertising and advertorial copy traditionally pays better than writing editorial copy—sometimes several thousand dollars better for the same number of words.

The drawback, in addition to potential conflicts of interest, is that you lose control over what you write. If an advertiser is paying you to produce a promotional piece, then the advertiser is going to have the final say in how that piece reads. It may be cheesy, it may stretch the truth, and at the end of the day, people may find out that you "wrote" it. Some writers—especially those with strong newspaper backgrounds who are not used to dealing with advertisers at all—simply can't stomach this idea of "selling out" by doing copywriting. That's a valid decision, and you can certainly choose to grow your writing business in other ways instead.

Partnering with Photographers and Illustrators

Remember what you learned in Chapter 12, about photographs often making a bigger impact on the page than your words? You can use this tactic to your advantage, too, when it comes time to expand your magazine-writing business.

Do some magazines select photographs first and then hire a writer to do a story that goes with them?
Yes, absolutely. For this reason, if your work is often used in conjunction with a certain photographer's work in one magazine, then the two of you can team up to pitch word-and-picture packages to additional magazines.

How Photographers Are Paid

Most photographers sign the equivalent of first North American serial rights agreements when it comes to letting magazines use their pictures. After the photos appear in print, the ownership and usage rights revert back to the photographer. This means that like you, the photographer who signs a first North American serial rights contract can repurpose and resell his photographs as many times as possible.

Smart magazine photographers know that most magazine editors want words to go along with photographs, so they look for writers they can work with to sell article-photo packages. Especially for magazines that are photo-heavy, these kinds of query letters are a blessing for editors to receive. You're basically placing an entire section of the magazine into the editor's lap, with no further reporting or photography oversight needed.

Sending a Joint Query

You can send joint photo-article queries a couple of different ways. If you know an editor at a certain magazine and can speak to her informally, then a good idea is to send an e-mail with a few terrific photos attached. Your note to the editor might read something like this: "This photographer shot some of the most beautiful photos I've seen of these soy-based snack bars that I wrote about for another magazine. I recently learned a few new things about the snack bars that would make for a terrific feature article, and I thought you might like to take a look at the kinds of photography that might run with it."

ESSENTIAL

Don't get into logistics in your query letter about who will be paid how much for repurposed word-and-photo packages. Simply present your story idea, get the editor to go for it, and negotiate your fee separately from the photographer's. Most magazines have separate art and copy budgets, so you and the photographer will each earn more if you negotiate with separate art and copy editors.

On the other hand, if you are sending a query to a magazine for which neither you nor the photographer has ever worked, you will likely have to use snail mail. (Most editors will not open e-mail attachments, especially large photograph files, for fear of viruses.) You can embed a few key photographs into the body of your query letter, or simply attach printouts of the photographer's contact sheets—small photo thumbnail samples—for the editor to peruse after reading your query letter.

One last note about working with photographers and illustrators: Don't forget to query magazines that are heavy on visuals but light on copy. You might be surprised at how much money you can earn by writing a really in-depth caption to go with a great shot that a photographer friend has available to re-sell.

Creating Alter Egos

When you expand your writing business into new markets, it's important to remember that you have to expand your image as well. Your business cards, your personal stationery, your Web site if you have one—all must be generic enough to fit multiple markets, or you'll have to create multiple versions.

FACT

Some magazine writers create actual alter egos for the different markets in which they work. A writer who works a lot on European political articles, for instance, is likely to adopt a nom de plume when writing celebrity gossip features for fear that working on such chatty and catty articles might hurt his reputation among serious world leaders.

Separate Your Genres

The easiest way to keep the various versions of yourself straight is to have a few separate folders on your computer. One may be titled "gardening magazines" while another may be labeled "home-improvement magazines." Within each folder, you can keep a separately tailored resume that highlights your accomplishments within each field. If you have the budget to do so, you can even make separate business cards and stationery, perhaps one version featuring a photograph of flowers and another showing carpenter's tools. Overall, your goal is to become the go-to writer of choice in all the magazine markets you enter. The more focused each of your editors believes you are in his or her field, the better your chances of landing the plum assignments.

Be the One for Everyone

Having separate identities for different markets means that the gardening-magazine editor may never even realize that you work for home-improvement magazines. This may be a good or a bad thing, depending on the markets you choose to work in, but it's nice to know the option is there if you want to take it.

Then, once you have your writing business organized and expanding the way you want it to, you can focus on enhancing your position as the go-to writer of choice in as many markets as you want—and earning more profits along the way. Chapter 14 shows you how.

Increasing Your Income

Expanding your base and increasing your income are two different things. You can write for dozens of different magazines if you want to, but if their pay scales don't work together to your benefit, you may end up creating more and more articles for the same amount of total annual pay. When it comes to earning more money, there are factors that you need to consider beyond just expanding your base of clients.

How Much Is Enough?

In Chapter 3, you considered what kind of magazine writer you want to become. You put yourself into one of four general categories:

- The occasional writer, selling three or four articles a year
- The part-time writer, selling an article or two every month
- The average full-time writer, selling three or four articles every month
- The serious full-time writer, selling as many stories as possible, perhaps branching out into books and other formats in the future

No matter which of these categories describes you best, you may eventually come to a point where you feel that you would like to increase your overall income. That could mean earning $500 or $5,000 more each month, and it could be done either by expanding your base to take on more work or by increasing the amount of money you earn from the clients that you already have.

What you need to think about at this point is not just the kind of magazine writer you want to be, but whether your goals also include making as much money as possible. You have to ask yourself the question: How much is enough?

It's Okay to Make a Little

A lot of people instinctively answer this question by saying, "As much as I can get!"

Of course you want to earn as much money as you can in your working life, and it would be wonderful if every magazine writer earned $50,000 for every 300-word article she produced. This obviously is a far cry from reality, though, and you have to understand your personal goals before you can decide how much income will really be enough to satisfy you.

The average freelance magazine writer in America earns between $30,000 and $60,000 a year, according to various surveys. Being average, then, may be perfectly fine for your goals. There's nothing wrong with admitting that you're happy with what you already have and focusing on the craft of writing instead of on increasing your annual income.

For many magazine writers, being published—not making big bucks—is the overall goal. There's nothing wrong with you if you fit that description. It's perfectly acceptable, even fulfilling in many cases, to sell an article here and there while collecting a bit of money for your efforts. You certainly don't have to spend every waking hour trying to figure out how to fatten your bottom line if you'll be just as happy fattening your file of magazine-article clips instead.

It's Serious Business to Make a Lot

You also need to keep in mind that if you do want to earn as much money as possible, you're going to have to go back into the mode of businessperson instead of creative writer. For many wordsmiths, this is a formidable challenge, one that sometimes just isn't worth all the effort and aggravation. A lot of magazine writers prefer to simply write great stories and take whatever money they can get. On the other hand, if you're the type of writer who is willing to knuckle down and scrape every last corner of the magazine-writing universe in search of dollars and pennies alike, then you certainly can find plenty of extra income out there.

How much money do top-earning freelance magazine writers make?
There are U.S.-based writers out there who earn well more than $100,000 a year. Some work exclusively for magazines, while others work for magazines and then repurpose their stories into books, advertorials, and other formats to boost their bottom-line income.

You'll have to think strategically about the kinds of assignments you're landing and the kinds of editors with whom you're building relationships, and you'll also have to do some soul-searching about how you can cut costs in your personal business—even if it means a little bit more work for you at first.

The $1-per-Word Question

As you do more and more magazine writing, you may come to hear what is commonly referred to as "the $1-per-word question." Basically, it boils down to the notion that "real" or "serious" magazine writers won't take less than $1 per word for anything they write, thus helping them to establish a general baseline of income no matter which magazine's assignments they accept.

These types of writers simply won't work for any editors who offer forty or fifty cents per word on an article. Some of them even refuse to work for editors who offer less than $2 or $3 per word on an article—the bulk of the magazine-writing universe.

The thing is, the more "real" and "serious" magazine writers you talk to, the more you will come to learn that there are plenty of ways to establish a general baseline of income, even if some of it comes from editors who pay forty or fifty cents per word on an article. You just have to make your contractual agreements on pay line up with your overall financial and professional goals as a magazine writer.

E ALERT!

Don't believe anybody who tells you that $1 per word is the financial standard by which you must write to earn a good living. Yes, that level of pay can mean a decent amount of annual income, depending on how long it takes you to write those $1-per-word articles, but there are other routes you can take to greater financial success as well.

There are two specific ways that you can earn more money without falling into the $1-per-word category: repurposing the content you own, and producing quick-hit articles that give you a high-quantity base of work as opposed to a high-quality base of work.

Repurposing What You Own

Try to recall everything you have learned so far about copyright ownership and reselling your stories. The general idea is that the more rights you retain to your magazine writing, the more you can repurpose, re-slant, and resell that writing to second, third, and even fourth or fifth magazines over time.

The point of reselling your stories, of course, is to make money. Now, even if your first editor paid you $1 per word for the article, you don't necessarily have to get that same pay rate in order to increase your income. As your article stands after its first printing, it's simply something you own, like a pair of old sneakers sitting in your basement. Only after you resell the article does it begin to pay you more dividends—and you shouldn't be preoccupied with the exact rate of those dividends.

Instead, try to focus on the idea that you're making more money for work you've already completed. Even if you get fifty cents a word for your reprint on a 1,000-word article, you'll have $500 in your pocket that you didn't have before—and you'll have to do very little work, if any, to get it.

Don't get caught up in exactly how much money editors are willing to pay you for reprints and rewrites of articles you've already published. Instead, try to remember that even if they'll only offer you a couple hundred dollars, the money is income you didn't previously have—and it will require very little of your time or effort to get it.

You will be surprised at how quickly income can pile up from resales and repurposing of stories. Think of it in terms of trying to earn $1,000 in a day. You can either sell an entirely new article—going through the query process, doing the reporting, fine-tuning the writing, and sending out an invoice—or you can re-sell two or three stories you already have completed and whose rights you retained. If you have networked properly and have a few editors who like your work, the odds are you can make that $1,000 faster on any given day through article resales than through new story assignments.

Quick Hits for Quick Cash

The same is true of taking less-than-$1-per-word assignments that you can produce quickly—so quickly that it would be a sin to turn the work down. For instance, there may be a trade magazine looking for 300-word articles about subject matter that you know well. Each article pays just $100, far less than $1 per word (which would be a $300 paycheck). However, since you know the subject matter well, you may be able to turn out that 300-word article in one hour's time.

If you can get four or five such assignments from that same trade magazine, you'll be earning $400 or $500 a day for working just four or five hours. If you can land those kinds of quick, easy assignments daily, then over the course of a year you could work five days a week with a couple of weeks off for vacation, and your overall income would be more than six figures.

FACT

When it comes to increasing your income, your time is as important as your pay rate. Yes, it's nice to land a $1-per-word assignment, but not if that assignment is going to take so long to complete that it's the only thing you can do for months on end. Sometimes, lower-paying but easier-to-complete articles are more financially productive.

Per-Project Versus Per-Hour Pay

The same kind of logic applies to the question of per-project versus per-hour pay. Normally, as a magazine writer, you will be asked to accept compensation on a per-project, or per-article, basis. An editor will offer you, say, $800 to write a story. You take as much time as you need, get the story done, and collect your paycheck. Case closed. Occasionally, though—primarily at nonconsumer titles and sometimes with custom publishers—an editor may ask you to work on a per-hour basis, perhaps assigning you an article and offering to pay you $20 per hour for the amount of time you need to get it written.

Should you take the hourly pay rate, or negotiate for a per-project fee instead? Nine times out of ten, the latter is the more lucrative answer. Here's why.

Knowing Your Pace

As you get better at the craft of magazine writing, you tend to do it faster. Be it reporting, writing, or self-editing, you will be able to cut to the chase a bit sooner as your career progresses. An article that took you three days to report and write during your first year in the business, for instance, may take you only a day to report and write just a year later. You'll just learn to do things quicker at the same level of quality.

QUESTION?

How can you tell what your pace is for writing articles?
Count the number of assignments you completed in the past year and divide that number into the total number of days you worked during the year. If you completed sixty-five articles during 300 days of work, then your pace for writing each article is about four and a half days.

Now, if you can make the same $1,000 for writing an article in one day that it used to take you three days to produce, you're going to be in much better financial shape overall. You can add two more articles to your workload over that same three-day time period, at an additional $1,000 apiece, and triple your income without tripling the amount of time you're working in general.

Making the Most of Your Time

On the other hand, let's say you charged $30 an hour for writing an article. If it took you three days to write the story, working eight-hour days, then you would earn $720—already less than the going per-project rate of $1,000 in the previous example. And, if you improved your skills enough to write that article in one day, you would actually be decreasing your income to $240 total.

True, you could add two more clients and charge each of them $30 an hour to write two more stories in the same amount of time, but you would still be making that same $720 after three days' worth of work—and you will have done three times the amount of work as if you'd simply asked for the $1,000-per-story fee in the first place.

ALERT!

Do not let editors take advantage of the fact that you are fast on the job. Don't accept comments such as, "It'll take you a day to write, so we'll pay you $250." Instead, explain that you want a per-story fee of at least $1,000 because that is the going rate for good stories—and the amount of time it takes you to write one is irrelevant.

The Bottom Line

So you see, finding ways to increase your income is as much about setting your own pace and payment terms as it is about landing high-paying assignments. Don't be afraid to negotiate a deal that earns you the most money for your particular set of expertise and skills—and remember to throw in as many little extras as you can to increase your income even more.

Adding Little Extras

The more that magazine writers become content providers for various forms of media, the more editors need things that they didn't used to. For instance, many magazines now have companion Web sites with "teaser" pages that refer to articles coming out in a soon-to-be-printed issue, or "exclusive" pages where the magazine posts information online that got cut out of the printed issue or that is simply too newsworthy to hold back until the issue hits newsstands.

Where does that online content come from? Often, your editor has to produce it herself. This adds to her workload (probably not to her liking) and leaves her searching for ways to get her own job done easier and faster.

Offering to help your editors with little extras that add to their daily workloads is a great way not just to earn a bit of extra money, but also to show your loyalty and commitment to being part of the magazine's team effort. Keep that attitude in mind when you're pitching add-ons to your feature article assignments.

Offer to Help Out

Just as you want to be every editor's go-to person when it comes to landing article assignments, you also want to be your editors' go-to person when it comes to helping solve these kinds of problems. Remember, you want your editors to think of you first—always—and there's no better way to cement that kind of relationship than by offering to help out with Web extras and other little items that will make your editor's life easier without making your own that much harder.

Many editors now require photographs to run on their Web sites alongside teasers for upcoming articles. If you own a high-quality digital camera, you can take photos during your interviews and offer them to your editor for an extra $25, $50, or $100 on top of your regular story fee. It's an easy way to add a little to your bottom line.

Perhaps your editor is offering you $2,000 for a 2,000-word article that will require a 500-word teaser item on the magazine's companion Web site. You could offer to write that teaser item for an extra $100. That's less than the per-word price for your article, but the job really won't take you much time to do since you'll likely be summarizing part of your article for the teaser item anyway. You gain an extra $100 pay for what probably will amount to less than an hour's worth of work, and you ease your editor's workload in the process. It's a win-win for both you and the magazine.

Think Long-Term

Now, it's true that little extras like these aren't going to add massive sums to your annual income right away, but over time, they do add up. An extra $200 or $300 a month from various magazines equals an extra $2,400 or $3,600 a year. That's not exactly chump change to most working magazine writers today. Also keep in mind that offering to help out on these kinds of little extras for a reasonable fee will help to cement your relationships with your editors over the long term. Anything you can do to enhance those relationships will lead to more work over time, which means more income overall. Be nice, offer reasonable options, and good things usually will come your way.

Getting Raises from Longtime Clients

When you work on staff for a magazine (or for most companies of any kind), you typically get some kind of annual performance review that includes the opportunity for a pay raise. A human-resources department keeps track of when you are "due" for a salary increase, and your performance since your last raise is taken into account as your boss decides whether, or how much, to add to your annual salary.

Magazine writers are not members of staffs, though, which means that nobody inside the magazine is keeping track of how long you've been writing for the title, how much you're earning, or when you might be entitled to start earning a bit more. It will be up to you, and you alone, to try to get raises from your longtime clients when you feel the time is right.

Don't Be Afraid to Ask

For a lot of writers, it's difficult to ask a longtime editor for a pay raise. Most writers are creative types at heart, and dealing with business matters can be off-putting. A lot of writers would simply continue accepting the same per-article fee for ten or fifteen years rather than have to have a dreaded conversation about money matters.

The thing is, that's no way to run your writing business—and it's just plain unfair to you as a member of the working class. The cost of living goes up every year, and you shouldn't have to work three, five, or ten times harder than you used to just to make ends meet.

FACT

Most editors value the writers who work for them over a long period of time. Just because they're not hurling money at you to keep you coming back doesn't mean they don't appreciate what you do for their readers. In a lot of cases, you simply need to remind them that you have earned the right to a higher pay scale than their newer writers.

When dealing with your longtime clients, you should think of yourself as a productive worker who deserves a raise just as much as anybody else on the magazine's team. After all, if an editor from a magazine continues to hire you for years on end, then you most likely *are* a productive worker who deserves a raise just as much as anybody else. Asking for a raise in this situation is not like asking for something that you don't deserve. It's simply asking for a financial acknowledgment of your continued commitment to the magazine's readers and editorial goals.

Make Your Case—Nicely

So how do you do pop that uncomfortable question? If you have a relationship with an editor that includes face-to-face meetings from time to time, then that's the best venue for a discussion about a raise. Always try to talk business in person when you can. Doing so will help your editor see the sincerity on your face as you outline the reasons you feel you deserve a pay increase.

Sometimes, a face-to-face meeting will be impossible, and in those cases there's nothing wrong with asking for a raise over the telephone. The principle discussion will be the same, and the editor will at least be able to hear the sincerity in your voice. The trick to the discussion—no matter how you have it—is to make a case for your request. You don't want to approach an editor by saying, "I've been working for you for five years without asking for a single extra cent, and I want what I'm entitled to now."

It's much, much more effective to outline your reasons nicely, perhaps saying something like, "I've been working for you for five years, always at the same pay rate, and I think I'm entitled to earn maybe a few cents more per word than your beginning writers. I know the magazine's tone, I know its needs, and I always bring my best material to you first. Do you think there's anything you can do to help me earn a bit more for my efforts?" Even if the editor doesn't have money in her budget to give you immediately, you're likely to win points for your attitude, which should translate into better pay when the new budget cycle comes around.

ALERT!

Discussions about pay raises should be just that—discussions. They should not be confrontations that result from you festering for years on end because an editor never offered you a raise. Ask for what you think you are entitled to, be prepared to make your case, and be as nice about it as possible if you want to succeed.

Dropping Your Lowest-Paying Clients

Another way to increase your income is by dropping your lowest-paying clients. This can be a tricky and even difficult decision to make, but it's one with which all top-earning magazine writers eventually are faced.

The plain truth is that there are only so many hours in your workday, and if money is your main priority, then you need to spend those hours crafting articles for the clients who will pay you the most. No matter how much you love working with an editor at a low-paying magazine, the time you are taking to work for him is eating into the time you could otherwise be using to land more lucrative story assignments.

If you find yourself turning down high-paying, high-quality assignments from great magazines so that you can spend your time writing for a longtime editor who just can't offer you half as much money, then you may have to make the hard choice to leave your longtime client and take your writing business to the next level. It will not be a fun decision, but it usually will be your smartest move.

Remember, magazine writing is a business. If your goal is to boost your income, then you will eventually have to say goodbye to time-consuming editors who pay less than you can earn by working for other magazines. It's not a personal slight to those editors. It's simply a matter of enhancing your bottom-line income.

Cutting Expenses

Yet another good way to increase your income is by cutting your expenses. It's a simple principle, really: If you spend less of the money you earn, then you keep more of it in your bank account over the long term. A lot of magazine writers look to cut expenses primarily in the areas of postage and copying. The amount of postage and photocopying required to send out query letters, resumes, and clips of previously published articles can add up quickly, sometimes to several thousand dollars a year.

Use the Web

One way to eliminate these expenses altogether is by posting your resume and clips online, at a Web site that serves as the online portal to your magazine-writing business. Instead of having to send paper copies of your work through snail mail, you can simply direct editors to your Web site and ask them to review your resume and clips online.

F A C T

More and more writers are building Web sites not only to cut down on expenses, but also to enhance their image of professionalism. Think about it: If one writer has gone to the trouble to build a Web site while another has not, the first writer is likely to look more established in the eyes of editors—and thus land more work.

Writers' Web sites don't have to be the fanciest thing online. In fact, most writers' Web sites are built in basic formats that allow editors to quickly scan pages and learn the writer's style, other clients, and recent awards. These kinds of sites usually can be built by a professional designer for a one-time fee in the range of $1,000 to $2,000, which, when compared to spending $2,000 or $3,000 annually for postage and photocopying, is not a bad investment.

Do It Yourself

If you have some publishing experience or a bit of the creative designer inside you, then you can often build a perfectly professional-looking Web site on your own. You can buy software programs such as Microsoft Publisher at any office supply store and use the templates that come pre-loaded in the program to build a Web site on your own. Many writers—especially those who have worked at magazines in the past and know the basics of layout and design programs such as Quark—can use these do-it-yourself programs to build nice Web sites over the course of a week. When you think about all the money you'll save for that small investment of time, it's easy to see how building a Web site is a good way to increase your overall income.

Chapter 15

Working with Editors

A good editor—a trusted, talented colleague—is a magazine writer's best friend. He is your lifeline to continued assignments, your intermediary when things go wrong with paychecks and contracts, your connection to other editors, your sounding board for story ideas, and your safety net for ensuring every article you write is as good as it can be. Knowing how to work well with editors is a key to magazine-writing success.

15

You're Part of a Stable

You have already learned that as a magazine writer, part of your job is forming a collection, or stable, of editors to whom you can continually pitch story ideas. What you need to keep in mind when working with editors is that from their perspective, they are not the ones who are part of a stable—you are. To understand why, you need to know a bit about the typical editor's day.

Ever-Increasing Tasks

You may think that an editor's job is, well, editing: assigning stories to writers like you, and then helping to ensure those stories turn out as good as they can for the magazine's readers. In reality, this is just one aspect of most magazine editors' work. Nowadays, many editors spend their days not just making assignments and editing copy, but also collecting accompanying artwork, coordinating photo shoots, dealing with invoices and accounting paperwork, addressing reader complaints and concerns, working on the magazine's Web site and custom-publishing projects, attending planning sessions for upcoming issues, promoting the magazine outside the office, and more.

The typical magazine editor is also a writer at many of today's publications. In some cases, budget cutbacks have forced even longtime, high-profile feature editors to help write front-of-book matter such as short news blurbs and quick-hit fun items, copy that used to be produced by freelance writers like you.

What all of those ever-increasing job duties means to you is that your editor is continually feeling frazzled about time. He probably is working far more than eight hours a day. Plus, his bosses are likely putting more and more pressure on him to do even more tasks as the magazine looks for additional ways to increase circulation and profits.

If you were in your editor's position, you surely would be looking for ways to make as many tasks as possible as easy as you could. This is exactly why editors create stables of magazine writers with whom they want to work on a regular basis.

Seeking Easy Solutions

Creating a stable of writers makes a magazine editor's life much easier. Most editors have a few favorite writers for different kinds of story assignments, such as two writers who are good at hard-hitting features, two writers who are great at humorous articles, two writers who excel at service and how-to assignments, and the like.

When an editor in the middle of a frantically scheduled day realizes that he has to make an assignment, the first writers he will go to—every time—are those in his stable. The odds are pretty good that if his first choice for a particular kind of assignment doesn't take the job, then the second, similar writer in his stable will.

QUESTION?

Is being a good writer enough to keep you in an editor's stable?
No. It's just the first step. You also have to be solid in terms of making your deadlines, making timely corrections and revisions to your copy, and in general being a pleasure to work with—even on rush jobs that come at the last minute.

For you, as a writer, the most important thing to keep in mind when working with editors is that you always want to be the number-one or number-two person in that stable. You want your editor to know that you understand how hard he works every day. Moreover, you want him to know that you are willing to do whatever it takes to help him by being an easy solution to whatever story problem or need may arise. If possible, you want your editor to think of you as more than just a favorite writer. You want him to think of you as an ally who will help him get through whatever crisis he may be facing.

Making and Keeping Allies

So, how do you make your editor an ally? You start by taking time to ask her what her day is like. Find out what challenges she is facing, and try to offer ways that you can work together to solve them.

Maybe there's a new section of the magazine that she's trying to figure out how to fill; well, you have writing talents she doesn't know about. Maybe her budget cutbacks mean she's looking for less-expensive ways to fill columns of type; you own photographs that you will sell to her at a reduced rate. Maybe she's having trouble with another writer who turned in a lousy story that needs to be completely rewritten; you can fix it for a fee much lower than your regular story rate.

Having editors as your allies is not only key to landing continual assignments, it's the best way of getting help when you need it and making broader contacts in the universe of magazines. Even if you don't have a pending assignment with an editor who is an ally, you should stay in touch regularly.

The more you work with your editor to solve problems such as these, the more you will become not just one of the top writers in her stable but also a trusted ally for whom she's willing to fight should the need arise.

The Importance of an Inside Advocate

Editors who are allies are more than people who fix your spelling and grammar mistakes. They are advocates who will work inside their magazine's system to help you, whether that means getting you paid on time, keeping your regular column in print, or offering your name to their bosses for potentially lucrative side projects that pop up from time to time. If you work hard to help your editor with whatever challenges she faces, then she will usually repay you by acting as this kind of an advocate on your behalf.

That's a huge boon to you in terms of immediate workload, and it can also reap big dividends at other magazines in the future.

Even editors who love your work can't always win battles on your behalf. Don't expect unrealistic dividends from a strong relationship with an editor—things that no writer, no matter how good, would get—but do expect the editors who are your allies to go to bat for you whenever they possibly can.

Editors Change Jobs

One reason that having an editor as an ally or advocate is so important is that editors change jobs. More often than not, if at all possible, they look to take their favorite writers with them.

Now, most people don't leave a good job to go to a bad one. Editors are no different: They look to go from working at good magazines to working at great (and better-paying) magazines. What better way for you to break into new, more lucrative markets than by being the golden child in the editor's existing stable when he lands at his new desk?

According to various surveys, most magazine editors will work at three or more titles during the course of their career. This means that having an editor who is an ally can help you break into at least three different areas of the business over the course of your own magazine-writing career.

Even if your editor has been with the same magazine for decades, the odds are that he will change jobs within the ranks—perhaps going from being a columns editor to a features editor. Again, if he's more than just your editor, he will want you to move with him as an ally as he tries to make a good impression. That kind of advocacy can take you from 500-word assignments to 5,000-word assignments faster than any query letters you might conceive.

Editors Have Friends

Another reason it's important to turn your editors into allies and advocates is that they will talk about you with their friends at other magazines.

QUESTION?

Where do editors talk about writers?
Everywhere. Sometimes over the telephone, sometimes at the local coffee shop, sometimes via e-mail, sometimes in online forums, and sometimes at networking events created specifically to help editors get together and compare notes. You want to be well spoken of in all cases.

Hopefully, when a friend asks one of your editors whether she "knows anybody who might be good for a job," your editor will put your name forward. This is what an ally does, both to help you as a friend and to make clear that she has a knack for finding and keeping talented writers around her.

Being Helpful Without Being Suckered

The sticky part about becoming an editor's ally is that, with the wrong kind of editor, offering to be helpful can turn into situations where the editor tries to take advantage of you. All editors are different people. Some are more ethical and honest than others. It's just a fact of life, the same as in any other business. You should always try to become your editor's ally and to make her your advocate, but you also need to look for warning signs that you are dealing with a less-than-scrupulous editor who will try to take advantage of your largesse.

Warning Signs

There are a few warning signs that you can look for to determine whether you're dealing with an editor who is trying to abuse your relationship. For the most part, if an editor is doing one of these things when she could be doing another, you should consider the behavior a red flag and ease away from offering to help her in the future.

- **Asking you to write for free to help stem budget cuts at the magazine:** She should at least offer you a reduced rate.
- **Asking you to add multiple sidebars to completed features without extra pay:** One idea once in a while is okay, but constant additions is an abuse of your relationship.
- **Asking you to take photographs to go with your article without extra pay:** You may not receive a professional photographer's day rate, but you should receive some compensation.
- **Asking you to withhold query letters from competing magazines even if she is not giving you any regular assignments:** She should make it financially worth your while to forgo working for her competitors.
- **Asking you to produce countless queries for stories that she later decides she does not want to publish:** You end up working for no pay, and her attitude shows that she does not value your time.

Should you find yourself trying to make an advocate or an ally out of an editor who works in these ways, you might want to reconsider the relationship. After all, you can take assignments from an editor like this from time to time without making her one of your favorite, go-to clients. At the end of the day, you want to be sure the editors with whom you choose to align yourself are high-quality people in the industry—because your name will be associated with them. Think twice about working hard to make allies of editors who are less than stellar in their business dealings.

How to Gently Back Off

The easiest way to untangle a budding relationship with an unscrupulous editor is to become too busy to help out on all the "little extras" the editor wants you to do for free. Whether you are up to your ears in other assignments or not, you can tell the editor that your plate is just too full to help him right now, but that you would be happy to do what you can for him in the future.

Never, ever make an enemy out of an editor—even if you believe she is the biggest cheater and liar in the business. You never know who her friends are, where she will work next, or what effect she might have on your career down the road. If you have a problem relationship, ease out of it as gently as possible.

Backing off from an editor in this way accomplishes two goals for you. First, you protect yourself without making an enemy, and second, you leave the editor with the impression that if he wants you to write for him in the future, he will have competition for your time. The latter is usually a good thing for these kinds of editors to know because they are less likely to try to push you around if they know you can earn your living elsewhere.

Protecting Yourself with New Editors

Working with an editor for the first time presents a different kind of challenge for you as a writer. You want to show a new editor that you are full of enthusiasm and excitement for whatever assignment you have landed, but you also have to be realistic about the fact that you are entering into a business relationship with somebody you don't know well. In other words, you need to be smart about protecting yourself while at the same time laying the groundwork for a relationship with a possible future ally and advocate.

Get That Paperwork

As you learned in previous chapters, the best way to protect your interests when working with any kind of editor is to get your assignment letter and contract in advance of doing your work. This is especially true with editors who are new to you. You have no way of knowing whether what they tell you about their payment dates, copyright purchases, and more is actually what will be outlined in print when it comes time for you to sign on the dotted line. Initial conversations can be misleading to both parties, and you need to make sure you understand exactly what you're agreeing to before you start a job.

Before you begin working for a new editor at a new publication, make sure you have an assignment letter and a signed contract in hand. If the editor doesn't offer them to you immediately, then you should politely ask for them by saying, "When can I expect the assignment in writing, so I can file the copies in my records?" A tone like this presumes that the paperwork is coming and is less likely to make the editor feel defensive or even suspicious about your desire to have all your t's crossed and i's dotted.

Few editors will intentionally mislead a new writer about payment and rights issues. However, not all editors are as well versed as others in their magazines' inner workings—including how and when writers get paid. Written agreements are all you will have to fall back on if something a new editor tells you turns out to be false.

Follow Through on Your End

Once you have that paperwork from your new editor, you can rest assured that you have taken the first step toward building what may someday become a relationship with an advocate or ally. It's now time for you to hold up your end of the agreement by writing a great story that fits all the requirements of the assignment, including word count and deadline. Show your new editors that if they follow through for you, then you will follow through for them. This kind of collegial approach is the seed of many a great writer-editor relationship.

When to Take the Kill Fee

A kill fee is a partial fee—usually ten to thirty percent—to which a writer may be contractually entitled if an assignment doesn't work out. For instance, you may write a piece in a way the editor doesn't like, and instead of paying you in full or asking for a rewrite, the editor may offer you a kill fee to end the assignment altogether. Any magazine writer who has been working in the field for any length of time will tell you that there are simply some occasions where you should take the kill fee, leave an editor behind, and move on without any second thoughts.

You should not feel like a failure if you find yourself having to take a kill fee for an assignment of any kind. A lot of times, kill fees are offered for reasons that have absolutely nothing to do with the quality of your work. In other instances, you and your editor may come to realize during the course of an assignment that you simply aren't a good working team.

In still other cases, you may actually request a kill fee because you feel an editor's demands have become too cumbersome.

Why You May Request a Kill Fee

Why would you give up a full-paying assignment in exchange for a kill fee? The most common reasons most magazine writers cite include these:

- Having an editor who can't make up her mind about how a story should be written, forcing you into countless rewrites that never seem to end
- Having an editor who rewrites your work and inserts errors that are embarrassing to your byline
- Having an editor who holds your story for so long without running it that you may never be able to publish it elsewhere because it will become untimely

Every one of these examples is a case where taking a partial payment as a kill fee will do you more financial good in the long run than hanging onto the full-paying assignment. In general, that should be the main criteria upon which you request a kill fee: You are spending too much time or losing too much money in trying to make a given assignment work out.

Why Your Editor May Request a Kill Fee

You may have the right to ask for a kill fee, but your editor usually has the right to insist on one. Common reasons editors force writers to take kill fees may be similar to those listed in the previous section, but additional reasons include the following:

- The magazine has changed direction and no longer wants your story, no matter how good it is
- Your assigning editor has left the magazine and the new editor wants to use his own writers
- A competing magazine ran a story just like yours right before your story was scheduled to go into print, and your magazine does not want to look like a copycat

All of these reasons are perfectly valid from the editor's business perspective, though they may leave you, the writer, feeling unsatisfied—especially if you've done the job you were asked to do. It's just a simple fact of the magazine-writing business, one you need to keep in mind as you work on building your relationships with the best editors.

QUESTION?

Does taking a kill fee mean you will never work for that same editor again?
Not necessarily. If an assignment ends badly with the editor hating your writing, then yes, your work for that editor is probably history. However, if an assignment simply doesn't pan out as planned, then offering to accept a kill fee will show your editor that you have the magazine's best interests at heart.

Five Tips for Keeping Editors Happy

When you do find editors with whom you work well—editors whom you want to keep as allies and advocates through good assignments and bad— you will want to do everything you can to help your relationship flourish.

The following five tips for keeping editors happy apply to editors you're working with for the first time as well as to longtime editors with whom you have exceptional relationships. Remember: There are always more writers out there trying to get into the editor's stable. Follow these five tips if you want to earn top billing and keep it for years to come.

Make Your Deadlines

There's nothing more troublesome to an editor than a writer who fails to make her deadlines. Even if you turn in the cleanest, most exciting copy the editor has ever seen, it won't do him very much good if the magazine is already rolling off the press by the time you actually send the story in. Do not take on work that you can't do on time, and always bust your tail to get your stories filed early if you can.

Announce Problems Early

If you suspect that you are going to miss your deadline—or if any other problem arises that will interfere with your living up to your end of the writing agreement—then be sure to tell your editor immediately.

ESSENTIAL

Don't abuse the notion of announcing problems early. Every story you write should not be accompanied by a deadline problem. The idea is that when you have a rare issue with making a deadline, you will handle it professionally by giving your editor as much advance warning as possible.

Most editors understand occasional problems that force writers to be a day or two late on an assignment. Maybe a key source is out of town, or your child becomes sick, or your research simply becomes more in-depth than expected. If you tell your editor at least a week in advance of a looming deadline problem, the odds are he will thank you for the head's up and try to adjust his own schedule to help you complete the story as best you can.

Make Your Word Count

If a writing assignment calls for a 2,000-word story, then you should turn in a story that is between 2,000 and 2,200 words long. That is the amount of space the editor will have reserved for you in the magazine, and that is the amount of space that will have to be filled whether you hold up your end of the deal or not.

Every editor will tell you that it is much easier to cut extra copy out than to add more copy in. If you turn in 1,200 words on a 2,000-word assignment, then the editor has to come up with a way to fill 800 words of space in the pages of the magazine—a frustrating task that will not bode well for you in terms of future assignments.

FACT

A good rule is to turn in about 10 percent more copy than is called for in your assignment letter. This shows the editor that you have thoroughly researched your topic and have additional information if he needs it, and it gives the editor a small cushion of word count for editing to make your piece fit the allotted space in the magazine.

By the same token, you don't want to turn in *too much* copy. Yes, cutting is easier than adding, but if you turn in 4,000 words on a 2,000-word assignment, you are basically telling your editor that you don't care about all the time it will take him to make your piece fit in the magazine. Again, this is not good for you in terms of getting future work.

Argue with Respect

If your editor makes changes in your copy that you dislike, be sure to question those changes respectfully. The editor always has the last say about what goes into the magazine. Still, if your editor learns that you can argue changes with respect for his authority, then he will be more likely to listen to your opinions and let you write things as you wish.

For instance, if an editor rewrites a sentence to include mistaken information, you should not open your conversation about the change by saying,

"You're destroying my hard work!" Instead, try something more along the lines of: "Perhaps I wasn't clear in my original, but what's there now is inaccurate. May I try again with that sentence?"

The latter shows that you are willing (and even happy) to be edited, but that you do want the story to be perfect—and that you will raise important questions that will help the editor look good in the long run, too.

See the Big Picture

No matter how minute a detail you may find yourself discussing with your editor, be it a verb choice or the hour a story must be filed, remember to always keep the big picture in mind. Every single assignment you get should, if possible, lead you to future assignments, whether at the same magazine with the same editor or with other editors to whom he recommends you.

Many a talented writer has lost out on future business because she could not step back from an argument about sentence structure and accept that even if she didn't love what the editor had done to her words on one particular story, she had earned the editor's respect and should just let the matter drop. Love every story you write, but remember that it's writing you love the most. You will have to let your editors have things their way more often than not if you want to continue working as a magazine writer at all.

Chapter 16

Collecting Your Due

The one thing most magazine writers dread the most is having to chase down paychecks for assignments they completed long ago. Most reputable magazines can be counted on to pay you for your work within a reasonable timeframe, but pretty much every writer out there can tell you a story about having had to fight with a magazine for months, or even years, to receive fair compensation for a writing assignment. Some writers even walk away penniless. Read on for helpful hints about collecting your due.

Money Matters

A lot of magazine writers will tell you that negotiating a good contract and a fair pay rate is the hardest part of the job, but even more magazine writers are likely to tell you that the toughest task is actually collecting what you've been promised. Virtually every writer working for magazines today has a horror story to tell about spending days, or even weeks, working on a writing assignment and then getting stiffed after turning in the final copy. It's never pleasant when it happens to you, but you're definitely not the first person in the business to experience this particular brand of aggravation.

QUESTION?

Why would a magazine fail to pay a writer?
Maybe the publication went out of print before the story editor signed off on the writer's invoice. Perhaps the writer's invoice got lost in the bowels of a massive accounts payable department. And, though it's sad, it's also true that editors are sometimes simply unscrupulous, and they want to get copy for free.

The most important things to remember if you find yourself dealing with these kinds of money matters are that you're a businessperson and that you must act like one—no matter how frustrating the situation becomes.

Remember, It's Just Business

Business of any kind is tough. Not everybody is cut out for it. When you have payment problems with a magazine, try to remember that you're experiencing the same kinds of issues that businesspeople of all stripes have to handle every day, all over the world. Their clients don't always come through with promised money or goods on time, either. It's a simple fact of doing business.

The important lesson is that the best businesspeople find ways to get their money in the end, or at least some of their money. You have to adopt that same attitude. Don't take the matter personally. Leave your emotions behind and try to think of nonpayment as a standard business transaction that needs to be rectified, like a lost bank statement.

The Right Attitude Is Key

Writing is such a passionate career choice that writers often have a hard time maintaining a decent attitude when handling anything having to do with their stories. You may get away with losing your cool when an editor changes your words around, but when it comes to getting paid, it's paramount that you keep calm.

More often than not, you will end up dealing not only with your editor, but also with the magazine's managing editor and perhaps its accounts payable department. The folks in those jobs don't have any patience for "passionate creative types," and they're more likely to help you if you act like the businessperson that they expect you to be.

FACT

At many magazines, your editor may not be the person responsible for ensuring you get paid. She may shuffle your invoices into the in-box of a managing editor or executive editor, who then sends them to the magazine's business manager, who then sends them to an accounts payable department. You can be mad at your editor—but nonpayment simply may not be her fault.

One thing that will help you stay focused during stressful discussions about money is having a plan of action to follow. If you know exactly what to do and how to do it when you realize your check isn't in the mail, you will have a far better chance of reconciling the problem.

When the Check Isn't in the Mail

The first thing you need to assess is whether your check *should* be in the mail. A common misconception is that the day you turn in your article, the editor approves your payment. This is not always the case. If you're not yet owed the payment, then you have no ground on which to stand when demanding it.

E ALERT!

The contract you sign will affect when you get paid. If you agree to be paid on acceptance, then the magazine should write your check as soon as your editor accepts your article. However, if you agree to be paid on publication, then your editor can accept your article and hang onto it—and your money—until the story's run date eventually comes around.

Some magazines pay within thirty days of accepting an article, while others can take as long as two or three months. If your contract entitles you to payment on acceptance and it's been more than six or eight weeks with no check in the mail, then it's probably time to pick up the phone and find out what's going on.

There are three things you'll need to have in hand when you make this initial phone call to your editor: your invoice, your patience, and your professionalism.

Have Your Invoice at Hand

Having a copy of your original invoice in hand can greatly smooth your first conversation about a missing paycheck. If nothing else, it alerts your editor to the facts that you have a bookkeeping system, that you keep track of what you're owed, and that you're organized about getting paid. Your level of seriousness may affect the delinquent magazine's level of seriousness if it typically counts on writers being disorganized and failing to follow up.

Your invoice should include the date you first sent it, the name of your article, the number of words you wrote, the amount you are owed, and your editor's name. Even if your editor has changed or the story has been cut, your invoice will show that you did what you agreed to in your contract. Sometimes, your invoice has simply been lost and all you need to do is resend it in order to get paid.

Check your bookkeeping system regularly for overdue invoices and notify your editors promptly about any problems. If you wait a few months to ask where your missing paycheck has gone, then nobody at the magazine will remember the details of your article. It's also possible that your editor may change, or the magazine may even go out of business.

Don't Be Nasty

Even if your situation becomes more complicated than resending an invoice, be sure to maintain a professional attitude. Remember: You want the person on the other end of the telephone to help you, not to dread talking with you. Try to make that person your teammate in solving the mystery of the missing money, not your enemy in a battle for every last cent.

When dealing with delinquent invoices, it's usually best to contact your editor by telephone instead of e-mail. You want to be sure that your tone is conciliatory and inquisitive, not demanding and nasty. Sometimes, those differences do not come through over the Internet, and you don't want to start off on the wrong foot when trying to track down lost money.

Be Clear: You Deserve to Be Paid

Being professional, however, does not mean that you should take on the role of fawning servant. It's not your job to find money that you're owed. It's the magazine's job, a regular part of doing business.

Keep in mind that your getting paid is not about *wanting* money. It's about being *owed* money for work that you have done. Think of yourself as a banker collecting on a loan. Have you ever known a banker to act squeamishly or feel bad about insisting on payment?

Again, you don't have to be nasty. Just be clear when you explain that you have met your end of the contract's terms, and that you now want the magazine to live up to its end of the deal.

Assuming the Best

One of the easiest ways to keep your cool is to assume the best: There has been a mistake. It happens all the time, and mistakes are just that. Nobody is out to get you or to sucker you out of your paycheck. Something just got out of whack with the paperwork.

FACT

Even at a smaller magazine, say one that has seventy editorial pages in each issue, a managing editor will likely have to handle invoices from at least a dozen different writers each month. Think of all those papers moving from desk to desk throughout the payment-system chain, and you can easily see how an invoice might get misplaced.

The most common reason that magazines fail to pay writers is that invoices get misplaced or incorrectly coded for the magazine's business manager. When this happens to you (and it eventually will), try to keep in mind that the magazine probably already has a system in place to track your invoice down, correct whatever accounting codes are wrong, or figure out that you need to resend your invoice and start again.

A Good Editor Is Working for You

In this situation, you'll usually have either your regular editor or a conscientious managing editor working on your behalf to track down the lost or incorrect paperwork. Keep in mind that these editors don't relish this part of the job, either; it usually involves frustrated writers screaming at them over the telephone and bean counters making their lives miserable from a distant corporate office. If you can be the pleasant writer who is willing to help them solve the problem, you will likely earn their respect and any additional help that you might need should your problem escalate later.

The point is that you should assume the best—a mistake or misunderstanding—and do everything that you can to help the editor rectify it, even if it's not your fault.

There's a Fast-Track System

Sometimes, magazines have a fast-track system for getting invoices paid much quicker than usual. These systems are often designed to compensate for time lost to misplaced invoices and the like. If you can resend your invoice immediately to an editor who is trying to help you, then you just may get lucky and have your "lost" paycheck within a week's time.

Understanding the Worst

Sadly, you are likely to encounter a situation where a mistake has not been made and where you are going to have to put up a bit of a fight if you want to get paid for work that you've completed. It happens to all magazine writers at some time during their careers, and it never gets any less frustrating.

QUESTION?

How can you tell when you're not likely to get paid?
The editor's tone on the telephone—if he even answers your calls—is one dead giveaway. Unanswered e-mails are another bad sign, as are telephone transfers that end up hanging up on you instead of placing you into the voice mail of yet another person with whom you've been asked to speak.

The first thing you need to do is determine why you're not getting paid. If a mistake hasn't been made, then the odds are you're either getting the runaround, being put on hold by your editor, or dealing with a magazine that is having serious financial issues.

You're Getting the Runaround

In the world of magazines, getting the runaround on payment usually means that you're being asked to speak with multiple people at multiple times, and that they're all directing you to speak with other people at other times. These people can be editors, business managers, accounts payable agents, or even vice presidents.

The titles of the people you're dealing with aren't the most important factor in terms of determining whether you're getting the runaround. Instead, look for a pattern in which you are shuffled from person to person without having anyone actually offer to help you get paid.

ALERT!

Some startup magazines with limited budgets, or magazines that are truly unscrupulous, will give writers the runaround on payment because they don't expect the writers to follow up. Many writers don't enjoy the confrontations that business can involve, and some magazines prey on that quality by assuming you will simply stop calling even if they don't pay you.

When you're getting the runaround, all you can do is make a pest of yourself and keep placing those calls. It's not an ideal situation, and it may not have a happy ending, no matter how hard you try.

Your Editor Isn't Happy

Sometimes, your payment will be withheld because the editor feels you have not lived up to your end of the contract or story assignment. In this case, your invoice usually sits on the editor's desk until you do whatever he feels you failed to do the first time around.

This can be difficult territory if you disagree and believe that, in fact, you have done everything requested of you. Especially if it's a magazine you would like to work with again, you often have to be an expert at diplomacy to argue your cause—and even then you may end up having to do more than your contract demands in order to finally get paid.

FACT

It's usually not a good idea to go above and beyond your contractual obligations when dealing with an editor who refuses to pay you. Most reputable editors will ask you to complete only the work you have agreed to do—while unscrupulous editors may try to squeeze lots of extra work out of you with no intention of ever paying you at all.

If you find yourself at odds with an editor over whether you have met your end of a contract for a writing assignment, your only option is usually going to the editor's boss to argue your case. You may win the paycheck in the end, but keep in mind that you'll probably never again land an assignment from that editor.

The Magazine Closes Shop

There are far too many cases of writers crafting beautiful articles for magazines that end up going out of business before the words can be published. It's one of the challenges that goes along with writing, and it can happen with a startup or with an established title that has fallen into financial distress.

If you find yourself in this situation, your only course of action may be to hire an attorney and file a legal action against the magazine's parent company. As the lawyer is likely to cost you more than the total amount you're owed, you will have to assess whether fighting to get your paycheck is truly worth the time and effort.

Is Fighting Worth Your Time?

It's sad to say, but sometimes it's just not worth it to fight for your right to be paid. Nobody likes to say so out loud—nobody likes to be a quitter or to be taken advantage of—but at the end of the day, fighting takes a great deal of time. And in the business of magazine writing, time is money.

Time Is Money

When you find yourself in a situation where it's going to require a lot of time, effort, and arguing to collect the paycheck that you're owed, you need to stop for a moment, gather your wits about you, and think like a business-person about whether the aggravation is really worth it. For instance, let's say you're owed $1,000 for a story, but it's going to take three weeks of your working hours to get that $1,000 paycheck. Perhaps you would be better off using that time to send query letters to other magazines that might be interested in buying the story, or a slightly modified version of it. Or, if your average income is $2,000 a week, you might be better served by using your time to complete assignments for magazines that *do* pay you after you've finished a job.

Of course, you have no way of knowing at first whether a paycheck disagreement is going to go on for weeks. But you can probably get a pretty good idea about where you stand after the first few days of dealing with the magazine. Just keep in mind that you shouldn't throw away your valuable time chasing ghosts when you could be chasing new assignments.

The exception here is if you're dealing with a repeat client. With editors from whom you typically get a lot of work—and with whom you've had no such payment problems in the past—your time may indeed be best spent resolving the problem, no matter how long it takes or how little the invoice amount.

To know whether it's worth your time to argue, you have to know how much income you're generating on a daily or weekly basis. Keep track of your average, and weigh that figure against the time you think it will take to get paid. If the invoice amount is small in the grand scheme of things, you might be better off letting it go and focusing on paying assignments instead.

Is It a Good Repeat Client?

The key in this type of situation is knowing whether you're dealing with any old repeat client or a *good* repeat client. What's the difference? In this situation, it's money.

A regular repeat client is any magazine you've worked for more than once. It could be two articles over the course of five years, or ten articles over the course of two months. A *good* repeat client, on the other hand, is a client you've worked for more than once who pays you well for the work that you do. It could be forty cents a word for assignments that take you an hour to write or $5 a word for assignments that take you a month to complete, but it's regular work that contributes to the majority of your income—which means it's work that you don't want to lose.

ALERT!

When you're dealing with a missing paycheck from a good repeat client, remember that your end goal is probably not getting this one issue resolved quickly, but holding onto the magazine's long-term business. Try to keep the big picture and future income in mind, even if receiving a missing paycheck takes months on end.

In some cases, you may be dealing with an unhappy editor who happens to be one of your best repeat clients. In this case, even if you believe that you've done everything in your contract, your smartest move might be taking the kill fee.

Taking the Kill Fee

Magazine writers accept kill fees for a variety of reasons, but on the whole, taking a kill fee simply means you're taking a shortcut to end a particular business deal. Whether your editor is unhappy or you think a magazine's financial situation looks so poor that you may never get your entire paycheck anyway, taking a kill fee can be a good route to ending the non-payment nightmare and moving on.

Can a writer request a kill fee?
Yes—but it's usually frowned on by editors, especially if they're counting on your article to fill pages in an upcoming issue. On the other hand, there's no danger in requesting a kill fee from an editor who you don't think is going to pay your previously agreed-upon fee in the long run.

Sometimes, if a nonpayment issue is dragging on endlessly, an editor will offer you a kill fee just to make the hassle go away. Again, you have to consider the time you're spending arguing about what you're owed and weigh it against this partial form of payment. In some cases, you'll be better off taking the reduced check and simply being done with the particular editor, and the particular magazine, forever.

There will be times, though, when you will want to hold out for the full amount. Your editor can send you a kill-fee check, but if you don't cash it, then you're legally not accepting it, and you have the right to continue fighting for your total due or to write off the total amount when tax time rolls around.

Writing Off Losses

As with anything tax related, you need to consult your personal accountant to find out exactly which write-offs apply to you. Generally speaking, though, unpaid invoices—partial or full amounts—can be used as tax write-offs.

If you find yourself in what you sense is becoming a protracted battle over, say, an unpaid $500 invoice for a story that didn't take you too long to write, call your accountant and ask whether you'll be able to write off the amount on your taxes. He should have a good idea of whether it will be worth your time to fight for the payment or to just chalk it up to a lousy business deal and move on.

Strategic Techniques

In addition to consulting an attorney, there are other strategies that you can use and people whom you can contact to try to get paid. None of these techniques will win you friends at the magazine you're fighting, and you'll probably never work for any of the editors—or their friends at other magazines—again. Still, if you feel it's worth the fight, you do have options.

Moving Up (and Off) the Masthead

A tried-and-true method for getting an editor's attention is by calling *his* editor. Nobody likes having their employees go over their head to their boss, but if you feel your relationship with your editor is shot anyway, then you have nothing to lose by escalating the situation and trying to put him in the hot seat. You can often figure out the name of your editor's editor by looking at the magazine's masthead. Call the general number, ask to be connected, and leave a voice mail if that's the option you are given.

Remember to keep your voice calm when dealing with your editor's boss. You may have been through days or weeks of arguing over a missed paycheck, but to your editor's boss, this is a new problem—and you don't want her to think you're a screaming shrew. You want her help, and you should ask for it as nicely as possible.

Usually, the editor's boss will at least want to find out what the disagreement is when it concerns a missed payment, so you'll have that going for you. In some cases, the boss will put pressure on your editor to resolve the problem simply to keep you from calling again.

Using Writers' Groups

One of the great things about magazine writers' groups is that they usually have forums or even databases that keep track of publications that give writers a hard time about payment. If you end up in an unsolvable situation, then you can always file a request with your writers' group of choice to make the dispute public. The American Society of Journalists and Authors, for instance, gets both sides of the story and then, if appropriate, publishes the magazine's title on its "Warning List."

Sometimes, this embarrassment is the straw it takes to break the magazine's back and finally get your paycheck. And even if that's not the case, you'll at least be helping your fellow magazine writers to steer clear of shysters in the business.

Legal Options

As a last resort, you can always consult an attorney and even file a lawsuit against a magazine to make it pay. The downside to this is, of course, that lawyers usually charge more for a day's worth of work than your writing fee, so you'll end up losing money in the long run by fighting with an attorney on your side.

Still, if you feel you've been taken advantage of and you see no other solution, you may want to give it a try. There may be other writers who have had the same problem with the same magazine, and a class-action suit could be the result of your refusing to give up.

Chapter 17

Managing Your Future

Now that you have plenty of magazine clients, a solid invoicing system, and a good routine established for your writing business, it's time to make sure your personal matters—and your future—are in order. Being a magazine writer comes with terrific freedom and the opportunity to follow your intellectual curiosities, but it also comes with additional responsibilities such as ensuring your own health care and retirement savings. You need to keep tabs on everything from your bank accounts to your personal time management.

A Life of Sporadic Cash Flow

One of the more challenging aspects of being a magazine writer is that your income is likely to be sporadic. You may have month after month of nonstop work—and paychecks—coming your way, only to wake up one morning and realize that you have no assignments on your to-do list for the next several weeks.

This actually is a fairly common occurrence, even among the most successful magazine writers. After all, if you're busy completing assignments, then you're not going to have time to send out as many query letters as you may like.

The thing is, though, if you're not writing, you're not getting paid. And even though your income will fluctuate, your mortgage and credit-card deadlines will not. It's important that you set yourself up financially to pay your bills even if all of your writing jobs dry up from time to time.

Having a Cushion

A lot of financial planners recommend that you have three months' worth of money in the bank at all times, in case of emergencies. That means having enough cash in your savings account to pay three months' worth of your rent or mortgage, car payment, health insurance premiums, food bills, taxes, utilities, and any other regular expenses.

When you're a magazine writer, that advice is good—but it does not take into account "dry spells" when there will be no income at all. For a magazine writer, especially one living on a single income, it's important to have *at least* three months' worth of money in the bank. Ideally, you would have twice that amount in your savings.

FACT

You don't have to limit yourself to a low-interest rate savings account when putting away money for a rainy day. If you can get a better return on your money by investing in a certificate of deposit, for instance, that might be a good option. They typically pay more interest than a regular account, but you can still access your money in an emergency.

Of course, saving up half year's worth of expenses is no short order, but as you learned in Chapter 2, financial considerations are a major part of deciding to become a magazine writer in the first place. Only you know your personal situation well enough to know exactly how much cash you should have in the bank for emergencies, but if you start out smart—say, with three or four months' worth of savings—then you can add to that nest egg during the months you have lots of assignments. Before you know it, you'll have six months' worth of savings, or even more, in your rainy-day fund.

Remember Your Taxes

Another major financial consideration for magazine writers is quarterly tax payments. When you work for a corporation, your income taxes are deducted from each of your paychecks. However, when you are a magazine writer, you are paid in full—a $1,000 check for a $1,000 assignment—and it is up to you to remember to pay a portion of your estimated taxes every quarter.

It's a smart idea to write quarterly tax payment dates into your work calendar, right alongside your assignment deadlines. That way, you won't be surprised in April, July, September, and January when your payments (possibly in the thousands of dollars) come due to the Internal Revenue Service.

This can be a challenging prospect for writers who have poor money-management skills. Basically, what happens during periods of good work is that your bank account gets very fat, very fast. If you fail to realize that a good percentage of that money is going to have to be paid out to the government later, then you can find yourself spending it—only to come up short when Uncle Sam's bill comes due.

Some magazine writers actually open a second savings account specifically for tax-payment purposes. That way, the money is clearly separated from your regular savings or checking accounts, and you'll know that it is not to be spent on things like clothes, restaurant meals, or the like.

Retiring Without a Pension or 401(k)

As if all that saving for rainy days and taxes weren't enough, as a magazine writer you'll also have to think about saving for your retirement. You will not have the corporate benefits of a matching-investment 401(k) or a pension to take care of you when you get old and can no longer work. Instead, you will have to save additional money and invest it wisely so that it will grow over time.

ALERT!

Don't shy away from setting your writing business up as a limited liability corporation or an S-corporation. If you do set up your business this way, then you can take advantage of more retirement savings options. For instance, you can open a SEP-IRA, the easiest form of retirement IRA to handle administratively and one that should help your savings grow.

Plenty of media coverage has been given in recent years to the idea that Americans, in general, are not saving enough for retirement. Sadly, magazine writers usually fall into this group. You would be wise to be the exception to that rule by opening at least a SEP-IRA or making additional investments if your income level allows them.

SEP-IRAs

SEP-IRAs allow you to put away as much as 25 percent of your annual income for retirement, up to a total amount of $40,000 each year. The thing that makes them a good choice for many writers is that you do not have to contribute the same amount every year, every quarter, or ever at all—you can adjust your contribution depending on what kind of year you're having in terms of workflow and income.

Still, a SEP-IRA offers you the benefit of compounding your savings over time. You could contribute $10,000 one year, $15,000 the next, and $7,000 in year three, and at the end of that third year, you will have a total of $32,000 working for you and compounding to generate interest income. With other forms of annual investments (such as certificates of deposit), you don't always get that benefit of increasing your total base of savings over time.

QUESTION?

How can you set up a SEP-IRA?
If you have formed an LLC or an S-corp with no other retirement savings plan, then you are eligible. Usually, you simply can call your regular bank and take advantage of the SEP-IRA programs it offers. If none is available, your accountant can point you toward the provider that will work best for you.

Other Investments

Interest income on the amounts of money that magazine writers typically earn is not always the best way to generate a strong return on your retirement investment. Face it: If your total savings is only $30,000, then you're not going to compound that savings very quickly at a return rate of 3 to 6 percent. For this reason, writers with the financial wherewithal often choose to diversify their retirement savings beyond IRAs and regular accounts, instead investing in things like real estate that have the potential to increase dramatically in value over time. Again, only you know your personal financial situation well enough to know whether this type of investment is a good option, but keep it in mind and work with your accountant to ensure you are maximizing whatever retirement savings you have.

Health Care

Perhaps the greatest expense that most magazine writers take on is paying for their own health care. As with all insurance rates, the cost of health insurance has skyrocketed in recent years. Without an employer to pick up part of that financial tab, the entire burden falls on you.

Nowadays, finding a plan with decent benefits that costs you $100 or $150 a month is considered a good deal—but can be a serious financial strain if you're only selling two or three articles a month that pay $500 or $1,000 apiece.

FACT

According to the Kaiser Family Foundation, the average cost for a single person's annual health insurance coverage in the year 2005 was $4,024. For a policy that covers an entire family, the average annual cost in that same year was $10,880. The average was based on health maintenance organization (HMO), preferred provider option (PPO), and point-of-service plans.

You need to assess your options for continuing health insurance, preferably looking for plans that include some form of disability coverage. Remember, if you can't work, you aren't going to get paid—and you will quickly run through your savings.

Your Spouse's Plan

If you are married, the easiest option may be to simply sign on with your spouse's employer-sponsored health insurance plan. There will be a cost, of course, but you may get a family discount, and you can usually be assured that the benefits will be at least decent, if not quite good, depending on what kind of employer your spouse has.

An additional benefit to getting onboard with your spouse's plan is that even without a family discount, your total costs are likely to be lower than they would be if you got an individual plan. This is because your spouse's employer will still be picking up a portion of the annual premiums, a benefit you will not have if you are forced to look into individual account options.

Individual Accounts

Another way to get health insurance is to open up an individual account with an insurance provider. This is actually a lot harder than it sounds, because most major providers choose to work only with large companies—which you, even as an LLC or an S-corp, most certainly are not.

Why do most health-insurance providers want to work only with large companies?
Because doing so limits their risk. When they insure a large group of people, the odds are good that most of them will be healthy. By contrast, most people who look for individual policies usually have some kind of health-care needs, which the insurers know will cost money.

In addition, if you do manage to find your way into an individual account with a major health-insurance provider, you're likely to have to pay through the nose for it. Some average premiums cost in the neighborhood of $400 to $700 per month, which is often simply too expensive for magazine writers. For this reason, a recent law created the option of health savings accounts, to which more and more writers are turning for coverage.

Health Savings Accounts

Health savings accounts are known as HSAs in insurance circles. They were created as part of the Medicare bill that President George W. Bush signed into law in 2003, and they are becoming a popular choice among writers because of the relatively low premiums attached to them.

Basically, an HSA is a bank account into which you deposit pre-tax dollars. You then use this money whenever you have a health-care need, with any remaining funds being saved for future health-care needs during your retirement. In addition, you pay premiums to the health-insurance provider, though they are typically far lower than the premiums you would have to pay for a traditional, single plan. You can go to any doctor you choose, at any time you like.

ALERT!

With an HSA, you typically pay 100 percent of your medical bills out of pocket, without the benefit of a co-pay, until you satisfy your deductible. This means that instead of getting a bill for, say, $75 for a blood test that your insurer has paid extra to cover, you very well may receive a bill for the entire $750 that the test actually costs.

Deductibles on HSAs are high. By law, you must carry a "high-deductible health plan" to qualify for an HSA, and as of 2006, the minimum deductible amounts were $1,050 for single coverage and $2,100 for family coverage. Many HSAs have deductibles that are twice those amounts or more.

You pay 100 percent of your medical expenses out of your health savings account until you satisfy that deductible. It sounds like a lot, but in reality, for healthy individuals, the overall annual expenses for an HSA are about the same as or even lower than annual expenses with a traditional plan. That's because with a traditional plan, the monthly premiums are far higher than they are for an HSA. What this new form of insurance does is help you to save on premiums, but force you to pay more for the care you decide you need.

ESSENTIAL

No matter what form of health insurance you choose, be sure to save all of your receipts for premiums and expenses. In many cases, those expenses are fully deductible for self-employed magazine writers at tax time. (Check with your accountant to determine whether you are eligible.)

Using Writers' Groups

Heatlh savings accounts and traditional forms of insurance are becoming more easily accessible through writers' groups. Some groups, like *www.mediabistro.com*, the National Writers Union, and the American Society of Journalists and Authors, use their large memberships the same way corporations use their large pools of employees to attract health-insurance providers. You can check out the health insurance options available through these groups by going to their Web sites, which are listed in Appendix A.

Your Network of Colleagues

While it is important to ensure that your retirement savings and health coverage are in order for the long haul, it's also important that you take into account the more personal facets of your long-term happiness. When managing your future, you want to think about more than just dollars and cents so that you can lead a fulfilling and interesting life.

That means making sure your network of colleagues stays intact and continues to grow. Though writers' groups can be a terrific source of support for you throughout your magazine-writing career, you will undoubtedly begin to create your own circle of industry friends to whom you can turn again and again for ideas, advice, and assistance.

Editors Can Be Friends

The creative and collaborative nature of magazine writing means that most writers end up becoming personal friends with their favorite editors. This is a wonderful thing when it happens. Not only do you gain a steady cheerleader for continuing work at a given magazine, you also come away with a colleague whose personal interests you share. What better friend could a writer ask for than someone who likes to go out and explore the same things from time to time, be they new speaker technology or new Broadway musicals?

Your Fellow Writers

Your fellow writers will also be a continuing source of inspiration and support to you throughout your career. You may meet them at writers' conferences, while on assignment, or at retreats sponsored by magazines for which you regularly work—but it will be up to you to continue the relationships, which are often just as personally fulfilling as they are professionally valuable.

FACT

Most magazine writers value their fellow writers more than any other types of longtime friends. The isolation and challenges that can go along with being a writer create a common bond, one that only fellow writers can understand. It sure helps to have a sympathetic ear when you're having a bad day full of denied queries and unpaid invoices.

Even if a writer friend doesn't work for the same genre of magazines that you do, he will likely still face many of the same challenges in terms of the business of writing. That alone is enough to fill a telephone conversation each week, which is the hallmark of many a thriving friendship.

Staying in Touch with Sources

Yet another form of relationship that you can cultivate over the long span of your magazine-writing career is friendship with your regular sources. If you write about, say, animals, then you are probably going to have a lot of sources who are veterinarians. You also are likely to be an animal lover yourself, which means that you and your sources will have tons of things in common.

There's absolutely nothing wrong with becoming friends with sources who share your interests—as long as you don't unethically promote their services or products above those offered by their colleagues and competitors. Make friends and keep them, for sure, but use your best judgment and tell your editors about any conflicts of interest when it comes to your writing.

Balancing Work and Play

One of the hardest things for magazine writers who work from home is finding a balance between work and play. The fact that you wake up in the morning mere steps from your desk, and that your computer is always available to you right before bedtime, means that you may be tempted to work far more than you should. Checking that e-mail one last time before you drift off to sleep can quickly turn into a few extra hours a day spent at the computer. That's not good for your health, not good for your work, and certainly not good for your personal relationships.

Get Out of Your Chair

The first thing that you can do to combat workaholic tendencies is to make a point of stepping away from your computer every couple of hours. Set an alarm clock to tell you when you've been typing for more than, say, three hours, and consider spending a half-hour doing something active, such as:

- Walking your dog
- Gardening
- Shopping
- Cooking
- Cleaning

Some of these activities definitely fall into the category of chores, but they're still good break-time ideas because they force you to move around. Even the most die-hard workaholic can see the value of taking a few minutes off to, say, do laundry, and the act of carrying the basket of clothes around will be good for your blood flow.

Get Out of Your House

On weekends or slow days when you have no assignments, it's important that you get out of your house. Simply being at a movie theater or a restaurant will be a good way to leave your home-office worries behind, and taking an actual vacation will be a rejuvenating change that should help you stay focused on your writing business for months to come.

Several 2006 studies show that only about 60 percent of Americans take a summer vacation, the least amount of people traveling on vacation in nearly three decades. Experts say it takes at least three days to start to unwind from your job—so being part of that 60 percent is paramount to your long-term health and happiness.

Budgeting time and money for a vacation is something many magazine writers fail to do, but it's important if you want to remain sane throughout your career. It's also important if you want to continue thriving creatively, since getting out into the world and experiencing new things will help you to become a better writer.

Get out of Your Routine

Even if you find that you can't get out of your house for a reasonable vacation, it's important that you at least break out of your routine from time to time. Otherwise, you can start to feel like a prisoner in your own home office—and your writing will suffer because of it.

If you usually work Mondays through Fridays, consider taking a Wednesday off and instead typing during the weekend. If you usually work from early morning till mid-afternoon, think about spending one morning reading a favorite book and then typing after dinner. The mere act of shaking up your schedule can sometimes be enough to help you feel like you've had a break, which every writer needs to remember to take.

Getting Help at Home

It bears repeating that just because you'll likely be doing your work from home, you are not a stay-at-home laborer. Your presence in your house should not translate into you doing all of the chores that you and your spouse used to split when you both worked in office jobs.

Hopefully, your spouse will be supportive of your writing and will understand that when you are home, you need to be sitting at your desk doing research and crafting query letters. Still, even the most supportive spouse may slip from time to time into thinking that because you're "around," you can handle everything from dealing with exterminators to mowing the lawn.

ESSENTIAL

It's imperative that you draw a line between your work time and your personal time at home. Just because you are physically in your house does not mean that you should have to do all the chores and work associated with home ownership. If your spouse doesn't understand this, then you need to bring in help around the house.

This is the kind of situation in which you should ask for—or demand—some in-home help. Many magazine writers working from home have in-home child care, landscapers, and housekeepers to help ease the tension between what they can handle themselves and what their spouses expect of them.

These types of assistants may seem like a financial luxury, but in reality, they are the people who will allow you to focus on your writing in your home office. It's not just your career at stake; it's your long-term sanity. Don't you think that's worth a few extra bucks a month?

Chapter 18

Dealing with the Doldrums

Being a magazine writer usually involves working quite a bit from home, and many writers lament the fact that this situation often leads to boredom and loneliness. Isolation is usually not good for the human spirit in general, and when you work from home as a writer, the feelings of isolation can close in on you fast. You will need ideas and techniques for keeping your spirits up so you can keep your writing on track.

Boredom and Loneliness

It's pretty easy to see how a person sitting in a home office typing day after day all by herself might succumb to feelings of boredom and loneliness. In fact, so many writers complain of these feelings that there is an industry phrase related directly to the phenomenon: writer's block. It's the temporary inability to write, usually caused by lack of imagination or creativity—two things very easily ground down by boredom and loneliness.

When you find yourself experiencing these feelings, remember that you are far from being alone. Boredom and loneliness afflict most magazine writers at some point, sometimes several times a year, a month, or even a week. You need to recognize that there are reasons for this suffering, and that you can get through them just like every other writer does every day, all over the world.

Procrastination: The Brakes of the Soul

A wise person once said that procrastination is the brakes of the soul. All of us can become so bogged down in our work that we forget to take a break, take a walk, or simply enjoy life for a few minutes. Americans are particularly adept at working themselves into regular tizzies, and writers—with nothing to stop their working at home except for power outages—fall squarely into this trap all the time.

So if you feel yourself becoming bored and lonely, consider the idea that perhaps it's just your soul's way of trying to get you to procrastinate a little, to maybe go read a book or visit with a friend down the street. If you try to keep yourself running on the productivity treadmill nonstop, your soul may simply have no other way of getting your attention than by making you feel bored and lonely.

What Is Your Soul Telling You?

This is the time to ask yourself *why* you feel bored and lonely. Some reasons that commonly befall writers include:

- You're writing too much about a topic that you don't like
- You're writing too much in general every day

- You're writing too often—say, seven days a week
- You're not leaving your office for frequent breaks
- You're not leaving your house for daily walks or other exercise

If you find that one of these descriptions fits you, then you'll know how to take action to help alleviate your feelings of loneliness and boredom. Perhaps you need to try sending query letters to magazines on new subjects, or maybe you just need to get up out of your chair and take your dog for a walk in the park (ideally, in the middle of a Wednesday afternoon). Shake up your routine, and your writer's block should soon subside, leaving you feeling productive again.

Adding Travel to Your Work

One way to shake up your routine is by adding travel to your work. This can be anything from landing an all-expenses-paid travel-writing assignment to simply driving an hour to conduct an interview that you might otherwise have done over the phone. The point is that sometimes, you need to force yourself to break out of your routine in your home office, and travel arrangements of any kind can be an excellent motivator.

ESSENTIAL

Remember that running errands, doing the grocery shopping, and picking up the kids from school does not count as getting out and breaking up your routine. It's important that, on occasion, you allow yourself time to go wandering or to the movies or to a friend's house for a glass of wine.

Making travel arrangements doesn't have to mean flying to Kenya to board a safari in a game preserve. It can simply mean making an appointment with another person to meet someplace at a certain time, thus giving you a little peer pressure to actually get up and go. If you can't see yourself taking a long vacation right away, at least consider planning a single day away from your home office when you don't turn on the computer at all.

A Day Out Can Do Wonders

If you decide to treat yourself to a day away from the home office, make sure it includes fun things that have nothing to do with chores or tedium. This is not the time to get your car detailed or your cat groomed. Instead, it's time to go see a cheesy movie or eat ice cream in a park on a hot summer's day.

You may feel a bit guilty during your first hour or two away, but by the end of the day, you're likely to be kicking yourself for failing to take the much-needed break from work sooner. Most writers find that simply seeing new sights, even if through the car windshield during a meandering drive, helps the creative side of their brain re-engage. And that's the first step toward getting back on track with your magazine-writing business.

A Few Days Away Are Even Better

If you have the ability to take a break for more than a single day, you should absolutely go for it—especially if you have felt bored and lonely for a long period of time. Consider turning off your cellular telephone and ignoring your e-mail completely, and instead focusing on the important work of getting your mood back in order.

ALERT!

If you find yourself feeling bored and lonely for longer than a week, consider consulting your family doctor or a psychologist. Sometimes, boredom and loneliness are symptoms of psychiatric problems such as depression, which can be far more serious than writer's block and require more treatment than just a day away from the computer.

Above all, remember that being in a bad mood is bad for your writing, and that being a bad writer is bad for your business. Thus, allowing yourself time to take a vacation is not goofing off; it's investing time in ensuring that you will be up to the task of completing future magazine-writing assignments.

Creating a Network of Writer Friends

You have read a lot in this book about the importance of creating a good network of colleagues in the magazine industry. Yet another reason this is so is because other writers will know exactly how you feel when you come down with feelings of boredom and loneliness. Who better to help you through a rough patch than a fellow writer who has been there himself?

A lot of times, your fellow writers will be your best motivators for getting back on track. Simply meeting for business lunches can be a great way to break the monotony of your life, while attending writing conferences can take you even a step farther.

Writing-Conference Roommates

If you find yourself wanting to attend the same writing conferences year after year, the odds are that you will make some friends there. Many writers end up becoming annual roommates with a favorite fellow writer from these conferences, thus cutting down on travel expenses while having a colleague at hand with whom you can toss around ideas.

QUESTION?

Is it possible to attend too many writers' conferences?
Yes. In fact, there is a small segment of "writers" who do nothing but attend conferences, making themselves feel as though they're writers when really, they're would-be writers who are too afraid to put what they've learned into practice. Don't become part of their clan!

The real benefit to befriending a fellow writer at an annual conference is that you will be more motivated to attend the following year. This means you'll have a built-in break in your writing schedule, which gives you a break to look forward to and a legitimate excuse to take a short vacation.

Lunches, Lunches, Lunches

Agents and authors in the book-publishing industry have been fans of the working lunch for many years. There's no reason that you can't be, too, even though you're writing 1,000-word pieces instead of 100,000-word tomes.

If you live even an hour or two away from a writer friend, there's nothing wrong with meeting for a long afternoon's lunch that you can spend catching up, discussing your writing assignments, and generally acting as sounding boards for one another's ideas and concerns. Again, think of this as part of your writing business—an investment in your knowledge of what's going on at other magazines—and don't forget to keep the receipt for your accountant to deduct come tax time.

Taking Small Vacations

If you decide that you can get away for a two- or three-day vacation, try to make it one that has absolutely nothing to do with writing, computers, telephones, e-mail, or typing in general. It can definitely be difficult to completely unplug yourself in today's high-speed information age, but boredom and loneliness often arise out of feelings of being overwhelmed. If your body is telling you that you need a break, that doesn't always mean simply slowing down. It sometimes means jamming on the brakes and getting out of the fast lane altogether.

FACT

Your editors, sources, and writing assignments will almost always still be there waiting for you even if you ignore them during a few days' vacation. Try to remember that you're not a nuclear scientist or a member of the president's cabinet. You can take a few days completely off, and the world as you know it will continue to spin.

Small vacations can be just the boost you need to bring you out of the doldrums and back into the writing mentality. However, they're not quite as rejuvenating as bigger, weeklong vacations—which should be your goal if you haven't had one in at least six months.

Taking Big Vacations

One of the biggest perks about being a magazine writer is that you get to make your own schedule. If you want to work Fridays through Wednesdays with Thursdays off, so be it. If you suddenly change your mind and want to take Tuesdays off, you can.

For some reason, many writers fail to translate this freedom into the ability to schedule a vacation into their calendar literally whenever the desire occurs. Yes, vacations cost money and time away from work, but they're an important part of your mental health—and of keeping you productive over the long run. You should be able to find at least two weeks each year to enjoy them, no matter how much work you are getting from various magazine editors.

Americans tend to take a tiny amount of vacation time compared with workers in other industrialized nations. The average two weeks off in the United States is a far cry from the typical twenty-five days of annual vacation that Japanese workers receive and the average forty-two days of annual vacation time that Italian workers enjoy.

Even if you can't take the vacation of your dreams, then you can at least take a "vacation" from your everyday routine, which is likely a major cause of your loneliness and boredom. The following tips for getting back on track may keep you away for a short time from the magazines and editors you know best, but they may just be the change of pace required to get your writing mojo back.

Ten Tips for Getting Back on Track

You know yourself and your habits better than anyone else. If there's a tip or technique that has worked for you in the past when trying to get back on track, you should definitely stick with it. For instance, if you're the type of person who can spend a day eating Haagen-Dazs ice cream and then feel right as rain, then by all means dive into that pint of Macadamia Brittle or Vanilla Swiss Almond.

On the other hand, if boredom, loneliness, and writer's block are new to you, then you might not know exactly what to do to jolt your system back into gear. Following are ten solid tips that many magazine writers say work for them. Hopefully, one of them will work for you, too.

Write Something Different

Taking a break from a style or topic of writing can sometimes be just the thing you need. If all you write is nonfiction articles, for instance, then consider taking a day or two to write poems or start work on a screenplay. The mere act of having to think about words and characters and phrases differently can sometimes be enough to get your creative juices flowing again. And hey, you never know about that screenplay—it could be the best new writing Hollywood has seen in years.

It's important to really change up your writing style and focus once in a while, if only to keep your writing from becoming monotonous. For instance, if you write regularly about the food-and-beverage industry, consider spending a day writing about the process of bookbinding or the life of a famous forefather. Truly go off in a new direction.

Read Something Different

Reading is an excellent diversion for writers, if only because you still feel as though you're contributing to your skills while in fact you are relaxing and letting another writer carry you away in thought. If you're already an eclectic reader with shelves full of fiction, nonfiction, graphic novels, and more, then you're ahead of the game. However, if you tend to read only one kind of book—say, political nonfiction from the bestseller lists—then you may start to feel that taking a break to read is more like taking a break to read the same old thing.

That's not conducive to helping you stave off feelings of loneliness and boredom. Change things up and grab a trashy summer novel or even a business how-to book once in a while. The different patter of language will push your brain in new and unique directions, and you may even get some ideas for pitching articles to magazines other than your usual clients.

Read an Old Favorite

All writers have favorite classic authors, be they Sylvia Plath or Charles Dickens or Truman Capote. Sometimes, reuniting with a favorite book by a favorite author can feel like getting together with an old friend—something that almost always warms the soul and helps you to feel better.

Classic novels and narrative nonfiction works have made a comeback in the publishing industry in recent years. Even if you don't own a copy of a favorite classic such as *The Scarlet Letter* or *Little Women*, you can usually find it on the bookshelves at your local bookstore (or of course online at Amazon.com).

Give Yourself a Mini-Vacation

You've read a lot in this chapter about the importance of taking vacations, but you don't have to go far in order to enjoy a getaway on a miniature scale. Sometimes, an hour-long bubble bath or a longer-than-usual lunch out on the front lawn is all you will need to kick-start your writing abilities. When you think vacation, don't always think "getaway." Sometimes, you just need an hour away from your e-mail inbox to help regain your sanity.

Give Yourself a Deadline

If you're not the type to go tiptoeing through the tulips in search of your-self, then go 180 degrees in the opposite direction and add *more* structure to your routine. Tell yourself that you have precisely two days until you need to get back to working at full capacity, and then hold yourself to that timetable. Write the deadline right into your regular calendar of writing-assignment deadlines, as if it were just another demand from an editor. Enlist the help of a spouse, relative, or friend to call you on the morning of your deadline and ensure that you are, indeed, back at your computer writing. This technique certainly isn't for everyone, but for writers who prefer structure to relaxation, it sure does work.

Exercise

You've probably heard more than your share in recent years about how important regular exercise is to your health. Whether you already pound the treadmill daily or you consider reaching for the television remote to be a form of stretching, you can change or increase your exercise routine as a way of breaking out of the writing doldrums.

QUESTION?

Why does exercise help to relieve writer's block?
Exercising causes your body to release endorphins, which are molecules your body secretes into your bloodstream. They bind to receptors the same way drugs like morphine do, thus creating an analgesic effect that lifts your mood. If you're in a better mood, you're more likely to want to start writing again.

Exercise doesn't have to be difficult or boring. In fact, it doesn't even have to be in a gym at all. You can decide to play instead.

Play

Playing is the oldest form of exercise in history, and you probably have plenty of playmates around just waiting for you to decide to join them. Kids, dogs, friends, neighbors, relatives—give your brain a break by thinking about who might be a good playmate, whether for a game of racquetball or a round of fetch. When you play, your body will release endorphins just as it would during a session of exercise, only your brain will sense less structure to the activity and perhaps relax even more.

Know how kids are always smiling? And how dogs always seem content? It's because they make time to play. Follow their example from time to time, and you'll be just as happy.

Watch a Good Movie

Okay, so it's not politically correct these days to advocate plopping down in front of the television or in a seat at the movie theater. Still, watching a good film with a big bucket of buttery popcorn can be downright therapeutic. The storyline will literally take your mind away from whatever has caused it to fade into neutral, and the mere act of having to sit still to watch the scenes will by definition break up your routine of writing, e-mailing, and doing interviews.

ESSENTIAL

If you decide to watch a movie as a respite, make sure it's a good one. There's nothing worse than wasting a couple of hours on a film that has bad dialogue, horrible special effects, and lousy actors. Remember, your goal here isn't to kill time by watching the movie. It's to become engrossed in the plot and characters, to take yourself away from reality.

Don't feel guilty about pulling out an old favorite and popping it into the DVD player, no matter how cheesy it is or how well you already know the lines by heart. If you enjoy watching it, the movie will serve its purpose and, hopefully, break you out of your writing slump.

Cook Something

Cooking has long been a way for people to reconnect with reality. The basic act of chopping a pepper or dicing a tomato forces you to concentrate, lest you lose a finger, and the tastes those vegetables and other freshly prepared foods provide create an instant reaction in your body that makes you think about nothing else.

Even if your primary recipes usually include defrosting frozen pizzas and microwaving meals, take an afternoon to prepare a dish from scratch, and then savor every bite while you eat it. Simply follow the instructions in a recipe that doesn't look too hard—maybe one requiring twenty minutes' worth of preparation time—and you should end up with something that's not only delicious to eat, but also satisfying in that you will have created it out of nothing.

FACT

If you want to find easy-to-follow recipes, forget about fashionable celebrity cookbooks and stick with an old standard such as *The Joy of Cooking*. Inside, you'll find recipes for everything from strawberry preserves to tuna casserole, with clear directions about not only the ingredients you'll need, but also how long it will take to cook them.

Remember: The goal here is not to create your first seven-course tasting menu at home. The goal is to take your mind off your day-to-day routine for a while. Choose a recipe that won't leave you hurling knives across the kitchen in frustration, no matter how skilled a cook you already are.

Go See What a Real Job Looks Like

The one tried-and-true way to get back on track as a magazine writer is to go to your local shopping mall, or the nearest Starbucks, or your regular grocery store. Only instead of being a shopper, as you usually are, spend some time watching the cashiers and counter attendants and butchers.

Watch them as they hustle around on their sore feet all day long, smiling at customers who don't always smile back and listening to the same Muzak playing in the background again and again. Look up and see the fluorescent lights that beam into their eyes day and night, and pay attention to the actual jobs they get paid to do, be it hanging clothes on racks or frothing lattes or determining the proper SKU number for a bag of fresh parsnips.

Nine times out of ten, you'll find yourself saying something like, "Being a magazine writer sure beats this." And then you'll be on your way back home, happy with the career choice you've made and eager to keep working hard in order to pay your bills by writing articles.

Chapter 19

Adding to Your Repertoire

One of the best things about being a magazine writer is the idea that you can follow whatever interests you. As your career progresses, you may start to feel that simply writing about some of your ideas is not enough. In this case, you can use your magazine-writing contacts and skills as a steppingstone to additional sources of fulfillment and revenue, doing everything from taking photographs to writing books and teaching new generations of writers the tricks of the trade.

Using Magazine Writing as a Launch Pad

Being a magazine writer has many benefits, but one of the best is the ability to change your job whenever you see fit. Had enough of writing for gardening magazines? Maybe you'd like to try querying a marine science magazine instead. You can learn as much as you'd like about whatever subjects you fancy at any given time, changing your subject matter wherever and whenever the mood strikes.

If you take the same approach to your writing business in general, then you will soon see that you can change your overall job whenever you see fit, as well. You don't have to be just a writer (though that's a darn good thing to be). If you want to, you can also learn to be an editor, an illustrator, a consultant, and more.

FACT

Using your magazine-writing business as a launch pad for other forms of work can be both personally and financially fulfilling. The more tasks you can choose among on a daily basis, the less likely you are to feel bored—and the more likely you are to have multiple streams of revenue.

Perhaps one of the easiest skills to add to your repertoire nowadays is photography. You don't need to be Ansel Adams to make a few extra bucks by taking pictures, and you can have a heck of a lot of fun playing with modern digital equipment.

Taking Photographs

Taking pictures to run in the pages of magazines alongside the stories that you write is easier now than it ever has been. Digital equipment continues to slide down the price scale while improving in quality. For an investment of about $1,000, you can get a digital camera of high enough quality that magazines will accept the photographs you supply.

Additional Income

Even for amateur shutterbugs, this not only is fun, but also can be quite lucrative. Digital photography has a built-in learning system, in that your camera immediately shows you the photograph you've taken. This means that you can see whether you "have the shot," as the professionals say, or whether you need to click the auto-focus button a few more times to get a better image.

QUESTION?

How much do magazines pay for photographs?
It depends on the magazine and the size of the published photograph, be it a quarter-page or a full page. In some cases, you can negotiate a package deal, say an extra $1,000 above your story fee for the magazine's art director to use as many of your photographs as she would like.

At the end of your picture-taking session, you will know whether you have usable accompanying artwork for your editors, and you can offer it to them for an additional fee above and beyond your story payment rate. If you get good enough at taking pictures, your writing assignments may begin to include a built-in clause that states that you automatically are the story's paid photographer as well.

Photographs fall under different contractual stipulations than the stories that you write, so even though you may have accepted a work-for-hire contract for your words, you almost always will be able to retain the copyrights to your photographs. This will become important if you decide to branch out and market the photos you collect in your personal stock library.

Your Own Stock Library

"Stock photographs" is magazine-industry lingo for any pictures that exist already, before or after a story is written, without the magazine having to assign and pay a photographer to go shoot accompanying artwork on site. There are entire companies devoted to selling stock photographs of everything from beautiful beaches to industrial machinery.

When you develop your own stock library, your editors will learn to start asking you for photographs to go along with stories their other writers produce. They'll know exactly which kinds of images you have, and you can even post new images on your Web site and direct photo editors to it as a marketing tool.

ESSENTIAL

If you want to make money from your stock library of photographs, you either have to continually market your images—just as you send query letters for your writing—or you have to sign on with an existing stock agency, which will sell your photographs for you in exchange for keeping a percentage of the sale prices.

You may not earn the same amount of money as professional photographers do for their stock images, but think about it this way: Any dollars you make are dollars you didn't have before, and you didn't have to do anything to earn them besides sending an editor a copy of a photograph you already had on hand. That's easy money.

Illustrating Your Work

The same thing goes for drawing illustrations. If you have drawing skills, then you can use them to your advantage by offering to produce illustrations that go along with your stories. As with photographs, you can often get package deals that will earn you a far better return on your time than simply writing the story alone.

Illustrations nowadays can be hand-drawn or created by computer programs, depending on the magazine's art direction and style. However, keep in mind that illustrations do differ from photographs in that they tend to be one-time use only. You can develop a stock library of illustrations, but unless they're technical or how-to in nature, you'll probably have a tougher time repurposing and reselling them than you would photographs.

FACT

Technical writers who can produce illustrations to help explain tricky concepts are especially in demand in most magazine genres. If, for instance, you typically write about waste-management systems, magazine art directors would thrill at the idea of your providing detailed computer drawings of how those systems work—thus saving in-house artists from having to figure out the concepts themselves.

Editing and Proofreading

Editing and proofreading are in some ways natural extensions of writing. As a magazine writer, you are always looking for the best ways to work with words. Editors and proofreaders do the same thing, just from different perspectives.

If you have no editing or proofreading experience, then you would be wise to take a class at a local college or through an online university to give you the basics on what's expected. Good writers are not necessarily good editors, and you'll need to understand how to break down stories by overall structure, paragraph, line, and word in ways that are different from writing those elements yourself.

ALERT!

Don't assume that just because you're a good writer, you'll be a good editor or proofreader. Your ability to work with words definitely gives you an advantage in learning editing and proofreading skills, but you will have a fair amount to study at a local college before you can try to earn money by editing or proofreading.

Once you master the main tasks involved, you can begin to ask your regular editors whether they need any freelance editing help. You may be surprised at how many say yes, especially if your hourly or day rate is reasonable.

Enhancing Your Expertise

Being a freelance editor in addition to a magazine writer can do a lot to enhance your expertise and reputation in your field. For instance, if you are a medical writer who can make the transition to medical editor, then you will by definition be doing more research in the field as you fact-check and enhance articles written by other writers. Your knowledge base will grow far more quickly than through writing alone, and you will undoubtedly come up with plenty of new ideas for story pitches of your own.

Improving Your Writing

Being a good editor or proofreader will also help you to improve your own writing, because you can apply the skills you learn to self-editing your articles before you submit them to your editors. This will make you even more valuable as a magazine writer, which in turn should land you ever more business when you send out your query letters.

Writers who take the time to self-edit almost always turn in cleaner copy than writers who don't know how to self-edit. Thus, being able to self-edit makes your editor's job easier, and of course makes the editor more likely to return to you with additional assignments in the future.

Writing Books

Many magazine writers seek to make the leap from articles to books at some point in their careers, especially magazine writers who have a well-developed reputation and platform in a particular industry. In part, the idea of having your name on a book's spine is a romantic notion that's hard to overcome. In addition, the more you learn about your chosen area of writing expertise, the more you will have to say to your readers, and the bigger platform you will want to use to herald your idea.

FACT

In book publishing, "platform" refers to how well you are known in your area of expertise and, more important, how many contacts you have that can help a publisher sell copies of your book. A good writer without a platform will have trouble landing a book deal, while a decent writer with a great platform usually can get published.

For most magazine writers, moving into the realm of authorship comes along with the desire to expand on ideas more than magazine space limitations allow. A good example is Bill Buford, a writer for *The New Yorker* who wanted to learn and write about food and the celebrity chef Mario Batali. Instead of simply doing interviews and producing an article for that magazine, Buford spent more than a year researching his subject matter—cooking in Batali's New York City restaurant and traveling to work for Batali's favorite teachers in Italy—and then wrote what he found into the book *Heat*, which became a bestseller in the summer of 2006. Parts of *Heat* could have just as easily been sold as separate magazine stories, but Buford simply had too much to say to be confined to ten- or even hundred-page articles.

Expanding on Your Ideas

You can take the same approach to expanding on your ideas in a book, no matter your field of expertise. Any subject that you cover for a long enough time will eventually reveal holes in its marketplace, and you can take the initiative to fill them with a book. It could be a how-to title or a personal memoir, but if you understand how to use your platform to sell it, the odds are that you will be able to interest a publisher in your idea.

Selling book ideas is harder than selling magazine article ideas, though. Instead of writing query letters, you will have to write entire proposals complete with sample chapters and marketing ideas. Then, most likely, you will have to find a literary agent who can help you take your proposal to a publishing house. If you're lucky, you'll get at least a small advance—say, somewhere in the $3,000 range—plus royalties on book sales if your title does well.

ALERT!

Should you decide to go into book writing, get the biggest advance that you can. It's a well-documented fact in the publishing industry that most books—especially those by first-time authors—fail to earn out their advances. That means no additional income in the form of royalties, ever.

Needless to say, unless you're a famous author, writing a whole book for a $3,000 advance doesn't sound too financially wise when you could probably earn the same amount writing just one or two magazine articles. The reason you might take on the job, though, is your desire to expand upon your ideas in print—especially if you know that there may be ways to expand your income, as well.

Expanding Your Income

Virtually all book authors, especially first-timers, will tell you that the money isn't in the book itself. It's in the articles that you can sell to various magazines based on the chapters in your book. Essentially, what happens is that you write the book and then repurpose its content to suit various editors, just as you might repurpose an article that you once sold to a magazine but now want to reshape and sell to another magazine.

FACT

When you sell a magazine an article based on a book, you can expect to earn the same amount of money as you would for an article that you wrote as part of your regular routine. The difference, of course, is that since your article is based on an already-completed book, you will have to do far less work to earn that magazine-writing paycheck.

In the process, you should earn enough money to make writing the book worthwhile, even if it doesn't hit the bestseller list in *The New York Times Book Review*. Plus, you will have the satisfaction of having expanded on your ideas in print and having your name on a spine in the local Barnes & Noble, which is a lifelong dream that goes unrealized for many writers the world over.

Building a Web Presence

Another way to expand your magazine-writing business is through your Web site. You learned about some of the benefits of having a Web site in Chapters 11 and 14; now comes the idea that you can use your site to enhance your bottom line, too.

Blogs

There's no doubt that blogs are a hot trend in writing nowadays, and plenty of Web hosting companies have package deals that will help you get your own blog up and running in no time. Usually, there is an additional fee involved, but it is nominal in comparison to the self-marketing that the blog will help you achieve.

The benefit of a blog to you is twofold. First, it allows you a forum to expand on ideas for your readers without an editor's red pen getting in your way. Second, it allows you a place to promote yourself and your magazine articles, which will drive business to those magazines and in turn make the editors want to give you even more assignments.

QUESTION?

Is it ethical to ask your regular magazine editors to help promote your personal Web site?
Yes. If the magazine has a contributors' page, ask to be featured on it with a mention of your Web site. If the magazine has no contributors' page, ask to have your Web site mentioned in a tagline at the end of your article.

Subscriber Fees

If you write on a topic that draws an audience of consumers—say, fine wines or dining—then you may even be able to charge subscriber fees on your Web site. Your weekly blog describing the best deals in wine, for instance, could become a for-paid-users-only feature that you charge a monthly fee to view.

In this business model, you can earn money from subscribers while also determining which of your ideas generates the best reader response. Then, you can use that knowledge to help you sell magazine articles on the same topic, thus using what you wrote at least twice to create two separate streams of revenue.

An additional benefit to having a subscription-based Web site is that you can capture the names of your subscribers and create a mailing list for any future books that you write or other projects that you take on. You will have a built-in fan base, so to speak, and that never hurts in terms of landing more work from editors.

ESSENTIAL

If you intend to charge a subscriber fee for viewing parts of your Web site, be sure to go through a company like PayPal so that subscribers will have a secure way to input their credit card information. Nobody will pay to view the writing on your Web site if they fear their personal information may be compromised.

Giving Speeches

Talking to groups of students, community residents, or even corporation employees can be an excellent way of building upon your magazine-writing business. Speakers at universities and especially at corporations can make several thousand dollars a day, depending on the institution and its budget allocations.

Even better, if you combine paid speaking engagements with signings for any books that you have written, then you can increase your book sales while earning a profit as a speaker, all the while building on your platform to help you land more magazine-writing and book-writing deals. In some cases, you will even be able to build book sales into a speaker's contract, say by insisting that the company buy a copy of your book for each member of the expected audience to take home. That cost, of course, should be in addition to your regular speaker's fee. Again, it's a way of creating two streams of income for one day's worth of work.

Is it a good idea to promote yourself as a speaker?

Absolutely—as long as you can do the job. If you have no previous speaking experience, then you should take a course at a local college before trying to earn additional income talking in front of large groups. You don't want to get a reputation as a bad speaker when you're just starting out.

Teaching

Teaching is similar to being a speaker in that you need to make sure you are up to the job before you go around offering to do it. Most community colleges will allow you to teach a course on writing without an actual teaching degree, but you will need to get special certification in order to teach at other higher-education institutions, high schools, and lower-level schools.

Still, teaching can be an excellent way to build on your magazine-writing business because it can lead to additional work. For instance, if you teach a class on creative writing, your students will need a good textbook. Your built-in audience of students means you will have guaranteed book sales, which should help you to land a deal with a publisher to write the textbook in the first place. Then, you can market yourself to educational and writing magazines as the author of a textbook on your subject of expertise, which should land you additional magazine-writing assignments and keep the wheel of ever-expanding work turning.

Consulting

If you are successful at any or all of the add-on skills described in this chapter, then you may also have a future in consulting for magazines. You can offer to help publications with everything from starting up new titles to polishing their processes for making copy better.

ESSENTIAL

To become successful as a consultant, you need to have a particular area of expertise beyond "being a writer." For instance, if you are good at taking photographs that go along with your articles, then you can market yourself as a consultant for magazines that want their writers to learn the craft of photography.

Consultants can earn beaucoup bucks compared with magazine writers, sometimes in the neighborhood of $600 or $1,000 a day. Of course, you won't make top dollar when you're starting out, but if you maintain a steady course and prove to several magazines that you can help them to make a difference in the quality of their editorial, then you will receive excellent word-of-mouth referrals. Those referrals will lead not only to more paid consulting gigs, but probably also to multiple magazine-writing assignments along the way.

Chapter 20

Writing Stronger Stories

The one thing that you can never lose sight of in the magazine-writing business is your responsibility for producing excellent articles. No matter how many clients you land over the years or how successful you become in the overall industry, your end goal should always be to craft accurate, beautifully written—even award-winning—features for your readers to enjoy. To that end, this chapter looks at a few of the tried-and-true ways to enhance any magazine article, in any genre.

Better Reporting

Good writers tend to say that they spend hours poring through dictionaries and thesauruses searching for the perfect nouns and adverbs. Great writers do that, too, but they also typically admit to poring over their notebooks for even longer periods of time.

Strong reporting is almost always the keystone to building a better magazine article. Your notes from research and interviews should be accurate, detailed, and far more complete than you need to write your article to its specified word count. The best magazine writers often have countless pages of notes on hand that they can't fit into their actual stories.

QUESTION?

Why should you report more than you actually need to fill your word count?
Because the more you know about your subject matter, the more authoritative your articles will be. Plus, interview subjects tend to reveal more toward the ends of interviews, not at the beginnings. If you quit asking questions too soon, you'll probably forgo taking home the best quote of the day.

The more notes you have, the more details and quotations from which you can choose for your article—and the more memorable those details and quotes are likely to be.

Strong Quotes

There's nothing like a well-turned phrase to keep a reader's attention. It's a good thing that people being interviewed tend to say the darndest things. If you can get their most colorful remarks into your notebook accurately, then your magazine article will practically write itself.

Over time, most magazine writers develop an ear for hearing memorable, usable quotes the minute they come out of a source's mouth. Most people speak in patterns to which you become accustomed after a few minutes; you can tell when a person is trying to gather her thoughts versus when she actually knows what she wants to say. These moments of clarity are usually your keeper quotes, the ones you want to be sure you have written down accurately in your notebook.

Even if a source is stammering with "uhs" and "hmmms," write those words into your notebook. If you don't, you risk forgetting the person's state of mind when he spoke, and describing a person's state of mind to your readers can add volumes of context. "He said cautiously," or "he revealed," are much stronger descriptors than a simple "he said."

The more direct quotes you have in your notebook, the better. You can always go back later and paraphrase something that a source told you, but you cannot go back in time and get the source to repeat the exact quote again. Learn shorthand or develop your own system for writing or recording as many quotes as possible, and save the best ones for the parts of your articles where they will make the most impact on readers (more on that later in this chapter).

Sweating the Small Stuff

Details are another key to excellent writing, and the reporting phase of the magazine-writing process is usually where you will collect the best ones. Unlike quotations, though, details usually don't get handed to you right out of the source's mouth. You will need to use your observation skills to record as much of the small stuff as you can.

Citing details when writing descriptive sentences and paragraphs can tell your readers a heck of a lot about your subjects without your having to offer editorialized opinions. This is one of the hallmarks of good journalism, and your reporter's notebook is the place to practice the skill of digging deeper and deeper into everything you see.

As with quotations, details are best collected the first time around. You should gather as many as you can, even if your notebook is so overflowing that you just know you will never get all of them into your actual magazine article. The idea, again, is that when it comes time to write, you can pare down your notes to the absolute best, most essential details that the reader needs to know. With your notebook full of them, you can bet they'll be incredibly memorable and meaningful.

If you find yourself writing that a source is wearing jeans, be sure to note their color. And whether they're torn. And what's showing through the torn patches. And what brand name is on the back pocket. And whether they are zip-ups or button-flies. And whether they have boot cut or narrow cuffs. And how low they ride on the hips and stomach . . . you get the idea.

Improving Your Leads

Your lead is the beginning of your magazine article, the opener that draws the reader in and makes her want to continue through the rest of your story. Think of it like the first bite of a sandwich. If it's lacking in flavor, nobody's going to want to finish the thing.

Improving your story leads is a major component of improving your stories on the whole. Not only will a strong lead help you nab the reader's attention, but it will also help you set up the structure of the story that you want to tell. If you know a good place to start, you can usually figure out where you want to end up, and you can bring the reader along on the journey with you.

Learning to craft better story leads will also help you land more story assignments. The beginnings of query letters are often used as the beginnings of actual stories, so the more you can hone your skills for creating a bang-up opening on paper, the more likely you are to get editors' attention and acceptance of your ideas.

There are two longtime tricks that magazine writers use to ensure their leads are stellar. The first involves scene-setting in the opening paragraphs, while the other involves leading up to a shocking or memorable quotation from a source.

The First Five Paragraphs

The "first five paragraphs" method works on the premise that you have five paragraphs to get the reader to the point, or nut graf, of your magazine article. You won't win any friends at *The New Yorker* or *The New York Times Magazine* with this method (they prefer much longer set-ups, sometimes going on for pages), but you can make a very good living using the technique to write 1,000- or 1,500-word articles for magazines that cover pretty much every subject there is.

In fact, this technique is ideal for articles in which you need to set a scene—articles where some writers have a tendency to wander off the path of the actual story itself. A good example is personality profiles, in which the reader really wants to get to the part about what the subject has to say, but where the writer spends six or seven paragraphs describing the subject's car or office or wardrobe. Those details may be useful in creating analogies— "the genius CEO's car is cluttered like the laboratory of a madman preparing for a science fair"—but if the colorful descriptions run on for too many paragraphs, you're going to lose the reader (and probably the point of your article).

QUESTION?

Do you always have to take five paragraphs to get to your nut graf?
No. Sometimes, such as in straight-news reporting, your first paragraph will be your nut graf. But if you are trying to set a scene, you can typically use as many as five paragraphs to do so before you will lose the reader's attention, along with your point.

If you typically open your articles with descriptive writing instead of straight news, then look for places where you can pare back your leads to five or fewer paragraphs, with the last paragraph being your nut graf. You will find that your openers are much stronger and that your story structures will follow in kind.

Leading to a Killer Quote

Another great trick for writing a terrific lead is isolating the most pertinent, most interesting, or most colorful quote in your notebook, and then writing an opening paragraph (or two) that leads directly to it.

An example might go something like this:

> Sean is the kind of golf pro who always seems as perfectly pressed as his pants. Quick with a smile and handshake, he has a social director's easy smile and a salesman's aura of trust. He's the son you always wanted, the brother you never had, the husband of your dreams. He could be lining up his shot on the ninth green when the sky begins to darken, and he'll play right through the sudden downpour without missing a millimeter on his back swing, or even rumpling his shirt.
>
> And yet year after year, in tournament after tournament, this dedicated professional falls just one or two shots short of making the PGA Tour. The reason, he believes, is the same for every would-be Phil Mickelson out there on golf courses across America.
>
> "I have mental problems," he confides with a chuckle. "One bad shot, and I lose my concentration like a patch of grass that forgets to sprout at springtime."
>
> Mental focus, experts say, is the key to netting good scores consistently on the golf course. . . .

Now, would a quote like that be good anyplace in your article? Perhaps. But by leading into it with a contrasting paragraph or two, you are setting a scene for the reader that the story's main source then suddenly cranks up to a new volume. You are creating conflict, so to speak, which on many levels can equal drama—the stuff of which many great stories are made. Even better, you're doing it in the first five paragraphs and getting right to your nut graf, which is the next thing you can work on improving.

Strengthening Nut Grafs

The nut graf is the paragraph in your magazine article that tells the reader why he is reading. In many journalism schools, students are taught to write nut grafs that always begin the same way: "This is important because . . ." In the previous section's example, the student's version of the nut graf might have begun, "This is important because experts say mental focus is the key to netting consistently good scores on the golf course." The lead sets the scene and draws the reader in, and the nut graf explains both what point the lead illustrates and why the reader should stick around to learn more.

The problem with most nut grafs is that they are written too loosely. Even in a 5,000-word magazine article, your nut graf should be concise—probably two paragraphs at most. After all, if you can't articulate in a paragraph or two why your article is important, then how can you expect the reader to figure it out as you ramble on from page to page?

Tighten, Tighten, Tighten

One time-tested technique for improving nut grafs is to write them, let them sit without looking at them for a few days, and then go back and try to tighten them through self-editing. Nine times out of ten, you will find a more concise way to phrase your point the second or even third time you type it.

This technique works especially well for writers who tend to have trouble boiling their nut grafs down into just one paragraph on the first try. If you fall into that category (and you know who you are), then give the self-editing process a try on your next story assignment. Your editors will love you, and so will your readers.

Remember to approach your nut graf in keeping with your story's style. If you're writing a narrative nonfiction piece, for instance, you may not have a nut graf at all. The same is true for an essay. On a straight-news article, your nut graf is probably going to be your first paragraph. On a profile, it's likely to come around paragraph four or five.

Keep in mind that nut grafs can be one sentence or two paragraphs, depending on the length of the magazine feature. (Remember, some magazines with a more literary bent don't want nut grafs in your articles at all.)

The point to take home here is that if you are going to write a nut graf, then you should do everything you can to ensure it makes a point—and makes it as concisely as possible.

Say It Out Loud

If you're not sure whether your nut graf packs enough punch, then you can read it out loud, either to yourself or to a friend. You can even read it to your dog if that's the only audience you have.

The idea is to see whether you can read the key sentences in your nut graf without having to take a second breath. If you can, then you've probably written a pretty concise message to your readers. If you can't, then you might want to think about self-editing again, and then reading aloud one more time.

Hansel and Gretel

Once you've grabbed your readers' attention with a strong lead and forceful nut graf, your task becomes maintaining their interest throughout the rest of your story. How do you do this? By packing in solidly reported information and interesting word choices, of course, but perhaps also by using a technique that some writers refer to as "leaving a trail of breadcrumbs."

The reference comes from the classic Hansel and Gretel fairy tale, in which two children leave themselves a trail of breadcrumbs in the woods so that they can find their way back home. The idea as it relates to writing is that you can leave readers a trail of breadcrumbs to follow to the end of your magazine article, only instead of actual breadcrumbs, you use things such as quotes and clues.

Using Quotes

When you're writing about interesting people who provide you with good quotes, you can almost always use those quotes as your breadcrumbs. Readers who are intrigued by a person you are profiling will start to wonder, "What the heck will this guy say next?" That's exactly what you want them to be thinking—because it means they will keep turning the magazine's pages and following your article to the end to find out.

The trick for you, as a writer, is to spread the subject's best quotes throughout the article instead of bunching them all up in your lead and your ending. A lot of magazine writers fall into this trap, and it's unfortunate, because if all the good quotes are at the beginning and the end of an article, most readers will stop somewhere in the middle and never even get to the big finale.

ALERT!

Don't assume that terrific quotes can act as breadcrumbs on their own. You must lead the reader to each quote along a logical path, keeping each quote in context and ensuring the reader understands why it is so great. Think of your best quotes as exclamation points and the writing you do in between them as the heart of sentences.

Using Clues

If your subject matter doesn't lend itself to using quotes as breadcrumbs, then you might be able to use the same philosophy as it applies to basic information. For instance, if you are writing about a scientific discovery, then you can literally leave clues throughout your article for the reader to follow along, as if solving a mystery.

Perhaps you start with a lab worker seeing something unusual in a Petri dish. A few paragraphs later, you describe how the lab worker is conducting tests to figure out the dish's contents. A few paragraphs later, you can say the worker got the results and was surprised, all leading up to your big ending where the worker reveals his scientific discovery. Again, the idea is to keep the reader going along with you until your article ends. Whether your bread-crumbs are clues or quotes, you can mark the trail to be followed.

Meaty Quotes

One of the best ways to improve your magazine articles is by ensuring that your quotes are as meaty as they can be. This is true whether you're using quotes to lead up to your nut graf, to finish your story, or as a trail of bread-crumbs for the reader to follow.

Loose, wordy quotes are a waste of space. Tightly edited, powerful quotes are a writer's best friend.

Edit, Edit, Edit

Typically, sources do not speak in succinct quotations. Most people tend to ramble a bit, eventually coming to a point. Your job as a writer is to edit the source's words down to as few as possible in order to make that point. Cut through the red tape, so to speak, and give the reader only the essential elements that make the quotation great.

FACT

If a quote does not break smoothly—say the best part of the quote is buried within an annoying run-on sentence—then you can cut out the beginning and forgo using every single word your source said. For instance, you might write: John said he thought the car manufacturer would "make great improvements in fuel technology despite the financial challenges."

The one caveat you must keep in mind is that you always must be faithful to your source's intent and context, especially when you break a quotation in mid-sentence. You have a responsibility as a journalist to make sure your sources are quoted accurately, and that responsibility extends beyond printing the exact words the person said. You also must be certain that you are being true to what the person meant overall.

Watch Your Attribution

Using attribution properly is another way to make sure your quotes have as much impact as possible. A lot of beginning writers believe you should let the source speak, and then attribute the entire quotation at its end with a phrase such as "Michelle said." In reality, if you truly want the reader to feel the weight of the quote, the "Michelle said" should probably come in the middle of the quotation itself.

Look at the following examples, and see for yourself which sentence construction leaves you with a stronger impression:

- "I thought the patient might die, so I did the procedure myself, without an attending in the emergency room. When I stuck the catheter into his skin, I knew I was putting my job on the line, but all I kept thinking was that his *life* was on the line," Michelle said, fidgeting and looking down.

- "I thought the patient might die, so I did the procedure myself, without an attending in the emergency room," Michelle said, fidgeting and looking down. "When I stuck the catheter into his skin, I knew I was putting my job on the line, but all I kept thinking was that his *life* was on the line."

What makes the second version so much more powerful is that the last thing the reader sees is the terrific quote itself—"his *life* was on the line"—and not your interpretation of how the speaker looked when she said it. Of course, how she looked—fidgety and nervous—is important to the context of the quote, but where you put the attribution in this case has just as much effect on the reader as the way you phrase it. The same is true of most quotes, something to keep in mind when looking to strengthen the ones you want to use.

Authority and Voice

Writing coaches talk a lot about authority and voice: your ability to write powerfully about whatever subject matter you choose. Authority and voice are important components in any well-written magazine article. How do you develop them? By doing your research and saying what you mean.

Know Your Stuff

Researching your subject thoroughly—be it carburetor maintenance or the beetle-farming industry—is key to writing about that subject with authority. If you don't know what you're talking about, the reader is going to sense it, and she'll probably stop reading somewhere along the way.

The best way to project an authoritative tone in your writing is to know far more than you're actually writing about. Again, this involves filling your notebook with vast amounts of information beyond what you actually need to put into your story. If you know twenty-five things about your subject, for instance, then you'll have a much easier time convincing your readers that the five things you've chosen to share with them are, indeed, the most important things they need to know.

Say What You Mean

Saying what you mean—at least in your first drafts—is the way that you develop a voice in magazine writing. A lot of writers have been trained to state just the facts, ma'am, leaving out all hints about their personalities and opinions. With magazine articles, you often are encouraged to include your personality and even your biases in your copy, which means that you are encouraged to say exactly what you mean as opposed to a watered-down version of your thoughts and ideas.

When trying to let your voice come through, it's important that you don't self-edit during the initial drafts that you write. Put your deepest, darkest opinions into your copy. Get them onto the page. Later, you can go back and edit out references that are too over-the-top, but only after you make a point of letting your voice speak freely at first.

Don't be afraid to let your voice come through loud and clear in your rough drafts, and to leave as much of your voice in as feels appropriate before you file your articles with your editors. It's the only way to ensure your voice will still be there at all after the editing process is complete.

Memorable Endings

So much attention gets paid to crafting the beginning of magazine articles—the leads and nut grafs—that relatively little time is spent working on story endings. This is a shame, because leaving the reader with a strong ending can be the best way to create a lasting impression or spur the reader to take action. The following sections look at a few styles of article endings that typically have powerful resonance.

Looking Forward

If your article is about a person or a program, sometimes the best way to end your tale is by looking forward to the future of that person or program. It could be a sentence as simple as, "Where exactly will Donna go from here? Nobody's quite sure, but it will definitely be far."

If there's information that may spur readers to action with your story's ending, you should include it. There's no better place than the end of a magazine article to ask a reader: "Can this dreaded disease be stopped? Doctors hope so, and they're relying on your blood donations to help them make a difference. Call now, 1-800-555 . . ."

The idea is to give the reader the lasting impression that your subject continues to live, or strive, or fester out there in the real world, that you may write about it again, and that the reader should care about what happens in the future.

Looking Back

Another classic way to connect with readers at the end of a magazine article is by harkening back to your story's lead. This technique brings a sense of closure to many magazine stories, a feeling of having come full circle on a topic.

A good example might be an article about a person fighting to change a government agency's way of doing things. Perhaps your story's lead is about the person stepping up to a microphone to discuss the problem at a town meeting, only to be dismissed by the town board members. Then, the body of your story could be about this same person's continuing struggle toward change. At the end of your story—whether the person succeeds or fails—you could go back to the town board meeting room, only end with yet another meeting where the person's voice is heard.

By using the "looking back to your lead" technique, you will make a connection with the reader, whether this story's subject succeeds or fails in the quest for change. That's the beauty of being a writer. Stories don't have to have happy endings in order to have interesting endings.

Summary Quote

Perhaps the most commonly used technique for crafting powerful story endings is the summary quotation. This is that gem of a quote that you have in your notebook summing up all of a source's thoughts and feelings and actions on a subject, the quote that highlights everything you want the reader to remember long after he puts down his magazine. The trick to using the summary quote ending is making sure you have a great quote. All too often, writers will end their articles with just any old quote, perhaps the last one they come across in their notebooks. This is a lame and lazy approach to writing that you should not follow.

Instead, when you're searching through your notes for great quotes to use as breadcrumbs, put a star next to the one or two quotes that you think might be the best. Save them for the end, like a favorite dessert. Your readers, and your editors, will thank you.

Appendix A
Magazine Writers' Organizations

There are countless professional organizations that you can join when you become a magazine writer. Some are general—welcoming writers from every genre and field—while others are more specifically tailored to subject matter or other considerations. The following list of primarily United States–based, nonfiction, magazine-oriented groups includes examples of each, and you will undoubtedly discover more associations that fit with your areas of expertise as you progress in your magazine-writing career.

General Writers' Organizations

American Society of Journalists and Authors

Founded in 1948 and known to its members as ASJA, this society is the leading organization of independent nonfiction writers in America. It has more than 1,100 members who write magazine articles, Internet features, books, and more.

www.asja.org

Association of Young Journalists and Writers

This group has evolved from Forum of Young Journalists, which was created in 1981. Writers can post articles on the association's Web site, which then makes the articles available for magazines and other media to consider.

www.ayjw.org

Authors Guild

The Authors Guild sounds like it's just for book authors, but you can become eligible for membership if you have published three articles in general-circulation publications within the past eighteen months. The guild was founded in 1912 and offers writers help with everything from health insurance to copyright protection to Web site creation.

www.authorsguild.org

National Press Club

This Washington, D.C.–based group has existed for nearly a century, hosting luncheons and providing members with networking opportunities. It also offers mentoring, awards, professional events, and more.

www.npc.press.org

National Writers Union

A trade union for freelance writers, this group has about 3,500 members in seventeen local chapters across the United States. It works with support from the United Automobile Workers Union to defend the rights and improve the working conditions of all writers.

www.nwu.org

Society of Professional Journalists

SPJ has been around since 1909, working primarily to help journalists who work for newspapers. It recently began incorporating more information and resources for freelance writers into its publications and membership offerings, making it a good networking environment for magazine writers who want to cross into newspaper writing.

www.spj.org

Ethnic- and Gender-Specific Organizations

Asian-American Journalists Association

AAJA, as its members know it, was founded in 1981 with three goals: to encourage Asian-Americans to enter the field of journalism, to work for fair and accurate coverage of Asian-American issues, and to increase the number of Asian-American journalists and news managers in the media. There are nearly 2,000 members in nineteen U.S. chapters.

www.aaja.org

Association for Women in Communications

The AWC promotes itself as recognizing the complex relationships that exist across communications and disciplines. Its membership includes magazine writers as well as broadcasters, advertisers, and other media professionals.

www.womcom.org

Association for Women Journalists

This group is organized by regional chapters, with two of its most active Web-based groups in Chicago, Illinois, and Dallas/Fort Worth, Texas. The group's mission includes promoting the fair treatment of women in the media, and it welcomes freelance magazine writers.

www.awjchicago.org
www.awjdfw.org

International Women's Writing Guild

Writers of any experience level are welcome to apply for membership in this group, which publishes a bimonthly journal listing publication, contest, and award opportunities along with news that is of interest to the guild's members. Dental and health insurance is available, as are reduced fees to writing workshops held all over the United States.

www.iwwg.com

National Association of Black Journalists

The largest association in America for journalists of color, the NABJ was founded in 1975. It started with just forty-four members and has grown to be more than 3,300 strong. The NABJ's annual programs include awarding more than $100,000 in scholarships, internships, and fellowships.

www.nabj.org

National Association of Hispanic Journalists

Since its founding in 1984, the NAHJ has grown to include about 2,300 members. The group's programs include regional workshops and seminars, a national convention and career expo, professional development programs, an online job bank, journalism awards, a newsletter, and more.

www.nahj.org

National Association of Women Writers

Regional chapters and events are among the membership benefits of this group, which promotes itself as the place "where women unite to write." Legal advice, discounted memberships to U.S. writers' conferences, and more are also available.

www.naww.org

Native American Journalists Association

Founded as the Native American Press Association in 1984, this group changed its name in 1990 and today offers a national convention, fellowships, mentoring programs, a newsletter, job alerts, and more.

www.naja.com

Topic-Specific Organizations

American Medical Writers Association

Known to its members as AMWA, this group was founded in 1940 and is the leading association for medical communicators. It has more than 5,000 worldwide members who write everything from magazine articles to clinical presentations.

www.amwa.org

Association of Food Journalists

Formed in 1974, this group was previously known as the Newspaper Food Editors and Writers Association. It changed its name to the current moniker in 1994 and now has close to 300 members from the United States and Canada. Members include magazine writers as well as broadcast and newspaper journalists.

www.afjonline.com

Boating Writers International

Nearly 400 active members comprise this group, which offers a monthly newsletter, a boating media directory, and about $20,000 each year in writing contest awards to marine journalists who cover the recreational boating industry. The group also has a writer's marketplace for magazine editors seeking knowledgeable writers.

www.bwi.org

Catholic Writers Online

The goal of this group is to help writers learn from and support one another when publishing works for the Catholic market. Its Web site has a forum where you can chat with other members, as well as information about writing in general.

www.catholicwritersonline.com

Christian Writers Group

This site's links include topics such as "Tips & Hints from Professionals," "Christian Writers' Conferences," and "Resources for the Christian Writer."

Members follow the group's belief that writing is both a privilege and a challenge, but writing for Christ is an honor and a responsibility.
www.christianwritersgroup.org

Construction Writers Association

Founded in 1958, this group works to lend prestige and professional status to journalists covering the construction industry, to help improve the quality of journalism in the construction press, and to provide a forum where construction journalists can communicate with one another.
www.constructionwriters.org

Council for the Advancement of Science Writing

The CASW, as its members know it, is committed to improving the quality of science news that reaches the general public. The group has existed since 1959 and today offers fellowships, scholarships, and more.
www.casw.org

Dog Writers Association of America

The DWAA was created in 1935 in the Westminster Kennel Club's meeting room in New York City. It holds an annual writing contest, produces a monthly newsletter, organizes an annual dinner before the Westminster dog show, and promotes its members' work in various ways.
www.dwaa.org

Educational Writers Association

This is the national professional association of education reporters, founded in 1947. It started out as a newspaper-only group, but today its more than 1,000 members also include broadcast and magazine journalists.
www.ewa.org

Garden Writers Association

More than 1,800 communicators in the lawn-and-garden industry comprise this group, which offers everything from health insurance to legal assistance to workshops and symposiums. The association hosts an annual writing contest as well, known as the GWA Media Awards.
www.gardenwriters.org

International Association of Business Communicators

There are more than 13,000 members of this group, which spans sixty nations worldwide. The IABC was founded in 1970 and continues to provide a professional network for anyone communicating about business for the general-interest media, public relations departments, the government, and more.

www.iabc.com

International Food, Wine and Travel Writers Association

Founded in Paris in 1954, this worldwide organization offers a newsletter that lists job leads, networking opportunities, and sponsored media trips. To become and remain a member, you must publish at least ten topically appropriate articles per year.

www.ifwtwa.org

Internet Press Guild

This group's mission statement is to promote excellence in journalism about the Internet, online services, and bulletin-board systems. To become and remain a member, you must submit eight articles from an electronic or paper publication, be on the masthead of an online-oriented publication, or cover the online world for the general media.

www.netpress.org

Investigative Reporters and Editors

IRE, as its members call it, was formed in 1975 as a forum for journalists worldwide to help foster excellence in investigative reporting and writing. The group publishes a bimonthly magazine, maintains a resource center with more than 20,000 archived stories, offers discounted fees for database purchases, and more. It also is affiliated with the National Institute for Computer-Assisted Reporting.

www.ire.org

National Association of Science Writers

This group came to be back in 1934. Today, its main mission is to fight for the free flow of science news, and its charter also includes fostering the

dissemination of accurate science information to the public through all forms of media. Among the membership benefits are awards and a newsletter.
www.nasw.org

National Conference of Editorial Writers

Founded in 1947, this group works to improve the quality of editorial pages and broadcast editorials, and to promote high standards among opinion writers and editors. Membership benefits include writing critiques, an annual convention, seminars and workshops, a job bank, an e-mail discussion group, and more.
www.ncew.org

Outdoor Writers Association of America

This group's mission includes improving its members' professional skills, encouraging public enjoyment and conservation of natural resources, and mentoring the next generation of professional outdoor communicators. Annual awards are offered along with other membership benefits.
www.owaa.org

Public Safety Writers Association

Formerly known as the Police Writers Club, this group was founded in 1997 and now has a membership that includes writers as well as police officers, firefighters, and security personnel. It hosts an annual conference that includes a writing contest, and members have access to helpful hints about getting published.
www.policewriter.com

Society for Technical Communication

The 18,000 members of this group include technical writers and editors, academics, Web designers, and more. The group's goals include educating its members and industry associates about issues concerning technical communication.
www.stc.org

Society of American Travel Writers

This group is more than fifty years old and 1,300 members strong. It works to promote responsible journalism, provide professional support, and encourage the conservation and preservation of travel sources worldwide. Its annual writing contest is among the many services it provides.
www.satw.org

Society of Environmental Journalists

As the only United States–based organization of working journalists dedicated to improvements in environmental reporting, the SEJ's mission includes helping the public better understand environmental issues. The group sponsors an annual writing contest, mentoring, a journal, and more.
www.sej.org

Truck Writers of North America

Promoting itself as trucking's Web resource for journalists and communicators, TWNA has existed since 1988. Its members are writers, editors, and public relations communicators who are involved with information about the trucking industry.
www.twna.org

Must-Have Reference Books

There are as many writers' guides out there as there are would-be writers. Of course you'll need an updated dictionary and thesaurus, but when it comes to selecting the rest of the reference books for your personal collection, you can pick and choose among titles that suit your personal goals best. Some of the books in the following list overlap in content, while others are unique. All have a proven record of helping magazine writers land more work, and you should at least browse through them once even if you don't buy a copy to take home.

AP Stylebook

The Associated Press Stylebook and Libel Manual includes entries on everything from Dr Pepper (no period) to metric conversions. While this book is primarily used for newspaper instead of magazine writing, it is a valuable reference to have at your fingertips. In addition to its many style entries, it also includes sections on punctuation, capitalization, and more.

Get a Freelance Life

Published in the spring of 2006, this book is branded as a companion to the popular writers' Web site *www.mediabistro.com*. It includes information about the magazine-writing lifestyle along with examples of resumes and query letters. A glossary of publishing jargon may be especially helpful to beginning writers.

How to Write Irresistible Query Letters

Author Lisa Collier Cool is a longtime magazine writer as well as the former president of the American Society of Journalists and Authors. She uses her personal experience and connections to offer professional, practical advice for hooking editors with tantalizing leads and strong story ideas.

National Writers Union Freelance Writers' Guide

This book includes solid, down-to-details information about how business is conducted between editors and writers in fields including magazine writing, technical writing, electronic publishing, corporate writing, and more. It is a good resource to have on hand for dealing with contractual disputes and paycheck problems.

Six-Figure Freelancing

A lawyer-turned-freelance-writer put together this book, which includes worksheets and templates that can help you determine a strong strategy for starting or enhancing your magazine-writing business. Plenty of real-life examples are included so that you can learn from the successes of writers who have gone before you.

The ASJA Guide to Freelance Writing

Written by members of the American Society of Journalists and Authors, this book includes chapters on everything from finding experts to protecting yourself through copyright law. Each chapter ends with an e-mail or Web site address where you can contact the writer with questions—a generous resource, and one to take advantage of.

The Best of the Magazine Markets for Writers

The 2006 edition of this book includes nearly 1,700 listings of places where you might be able to sell magazine articles, ranging from consumer and special-interest titles to trade and regional publications. Articles are included throughout the book on general topics as well.

The Chicago Manual of Style

Subtitled "the essential guide for writers, editors, and publishers," this book is now in its fifteenth edition. It is primarily concerned with style, grammar, and usage as they pertain to book publishing, but many magazine editors rely on this title to make daily decisions about usage distinctions such as "different than" versus "different from."

The Elements of Style

This longtime college-course staple is now in its fourth edition, having been used by grammar and English teachers since it was first published in 1957. It continues to be a favorite among professional magazine writers as well, perhaps because it's compact: about one-fifth the length of most other grammar and style guidebooks.

The Renegade Writer

After you finish reading reference books that all tell you how to land writing jobs the same way, you can pick up this "totally unconventional guide to freelance writing success" and consider the authors' advice for trying new approaches. Both authors are professional writers themselves, and the book includes examples of successes they found by breaking with conventional wisdom.

Words into Type

First published in 1974, this style and usage guide is now in its third edition. It is marketed as being less cumbersome than the *Chicago Manual of Style*, but has a similar purpose: to help you make the best word choices, avoid usage mistakes, and in general file cleaner articles to your editors.

Writer's Digest Handbook of Magazine Article Writing

More than 100,000 copies of this book have been sold, and it's now in its second edition. It includes original content as well as articles taken from the magazine *Writer's Digest* and has a strong focus on the magazine market (as compared with other reference books that discuss magazine writing as well as book publishing and screenwriting).

Writer's Market

The 2006 edition of this annually updated book was nearly 1,200 pages long—offering page after page of listings that tell you what magazines want your work, how much they typically pay, and whom you need to query to land an assignment. There are also sections on book publishers, writing contests, and awards.

Magazine Marketplace

You learned in Appendix B that some of the best must-have reference books for magazine writers are titles such as *Writer's Market*, which are updated annually and include contact information for literally thousands of magazines in multiple genres. This appendix is an abridged version of those types of titles, providing you with the Web sites of titles within various genres so that you can get submission guidelines, editors' names, and additional information about each.

Consumer Titles

Magazines written for consumers come in all sizes and styles. There are countless magazines that you can query; the following is a sampling of titles that accept freelance queries.

Architectural Digest
www.archdigest.com

The Atlantic Monthly
www.theatlantic.com

Bon Appetit
www.epicurious.com

Car and Driver
www.caranddriver.com

Child
www.child.com

Highlights for Children
www.highlights.com

Men's Health
www.menshealth.com

Mother Jones
www.motherjones.com

Prevention
www.prevention.com

Reader's Digest
www.readersdigest.com

Town & Country
www.townandcountrymag.com

Trade Titles

Trade magazines are also known as trade journals or professional journals. They are written for people working in a given field, as opposed to being written for a general consumer audience.

Air Line Pilot: The Magazine of Professional Flight Deck Crews
www.alpa.org

Beer, Wine & Spirits Beverage Retailer
www.beverage-retailer.com

The Business Journal: Serving San Jose and Silicon Valley
www.amcity.com/sanjose

DiabetesInterview
www.diabetesinterview.com

Directed By: The Cinema Quarterly
www.directed-by.com

InstructorMagazine: For Teachers of Grades K-8
www.scholastic.com/instructor

Massage Magazine
www.massagemag.com

National Petroleum News
✐*www.npn-net.com*

Rental Management
✐*www.rentalmanagementmag.com*

Textile World
✐*www.textileindustries.com*

Today's Catholic Teacher
✐*www.catholicteacher.com*

Academic Titles

Academic magazines are also known as scholarly journals. For the most part, they are used as research tools, and they are written with a more serious tone than most consumer and trade magazines.

American Journal of Political Science
✐*www.ajps.org*

Artificial Life
✐*www.mitpressjournals.org/loi/artl*

Bulletin of the Atomic Scientists
✐*www.thebulletin.org*

Foreign Affairs
✐*www.foreignaffairs.org*

International Security
✐*www.mitpressjournals.org*

Journal of Cold War Studies
✐*www.mitpressjournals.org/loi/jcws*

Journal of the American Mathematical Society
✐*www.ams.org/journals/jams*

Latin American Research Review
✐*www.larr.lanic.utexas.edu*

Political Science Quarterly
✐*www.psqonline.org*

Social Science Computer Review
✐*www.hcl.class.ncsu.edu/sscore/sscore.htm*

The Washington Quarterly
✐*www.mitpressjournals.org/loi/wash*

Technical Titles

Technical magazines, like academic journals, are read by experts in virtually every chosen field. However, the content of technical magazines is more geared toward practical applications than scholarly research.

AmericanMachinist
✐*www.americanmachinist.com*

Business Communications Review
✐*www.bcr.com*

Computer Graphics World
✐*www.cgw.com*

Environmental Protection Magazine
✎*www.eponline.com*

Genetic Engineering News
✎*www.genengnews.com*

Industrial Laser Solutions
✎*http://ils.pennet.com*

Journal of Experimental Medicine
✎*www.jem.org*

Ocean News & Technology
✎*www.ocean-news.com*

Pollution Engineering
✎*www.pollutioneng.com*

Robotics World
✎*www.roboticsworld.com*

Wireless Design and Development
✎*www.wirelessdesignmag.com*

Online Titles

Online magazines can be standalone publications or electronic versions of a printed magazine. More and more online-only titles are becoming viable every day.

American Atheist
✎*www.americanathiest.org*

Ape Culture
✎*www.apeculture.com*

Asiaweek Online
✎*www.asiaweek.com/asiaweek*

Blender
✎*www.blender.com*

BYTE
✎*www.byte.com*

Carnegie Magazine Online
✎*www.carnegiemuseums.org/cmag*

Education Week
✎*www.edweek.org*

MedicalComputing Today
✎*www.medicalcomputingtoday.com/index.html*

Salon
✎*www.salon.com*

Science Online
✎*www.sciencemag.org*

Vet On-Line
✎*www.priory.com/vet.htm*

Index

A

Academic magazines, 49–50, 297
Accounting issues, 35–37, 41. *See also* Taxes
Administrative materials, 37–38
Agents, 112–13
American Society of Journalists and Authors (ASJA), 8, 22, 144, 162, 225
Artwork, 68–69
Assignment letters, 85–97
    contents, 86–87, 91–95
    deadline section, 89–90, 93
    defined, 86
    editor not providing, 95–97
    evolution of assignments and, 86
    filing instructions in, 94
    kill fees and, 89–90, 207–9, 223–24
    payment details in, 94
    reasons for, 87–91, 95, 206–7
    story content section, 92–93
    taking initiative for, 96–97
Assignments, managing. *See* Deadlines; Managing assignments
Attorneys
    for collections, 221, 226
    for contracts, 7, 112–13
    for copyright infringements, 131, 133, 140–41
    indemnity clauses and, 104–5
Attribution, watching, 276–77
Authority and voice, 277–78
Awards, 22–24

B

Blogs, 263
Books, for reference, 291–93
Books, writing, 260–62
Boredom and loneliness, 242–43
"Brand You," 77
Breaks. *See* Downtime
Business of writing, xii. *See also* Finances; Home-based business; Networking; Roles of magazine writer
    accounting issues, 35–37, 41. *See also* Taxes
    administrative materials, 37–38
    balancing downtime/play with, 236–38, 242, 243–44, 250–51
    business skills required, 30–31
    changing focus of, 256. *See also* Skills, adding
    changing routine, 238, 243–44
    choosing business name, 42
    commitment level (part-/full-time), 31–32
    expanding. *See* Expanding your base; Marketing yourself
    freedom from details of, 158, 159
    marketing materials, 38–39
    materials/equipment needed, 33, 34
    plan for, 33
    S-corps and LLCs, 41–42
    starting, overview, 29, 32–34, 42
    staying on top (ahead) of things, 10–11
    tricks of trade, 11–13
    varying workloads and, 26–27
    working independently, 24–27

C

Calendar
    downtime in. *See* Downtime
    editorial, learning, 11
    structuring work time with, 250
    for tracking assignments, 123–25
    for tracking tax payments, 136, 229
Cementing base, 73–84
    being go-to writer, 74, 193
    mastheads and, 74–77
    to specialize or not, 78–80
    through networking. *See* Networking
    top-quality customer service, 118–20

Clues, using, 161, 275

Collecting receivables, 213–26
  assuming the best and,
      218–19
  attitude in, 214–15, 217–18
  from closed business, 221
  fast-track system for, 219
  getting runaround in, 220
  initial call for, 216–18
  kill fee instead of, 223–24
  legal options for, 221, 226
  need for, 214
  standard payment time
      and, 215–16
  strategic techniques for,
      224–26
  time consideration in,
      221–23
  understanding why no
      payment, 219–21
  using writers' groups for,
      225–26
  writing off losses and, 224

Compensation. See also
    Collecting receivables
  assignment letters
      clarifying, 89
  contracts and. See
      Contract(s)
  for copyrighting, 180–81
  future assignments as, 81
  income expectations, 19
  increasing. See
      Compensation,
      increasing
  kill fees, 89–90, 207–9,
      223–24
  okay to make little, 186–87
  per-project vs. per-hour,
      190–92

for photography, 181–82,
      257
  for repurposing content,
      177, 189
  trading services/time,
      80–82

Compensation, increasing, 185–
    98. See also Skills, adding
  adding little extras for,
      192–94, 204–6
  consulting for, 265–66
  cutting expenses for,
      197–98
  determining increase
      goals, 186–87
  dropping lowest-paying
      clients, 196–97
  giving speeches for, 264–
      65
  making a lot and, 187–88
  $1-per-word question,
      188–90
  quick hits for quick cash,
      190
  raising longtime client
      rates, 194–96
  repurposing content for,
      177, 189
  teaching for, 265
  Web site fees, 263–64
  writing books for, 262

Competition
  enormity of, 144–46
  for high-paying
      magazines, 45
  between magazines,
      monitoring/researching,
      12, 13, 53–54
  staying ahead of, 7–10
  writing for, 67, 76, 205

Conferences, 144, 152–53, 162–
    64, 245

Conflicts of interest, 84, 180, 236

Consolidation, of publishers,
    55–56

Consulting, 265–66

Consumer magazines, 44–47, 296

Contacts, making, 8, 83–84. See
    also Networking

Content providers, 2–4, 13, 192

Contract(s), 99–113
  attorneys or agents for,
      112–13
  basics, 100
  common issues, 6–7
  credit clauses, 109–10
  expanded usage
      considerations, 111
  first North American serial
      rights, 101–2, 103, 104,
      110, 176
  hybrid, 103
  increasing demands and,
      4–5
  indemnity clauses, 39,
      104–5
  limited exclusivity
      considerations, 111
  negotiating effectively,
      110–11
  repurposing content and,
      176–77
  scary clauses, 39, 104–10
  superseding previous
      contracts, 109
  third-party promises, 39,
      106–7
  time limits, 101
  using your likeness and, 6,
      107–8
  when to walk away, 112

work-for-hire, 102–3, 110, 111, 131, 176, 257
Copyrighting, 179–81
Copyrights, 129–42
  basics of, 130–32
  changes in law, 131
  filing quarterly, 135–37
  forms for, 134–35, 136
  infringements/remedies, 137–42
  legal help for infringements, 140–41
  length of, 131
  meeting time limits for, 137
  right to sue with, 133
  saving money filing for, 136
  symbol for, 130
  value of, 132–33
Cover blurbs, 70
Creative-writing exercises, 164–67
Credit clauses, 109–10

D

Deadlines. See also Managing assignments
  announce problems early, 210
  assignment letters delineating, 89–90, 93
  giving yourself, 120–23, 250
  keeping editors happy, 210
  keeping updated to-do lists, 123–25
  kill fees and, 89–90, 207–9, 223–24
  managing, 120–23, 210

when overloaded, 122–23
Details, for stronger stories, 269–70
Distractions, 27, 35, 118, 158–59
Doldrums, 241–53. See also Downtime
  balancing work with play, 236–38, 242, 243–44, 250–51
  cooking something for, 251–52
  exercise for, 250
  getting back on track, 248–53
  loneliness and boredom, 241–53
  procrastination and, 242
  reading for, 248–49
  seeing what real jobs are for, 252–53
  traveling for, 243–44
  watching movies for, 251
  writer's block and, 242
  writing something different for, 248
Downtime
  balancing work with, 236–38, 242, 243–44
  getting out of chair, 236–37
  getting out of house, 237
  getting out of routine, 238, 243–44
  importance of, 169–70, 244
  travel and, 243–44
  vacations, 246–48, 249

E

Editing and proofreading, 259–60
Editorial calendar, 11
Editors, 199–212
  as allies/advocates, 202–4
  assignments from. See Assignment letters
  being go-to person for, 74, 193
  changing jobs, 203–4
  competition of, monitoring, 12, 13, 53–54
  contacting. See Query letters
  developing relationships with, 8–10, 12, 18, 235
  disputing changes by, 211–12
  ever-increasing duties of, 200–201
  as friends, 235
  getting attention of, 60
  going over head of, 225
  helping with collections, 218–19
  keeping them happy, tips, 209–12
  kill fees and, 89–90, 207–9, 223–24
  maintaining big picture with, 212
  new, 88–89, 206–7
  number of, for magazines, 118
  pitching stories to, 11–12
  protecting yourself from, 206–7
  references from, 56
  stable of writers, 200, 201

taking advantage of you, 204–6

treating as only client, 118–20

unhappy with work, 220–21

warning signs from, 205

Endings, memorable, 278–80

Exercising, 250

Expanding your base, 171–84. *See also* Marketing yourself

appealing to range of clients, 183–84

assessing pros/cons of, 172–73

by copywriting, 179–81

by entering new markets, 177–79

by partnering with photographers/ illustrators, 181–83

realistic approach to, 173

by repurposing content, 174–77

F

Fiction, reading, 160–61

Filing instructions, 94

Finances. *See also* Compensation; Compensation, increasing; Taxes

business entity types and, 41, 230

health care and, 19–20, 231–34

managing sporadic cash flow, 228–29

reducing expenses, 197–98

retirement savings, 20, 230–31

self-reliance and, 21

separating assets, 40–41

SEP-IRAs, 230–31

startup budget, 33–34

First North American serial rights, 101–2, 103, 104, 110, 176

Friendships, 235–36, 245–46. *See also* Networking

Full-time writing, 32

G

Goals

plan for achieving, 33

recognizing limitations and, 31

setting, 31–32

Growing business. *See* Expanding your base; Marketing yourself

H

Health insurance, 19–20, 231–33

Health savings accounts (HSAs), 233–34

Home-based business. *See also* Business of writing; Roles of magazine writer

help around house and, 238–39

intangibles of, 35

managing distractions, 27, 35, 118, 158–59

materials/equipment needed, 33, 34

separating work from home, 238

setup for, 34–35

working independently, 24–27

Hybrid contracts, 103

I

Illustrations, producing, 258–59

Illustrators, partnering with, 181–83

Improving your craft, 157–70. *See also* Skills, adding

attending conferences, 144, 152–53, 162–64, 245

controlling distractions, 27, 35, 118, 158–59

creative-writing exercises, 164–67

downtime and. *See* Downtime

editing/proofreading and, 260

incorporating photography, 167–69

reading for fun, 159–62, 248–49

reading top writers/ publications, 161–62

writing stronger stories. *See* Stronger stories

Income. *See* Compensation; Compensation, increasing

Indemnity clauses, 39, 104–5

Insurance

errors-and-omission, 40, 112–13

health, 19–20, 231–33

HSAs and, 233–34

Introductory letters/e-mails, 149–50

K

Kill fees, 89–90, 207–9, 223–24

L

Last-minute work, 125–26, 127
Leads
  defined, 270
  first five paragraphs, 271
  harkening back to, in
    endings, 279–80
  improving, 166, 270–72
  into killer quotes, 272
  leading to killer quote, 272
  for query letters, 62–63
Legal issues, 39–42. *See also*
  Attorneys; Contract(s);
  Copyrights
  business entity types, 41,
    230
  business name, 42
  protecting yourself, 40–42.
    See also Insurance
  using your likeness, 6,
    107–8
Likeness (your), using, 6, 107–8
LLCs (limited liability
  corporations), 41–42
Logos, 38, 42
Loneliness and boredom, 242–43
Lunches, working, 246

M

Magazine staff meetings, 153–54
Magazine titles, 295–98. *See also*
  Markets
Managing assignments, 115–27.
  See also Deadlines

controlling distractions,
  27, 35, 118, 158–59
handling last-minute work,
  125–26, 127
having resources ready,
  127
juggling projects, 116–17
keeping updated to-do
  lists, 123–25
listing assignments by
  categories, 124–25
not getting caught in
  business details, 158,
  159
time management, 117–18
top-quality customer
  service, 118–20
typical writer's day, 116–18
when overloaded, 122–23
Marketing yourself, 143–55. *See
  also* Expanding your base;
  Query letters
  to broad range of clients,
    183–84
  challenge of, 146–47
  competition demanding,
    144–46
  by creating Web site,
    154–55
  at industry conferences,
    144, 152–53, 162–64
  in introductory letters/e-
    mails, 149–50
  by joining magazine staff
    meetings, 153–54
  materials for, 38–39
  on the Web, 154–55,
    197–98
  in writers' groups, 151–52
  in writing contests, 150–51
Markets, 43–57

academic titles, 49–50,
  297
competing titles, 53–54
consolidated, using to
  advantage, 55–56
consumer titles, 44–47,
  296
creating stable of titles,
  54–55
expanding. *See*
  Expanding your base;
  Marketing yourself
magazine titles/Web sites,
  295–98
multiple, maintaining,
  178–79
online titles, 51–53, 298
specializing in, or not,
  78–80, 178
technical titles, 50–51,
  297–98
trade titles, 47–48, 296–97
universe of magazines, 44
Writer's Market for, 46
Mastheads
  getting on, 74–75
  inclusion without
    permission, 77
  pros/cons, 76–77
  protocols for, 75
  typical deals for, 75–77
Mistakes to avoid, x, 70–72

N

Name of business, 42
National Writers Union, 151, 234
Networking
  with editors, 56–57, 204
  friendships from, 235–36,
    245–46

importance of, 7–8, 82
making contacts, 8, 83–84
organizations for, 281–89
with writer's groups,
     151–52
Nut grafs, 17–18, 167, 271, 272–74
$1-per-word question, 188–90

O

Online magazines, 51–53, 298
Organizations, 281–89

P

Part-time writing, 31–32
Photographers, partnering with,
     181–83
Photography, 167–69
   additional income from,
        257
   compensation for, 181–82,
        257
   developing stock library,
        257–58
   endearing editors with,
        169
   power of, 167–68
   practicing, 168–69
   taking photos, 256–58
Plan, for business, 33. *See also*
     Goals
Procrastination, 242
Proofreading and editing, 259–
     60
Publicity/promotion. *See also*
     Marketing yourself; Mastheads
   free, with writing contests, 151
   using your likeness and,
        6, 107–8
   working for, 80–81

Q

Query letters, 59–72
   artwork accompanying,
        68–69
   changing losses to wins,
        148–49
   components, 62–66
   contact information in,
        65–66
   cover blurbs in, 70
   following up on, 71–72,
        148–49. *See also*
        Marketing yourself
   format, 61
   getting editor attention,
        60, 62–63
   helpful suggestions, 68–70
   joint, with photographer,
        182–83
   key points to make, 66–68
   leads, 62–63
   mistakes to avoid, 70–72
   qualifications in, 64–65
   supporting paragraphs,
        63–64
Quotes, using, 161, 268–69, 272,
     274–77, 280

R

Reading for fun, 159–62, 248–49
Recognition, 21–22. *See also*
     Awards; Publicity/promotion
Relationships. *See also*
     Networking
   developing, with editors/
        magazines, 8–10, 12, 18,
        235
   friendships, 235–36, 245–
        46

with other writers, 235–36,
     245–46
   with sources, 236
Reporting skills, 16–17
Repurposing content, 174–77, 189
Research
   ability to perform, 17
   enhancing expertise, 260
   generating authority with,
        277–78
   Internet access for, 33
   knowing time required
        for, 127
   ownership, 108
   paring down, 158–59
   repurposing content and,
        174–77
Researching magazines, 8–10
Resources
   magazine titles/Web sites,
        295–98
   organizations, 281–89
   reference books, 291–93
Retirement savings, 20, 230–31
Revisions
   repurposing content and,
        174–77
   unreasonable requests for,
        90–91
Roles of magazine writer, 1–13.
     See also Business of writing;
     Networking
   competing with other
        writers, 7–10
   content provider, 2–4, 13,
        192
   developing editor
        relationships, 8–10
   knowing submission
        guidelines, 9, 92

meeting increasing
demands, 4–5
staying on top (ahead) of
things, 10–11
using tricks of trade, 11–13
Routine, changing, 238, 243–44

S

S-corps and LLCs, 41–42
SEP-IRAs, 230–31
Skills
assessing, 16–18
entrepreneurial, 30–31.
See also Business of
writing
reporting, 16–17
working with editors, 18
writing, 17–18
Skills, adding, 255–66. *See also*
Improving your craft
building Web presence.
See Web sites
changing job focus and,
256
consulting, 265–66
editing and proofreading,
259–60
illustrating work, 258–59
making speeches, 264–65
photography, 167–69,
256–58
teaching, 265
writing books, 260–62
Software
accounting, 36, 37
optimizing, for stationery,
38
upgrading, 33–34, 136
Web-site, 198
Specializing, 78–80, 178

Speeches, giving, 264–65
Staff meetings, joining, 153–54
Starting business. *See* Business
of writing; Finances; Home-
based business
Stationery, 37–38, 39, 183
Stronger stories, 267–80
authority and voice for,
277–78
better reporting for, 268–
70
clues for, 275
details for, 269–70
improving leads for, 166,
270–72
keeping reader engaged,
274–75
memorable endings for,
278–80
quotes for, 268–69, 272,
274–77, 280
strengthening nut grafs
for, 272–74
Submission guidelines, 9, 92
Suing, for copyright violations,
133, 140, 176
Summary quotes, 280

T

Taxes
business entity types and,
41, 230
deductions, 36–37
quarterly payments, 292
tracking payments, 136,
229
Teaching, 265
Teaser articles/pages, 2, 192, 193
Technical magazines, 50–51,
297–98

Third-party promises, 39, 106–7
Titles of magazines, 295–98. *See
also* Markets
Topic(s)
expanding, in books,
261–62
pitching stories by, 11–12
Trade magazines, 47–48, 296–97
Trading services/time, 80–82
Traveling, with work, 243–44
Tricks of trade, 11–13

V

Vacation. *See* Downtime
Voice and authority, 277–78

W

Web sites. *See also* Online
magazines
blogs and, 263
creating, 154–55, 198,
263–64
of magazines, 295–98
posting resume/clips on,
197–98
subscriber fees for, 263–64
Word count, 92, 166–67, 168, 207,
211
Work-for-hire contracts, 102–3,
110, 111, 131, 176, 257
Work routine. *See* Business of
writing; Home-based business
Writer's block. *See* Doldrums
Writers' groups, 151–52, 179, 225–
26, 234, 235
Writing contests, 150–51

The EVERYTHING Series!

BUSINESS & PERSONAL FINANCE

Everything® Accounting Book
Everything® Budgeting Book
Everything® Business Planning Book
Everything® Coaching and Mentoring Book
Everything® Fundraising Book
Everything® Get Out of Debt Book
Everything® Grant Writing Book
Everything® Guide to Personal Finance for Single Mothers
Everything® Home-Based Business Book, 2nd Ed.
Everything® Homebuying Book, 2nd Ed.
Everything® Homeselling Book, 2nd Ed.
Everything® Improve Your Credit Book
Everything® Investing Book, 2nd Ed.
Everything® Landlording Book
Everything® Leadership Book
Everything® Managing People Book, 2nd Ed.
Everything® Negotiating Book
Everything® Online Auctions Book
Everything® Online Business Book
Everything® Personal Finance Book
Everything® Personal Finance in Your 20s and 30s Book
Everything® Project Management Book
Everything® Real Estate Investing Book
Everything® Retirement Planning Book
Everything® Robert's Rules Book, $7.95
Everything® Selling Book
Everything® Start Your Own Business Book, 2nd Ed.
Everything® Wills & Estate Planning Book

COOKING

Everything® Barbecue Cookbook
Everything® Bartender's Book, $9.95
Everything® Cheese Book
Everything® Chinese Cookbook
Everything® Classic Recipes Book
Everything® Cocktail Parties and Drinks Book
Everything® College Cookbook
Everything® Cooking for Baby and Toddler Book
Everything® Cooking for Two Cookbook
Everything® Diabetes Cookbook
Everything® Easy Gourmet Cookbook
Everything® Fondue Cookbook
Everything® Fondue Party Book
Everything® Gluten-Free Cookbook
Everything® Glycemic Index Cookbook
Everything® Grilling Cookbook

Everything® Healthy Meals in Minutes Cookbook
Everything® Holiday Cookbook
Everything® Indian Cookbook
Everything® Italian Cookbook
Everything® Low-Carb Cookbook
Everything® Low-Fat High-Flavor Cookbook
Everything® Low-Salt Cookbook
Everything® Meals for a Month Cookbook
Everything® Mediterranean Cookbook
Everything® Mexican Cookbook
Everything® No Trans Fat Cookbook
Everything® One-Pot Cookbook
Everything® Pizza Cookbook
Everything® Quick and Easy 30-Minute, 5-Ingredient Cookbook
Everything® Quick Meals Cookbook
Everything® Slow Cooker Cookbook
Everything® Slow Cooking for a Crowd Cookbook
Everything® Soup Cookbook
Everything® Stir-Fry Cookbook
Everything® Tex-Mex Cookbook
Everything® Thai Cookbook
Everything® Vegetarian Cookbook
Everything® Wild Game Cookbook
Everything® Wine Book, 2nd Ed.

GAMES

Everything® 15-Minute Sudoku Book, $9.95
Everything® 30-Minute Sudoku Book, $9.95
Everything® Blackjack Strategy Book
Everything® Brain Strain Book, $9.95
Everything® Bridge Book
Everything® Card Games Book
Everything® Card Tricks Book, $9.95
Everything® Casino Gambling Book, 2nd Ed.
Everything® Chess Basics Book
Everything® Craps Strategy Book
Everything® Crossword and Puzzle Book
Everything® Crossword Challenge Book
Everything® Crosswords for the Beach Book, $9.95
Everything® Cryptograms Book, $9.95
Everything® Easy Crosswords Book
Everything® Easy Kakuro Book, $9.95
Everything® Easy Large Print Crosswords Book
Everything® Games Book, 2nd Ed.
Everything® Giant Sudoku Book, $9.95
Everything® Kakuro Challenge Book, $9.95
Everything® Large-Print Crossword Challenge Book

Everything® Large-Print Crosswords Book
Everything® Lateral Thinking Puzzles Book, $9.95
Everything® Mazes Book
Everything® Movie Crosswords Book, $9.95
Everything® Online Poker Book, $12.95
Everything® Pencil Puzzles Book, $9.95
Everything® Poker Strategy Book
Everything® Pool & Billiards Book
Everything® Sports Crosswords Book, $9.95
Everything® Test Your IQ Book, $9.95
Everything® Texas Hold 'Em Book, $9.95
Everything® Travel Crosswords Book, $9.95
Everything® Word Games Challenge Book
Everything® Word Scramble Book
Everything® Word Search Book

HEALTH

Everything® Alzheimer's Book
Everything® Diabetes Book
Everything® Health Guide to Adult Bipolar Disorder
Everything® Health Guide to Controlling Anxiety
Everything® Health Guide to Fibromyalgia
Everything® Health Guide to Postpartum Care
Everything® Health Guide to Thyroid Disease
Everything® Hypnosis Book
Everything® Low Cholesterol Book
Everything® Massage Book
Everything® Menopause Book
Everything® Nutrition Book
Everything® Reflexology Book
Everything® Stress Management Book

HISTORY

Everything® American Government Book
Everything® American History Book, 2nd Ed.
Everything® Civil War Book
Everything® Freemasons Book
Everything® Irish History & Heritage Book
Everything® Middle East Book

HOBBIES

Everything® Candlemaking Book
Everything® Cartooning Book
Everything® Coin Collecting Book
Everything® Drawing Book
Everything® Family Tree Book, 2nd Ed.
Everything® Knitting Book
Everything® Knots Book
Everything® Photography Book

Everything® Quilting Book
Everything® Scrapbooking Book
Everything® Sewing Book
Everything® Soapmaking Book, 2nd Ed.
Everything® Woodworking Book

HOME IMPROVEMENT

Everything® Feng Shui Book
Everything® Feng Shui Decluttering Book, $9.95
Everything® Fix-It Book
Everything® Home Decorating Book
Everything® Home Storage Solutions Book
Everything® Homebuilding Book
Everything® Organize Your Home Book

KIDS' BOOKS

All titles are $7.95

Everything® Kids' Animal Puzzle & Activity Book
Everything® Kids' Baseball Book, 4th Ed.
Everything® Kids' Bible Trivia Book
Everything® Kids' Bugs Book
Everything® Kids' Cars and Trucks Puzzle
   & Activity Book
Everything® Kids' Christmas Puzzle
   & Activity Book
Everything® Kids' Cookbook
Everything® Kids' Crazy Puzzles Book
Everything® Kids' Dinosaurs Book
Everything® Kids' First Spanish Puzzle and
   Activity Book
Everything® Kids' Gross Cookbook
Everything® Kids' Gross Hidden Pictures Book
Everything® Kids' Gross Jokes Book
Everything® Kids' Gross Mazes Book
Everything® Kids' Gross Puzzle and
   Activity Book
Everything® Kids' Halloween Puzzle
   & Activity Book
Everything® Kids' Hidden Pictures Book
Everything® Kids' Horses Book
Everything® Kids' Joke Book
Everything® Kids' Knock Knock Book
Everything® Kids' Learning Spanish Book
Everything® Kids' Math Puzzles Book
Everything® Kids' Mazes Book
Everything® Kids' Money Book
Everything® Kids' Nature Book
Everything® Kids' Pirates Puzzle and Activity Book
Everything® Kids' Presidents Book
Everything® Kids' Princess Puzzle and Activity Book
Everything® Kids' Puzzle Book
Everything® Kids' Riddles & Brain Teasers Book
Everything® Kids' Science Experiments Book
Everything® Kids' Sharks Book
Everything® Kids' Soccer Book
Everything® Kids' States Book
Everything® Kids' Travel Activity Book

KIDS' STORY BOOKS

Everything® Fairy Tales Book

LANGUAGE

Everything® Conversational Japanese Book with
   CD, $19.95
Everything® French Grammar Book
Everything® French Phrase Book, $9.95
Everything® French Verb Book, $9.95
Everything® German Practice Book with CD,
   $19.95
Everything® Inglés Book
**Everything® Intermediate Spanish Book with
   CD, $19.95**
**Everything® Learning Brazilian Portuguese
   Book with CD, $19.95**
Everything® Learning French Book
Everything® Learning German Book
Everything® Learning Italian Book
Everything® Learning Latin Book
**Everything® Learning Spanish Book with
   CD, 2nd Edition, $19.95**
Everything® Russian Practice Book with CD, $19.95
Everything® Sign Language Book
Everything® Spanish Grammar Book
Everything® Spanish Phrase Book, $9.95
Everything® Spanish Practice Book
   with CD, $19.95
Everything® Spanish Verb Book, $9.95
Everything® Speaking Mandarin Chinese Book
   with CD, $19.95

MUSIC

Everything® Drums Book with CD, $19.95
**Everything® Guitar Book with CD, 2nd
   Edition, $19.95**
Everything® Guitar Chords Book with CD, $19.95
Everything® Home Recording Book
Everything® Music Theory Book with CD, $19.95
Everything® Reading Music Book with CD, $19.95
Everything® Rock & Blues Guitar Book
   with CD, $19.95
**Everything® Rock and Blues Piano Book
   with CD, $19.95**
Everything® Songwriting Book

NEW AGE

Everything® Astrology Book, 2nd Ed.
Everything® Birthday Personology Book
Everything® Dreams Book, 2nd Ed.
Everything® Love Signs Book, $9.95
Everything® Numerology Book
Everything® Paganism Book
Everything® Palmistry Book
Everything® Psychic Book
Everything® Reiki Book

Everything® Sex Signs Book, $9.95
Everything® Tarot Book, 2nd Ed.
Everything® Toltec Wisdom Book
Everything® Wicca and Witchcraft Book

PARENTING

Everything® Baby Names Book, 2nd Ed.
Everything® Baby Shower Book
Everything® Baby's First Year Book
Everything® Birthing Book
Everything® Breastfeeding Book
Everything® Father-to-Be Book
Everything® Father's First Year Book
Everything® Get Ready for Baby Book
Everything® Get Your Baby to Sleep Book, $9.95
Everything® Getting Pregnant Book
Everything® Guide to Raising a One-Year-Old
Everything® Guide to Raising a Two-Year-Old
Everything® Homeschooling Book
Everything® Mother's First Year Book
**Everything® Parent's Guide to Childhood
   Illnesses**
Everything® Parent's Guide to Children
   and Divorce
Everything® Parent's Guide to Children
   with ADD/ADHD
Everything® Parent's Guide to Children
   with Asperger's Syndrome
Everything® Parent's Guide to Children
   with Autism
Everything® Parent's Guide to Children with
   Bipolar Disorder
**Everything® Parent's Guide to Children with
   Depression**
Everything® Parent's Guide to Children
   with Dyslexia
**Everything® Parent's Guide to Children with
   Juvenile Diabetes**
Everything® Parent's Guide to Positive Discipline
Everything® Parent's Guide to Raising a
   Successful Child
Everything® Parent's Guide to Raising Boys
Everything® Parent's Guide to Raising Girls
Everything® Parent's Guide to Raising Siblings
Everything® Parent's Guide to Sensory
   Integration Disorder
Everything® Parent's Guide to Tantrums
Everything® Parent's Guide to the Strong-Willed
   Child
Everything® Parenting a Teenager Book
Everything® Potty Training Book, $9.95
Everything® Pregnancy Book, 3rd Ed.
Everything® Pregnancy Fitness Book
Everything® Pregnancy Nutrition Book
Everything® Pregnancy Organizer, 2nd Ed., $16.95
Everything® Toddler Activities Book
Everything® Toddler Book

Everything® Tween Book
Everything® Twins, Triplets, and More Book

PETS

Everything® Aquarium Book
Everything® Boxer Book
Everything® Cat Book, 2nd Ed.
Everything® Chihuahua Book
Everything® Dachshund Book
Everything® Dog Book
Everything® Dog Health Book
Everything® Dog Obedience Book
Everything® Dog Owner's Organizer, $16.95
Everything® Dog Training and Tricks Book
Everything® German Shepherd Book
Everything® Golden Retriever Book
Everything® Horse Book
Everything® Horse Care Book
Everything® Horseback Riding Book
Everything® Labrador Retriever Book
Everything® Poodle Book
Everything® Pug Book
Everything® Puppy Book
Everything® Rottweiler Book
Everything® Small Dogs Book
Everything® Tropical Fish Book
Everything® Yorkshire Terrier Book

REFERENCE

Everything® American Presidents Book
Everything® Blogging Book
Everything® Build Your Vocabulary Book
Everything® Car Care Book
Everything® Classical Mythology Book
Everything® Da Vinci Book
Everything® Divorce Book
Everything® Einstein Book
Everything® Enneagram Book
Everything® Etiquette Book, 2nd Ed.
Everything® Inventions and Patents Book
Everything® Mafia Book
Everything® Philosophy Book
Everything® Pirates Book
Everything® Psychology Book

RELIGION

Everything® Angels Book
Everything® Bible Book
Everything® Buddhism Book
Everything® Catholicism Book
Everything® Christianity Book
Everything® Gnostic Gospels Book
Everything® History of the Bible Book
Everything® Jesus Book

Everything® Jewish History & Heritage Book
Everything® Judaism Book
Everything® Kabbalah Book
Everything® Koran Book
Everything® Mary Book
Everything® Mary Magdalene Book
Everything® Prayer Book
Everything® Saints Book, 2nd Ed.
Everything® Torah Book
Everything® Understanding Islam Book
Everything® World's Religions Book
Everything® Zen Book

SCHOOL & CAREERS

Everything® Alternative Careers Book
Everything® Career Tests Book
Everything® College Major Test Book
Everything® College Survival Book, 2nd Ed.
Everything® Cover Letter Book, 2nd Ed.
Everything® Filmmaking Book
Everything® Get-a-Job Book, 2nd Ed.
Everything® Guide to Being a Paralegal
Everything® Guide to Being a Personal Trainer
Everything® Guide to Being a Real Estate Agent
Everything® Guide to Being a Sales Rep
Everything® Guide to Careers in Health Care
Everything® Guide to Careers in Law Enforcement
Everything® Guide to Government Jobs
Everything® Guide to Starting and Running a Restaurant
Everything® Job Interview Book
Everything® New Nurse Book
Everything® New Teacher Book
Everything® Paying for College Book
Everything® Practice Interview Book
Everything® Resume Book, 2nd Ed.
Everything® Study Book

SELF-HELP

Everything® Dating Book, 2nd Ed.
Everything® Great Sex Book
Everything® Self-Esteem Book
Everything® Tantric Sex Book

SPORTS & FITNESS

Everything® Easy Fitness Book
Everything® Running Book
Everything® Weight Training Book

TRAVEL

Everything® Family Guide to Cruise Vacations
Everything® Family Guide to Hawaii
Everything® Family Guide to Las Vegas, 2nd Ed.
Everything® Family Guide to Mexico
Everything® Family Guide to New York City, 2nd Ed.
Everything® Family Guide to RV Travel & Campgrounds
Everything® Family Guide to the Caribbean
Everything® Family Guide to the Walt Disney World Resort®, Universal Studios®, and Greater Orlando, 4th Ed.
Everything® Family Guide to Timeshares
Everything® Family Guide to Washington D.C., 2nd Ed.

WEDDINGS

Everything® Bachelorette Party Book, $9.95
Everything® Bridesmaid Book, $9.95
Everything® Destination Wedding Book
Everything® Elopement Book, $9.95
Everything® Father of the Bride Book, $9.95
Everything® Groom Book, $9.95
Everything® Mother of the Bride Book, $9.95
Everything® Outdoor Wedding Book
Everything® Wedding Book, 3rd Ed.
Everything® Wedding Checklist, $9.95
Everything® Wedding Etiquette Book, $9.95
Everything® Wedding Organizer, 2nd Ed., $16.95
Everything® Wedding Shower Book, $9.95
Everything® Wedding Vows Book, $9.95
Everything® Wedding Workout Book
Everything® Weddings on a Budget Book, $9.95

WRITING

Everything® Creative Writing Book
Everything® Get Published Book, 2nd Ed.
Everything® Grammar and Style Book
Everything® Guide to Magazine Writing
Everything® Guide to Writing a Book Proposal
Everything® Guide to Writing a Novel
Everything® Guide to Writing Children's Books
Everything® Guide to Writing Copy
Everything® Guide to Writing Research Papers
Everything® Screenwriting Book
Everything® Writing Poetry Book
Everything® Writing Well Book